The INNER WORK

of

RACIAL JUSTICE

HEALING OURSELVES AND TRANSFORMING
OUR COMMUNITIES THROUGH MINDFULNESS

RHONDA V. MAGEE

A TARCHERPERIGEE BOOK

**tarcher
perigee**

AN IMPRINT OF PENGUIN RANDOM HOUSE LLC
penguinrandomhouse.com

TarcherPerigee with tp colophon is a registered trademark of Penguin Random House LLC.

Most TarcherPerigee books are available at special quantity discounts for bulk purchase for sales promotions, premiums, fund-raising, and educational needs. Special books or book excerpts also can be created to fit specific needs. For details, write: SpecialMarkets@penguinrandomhouse.com.

Library of Congress Cataloging-in-Publication Data
Names: Magee, Rhonda V., author.
Title: The inner work of racial justice: healing ourselves and transforming our communities through mindfulness / Rhonda V. Magee.
Description: New York: TarcherPerigee, 2019. | Includes bibliographical references and index.
Identifiers: LCCN 2019010665 | ISBN 9780593083925 (hardcover) | ISBN 9780525504702 (ebook)
Subjects: LCSH: Racism—Psychological aspects. | Mindfulness (Psychology)
Classification: LCC HT1523 .M325 2019 | DDC 305.8—dc23
LC record available at https://lccn.loc.gov/2019010665

Printed in the United States of America
4th Printing

Book design by Lorie Pagnozzi

Some names and identifying characteristics have been changed to protect the privacy of the individuals involved.

IF THE PATH COULD SPEAK

Beneath these words rests the awareness of generations.

And of generations.

And of generations that have come before.

The awareness that each one of us is a vital part of the
earth that we call home,

is of the wind, the rain, the fire.

And so inherently belongs.

If the path could speak, it would say:

"We must assert that which exists deep within us,

namely, a sense of kinship with all those with whom we
share the earth."[1]

On repeat.

In every language.

Unceasingly.

—Rhonda V. Magee

Contents

Foreword

In terms of our DNA, we humans are 99.7 percent the same. This sameness doesn't negate or belie the reality and beauty of our differences. Yet we persist to a large degree in overt and unconscious disregard and "othering," both of which make it extremely hard for us to see our own implicit biases and the toxic effects these can have on others and, ironically, on ourselves as well. Often, it is even harder for us to *want* to see and disentangle ourselves from such automatic and unexamined biases, especially since they are usually supported by laws and social customs favoring some at the expense of others. Such asymmetries have wide-ranging consequences, especially for those individuals who are most at risk and vulnerable to endemic injustices. At the same time, they also erode the short- and long-term health and well-being of all of us, our societies, and our entire species.

If we humans are going to make it on this planet, sooner or later—and hopefully it will be sooner—this form of mindlessness has got to be met with the openhearted clarity, wisdom, and selflessness of mindfulness, an awareness that calls into question, investigates, and ultimately reveals the limitations of narrow identifications with any sense of self as a fixed and enduring entity. With seven billion people on the planet and counting, and the extent of the violence we are capable of with our weapons and our intellects, our well-being as a species is unsustainable unless we wake up and learn to love our differences, celebrating them rather than fearing them, as we come to recognize our commonalities. Obviously, this is a work in progress in our country and around the world, and very much in the forefront of public conversations about what kind of society we want to be and what kind of world we want to inhabit. This book is a major contribution to that conversation.

It wasn't until I was in my seventies that I began to realize—listening to people of color giving voice in recent years to what was obvious to them but opaque to me—that my own life trajectory had benefited in major ways from my skin color, family, and openings not afforded to all, in spite of the rhetoric about us all being created equal and the implicit suggestion that that "equality" carried forward through life as "equal opportunity." Over time, I have come to welcome this hard-to-absorb lesson, and I am grateful for the voices of colleagues and friends who helped me tune my ear and my heart to this level of ignorance and to recognize a tendency to not quite let the enormity of it register fully at a visceral level. Various presentations at conferences over the years, as well as books by brave and empowered voices, revealed levels of outright blindness in myself that cut me off from a sense of commitment—beyond my merely intellectual and thought-based abstractions—to learning from those whose trajectories through life were totally different from my own as a result of legalized and normalized injustice.

Now, with this book, Rhonda Magee offers the world a wise and caring way of recognizing, through the lens of mindfulness, these harmful and imprisoning patterns in ourselves. Mindfulness has the potential to catalyze transformation at the individual, societal, and legal levels when applied to these very issues and to the forces of asymmetric power and misconstrued "self" interest that keep them alive. This book is an invitation to join a conversation that is uncomfortable at times, but ultimately freeing—not only for ourselves, but for the world—because it shows us a viable approach to living together on this planet in ways that minimize harm and maximize well-being for all of us, while we still have the chance. In that regard, this inner work of which Rhonda speaks rests on a profoundly ethical and moral foundation.

The beauty of mindfulness is that through its practice, no matter who we are, simply by being human, we learn to cultivate a gentle intimacy with awareness itself. From an evolutionary perspective, we might say that our innate capacity for awareness is the final common pathway of what makes us human. When we learn through the ongoing cultivation of mindfulness to inhabit the space of awareness itself, we come into creative relationship with the full range of our experiences, even in the face of the unwanted, the toxic, and the painful. In awareness, we have the opportunity to name, investigate, and discern both inner and outer conditions as they actually are rather than as we would like them to be. And out of that awareness, we can learn and grow from our very willingness to bravely place our attention—with gentleness, openness, and kindness— where we usually don't, and to keep it there (or maybe I should say "here") for longer than we might at first feel comfortable doing, and bring it back over and over again when it drifts off or gets overwhelmed.

Indeed, such an intentional cultivation of intimacy with our own awareness and capacity for wakefulness is nothing less than a love affair with life itself. In the end, it can be hugely healing, even in the face of the unwanted and the horrifically painful—and where race is concerned, from a constellation of overt or implicit bias, unconscious microaggressions, and institutionalized injustice. What is more, these biases and other forms of disregard and harm are often invisible to those of us who benefit most from the status quo, only compounding the pain and frustration of those who are experiencing every day the brunt of the disregard, the toxicity, and the harm.

Cultivating mindfulness is not and cannot be merely an individual pursuit. Because we can be so blind to our own mental processes, biases, and racialized identities, we need one another to point out what we can't or won't see, and what we don't even know we don't know. That ignorance is at the root of our own imprisonment and isolation, and at the root of the harm we can so easily cause others, wittingly or unwittingly.

This is one of the fundamental challenges of being human: that we often have no inkling that we don't know what we don't know. We create stories in our minds that separate us from others, and often separate us from our own wholeness as well. We easily assume that we know the other, when we don't. In actuality, we don't even know ourselves. This is where learning how to default to and inhabit the domain of pure aware-ness comes in—an awareness that transcends our highly conditioned patterns of unawareness and therefore our blindnesses. Knowing that we don't know is itself transformative. It invites us to be open, to look, and to see, as best we can, beyond our own attachments and the ways in which we might be benefitting from the status quo.

The practice of mindfulness ultimately involves a willingness to en-gage up close and personal with your moment-by-moment experience, no matter what arises. This attitude itself changes everything. It changes things in ways that might seem tiny but in fact are anything but. Such a process is hugely uncomfortable at times, as you will see from Rhonda's candor about her own experience and her descriptions of various dia-logues about race in her law school classes.

We are faced with the paradox that we have to do our own inner work if we hope to wake up to and embody the fullness of who we really are. No one can do it for us. Yet at the same time, we need one another to function as mirrors to point out where we are most unaware, most blind. Our lenses are often too clouded over with unexamined opinions, inherited prejudices, biases of all kinds (and if you identify as white, then with what some call "white fragility"), and stories about who each of us is as a person—usually a good, well-meaning, kind, and aware person. We need a community of folks to challenge us at times and reveal our most stub-born and opaque blindnesses.

The ultimate responsibility is ours. We can't rely on others to do our own inner exploration for us, or even to repeatedly point out where we go blind. That said, once we start to inquire and investigate along these lines for ourselves, plenty of allies and opportunities are likely to appear to help orient and sustain our efforts to understand and work to disman-tle the constraining realities that perpetuate injustice and suffering.

Instances of human caring and connectedness across differences are everywhere, if we are willing to look. We may find them at work and in our families. They occur everywhere people gather and interact, especially face-to-face. Rhonda's teachings create such environments. Her accounts of her students' experiences with racism and mindfulness provide a lens and a compass for doing the inner work ourselves. Ultimately, it is unawareness of greed, hatred, and delusion in ourselves, as well as in our institutions, that is the root disease, and the source of our dis-ease.

Communities of belonging, deep listening, inquiry into the actuality of things, and attempts at truth-telling can and should draw inspiration from history, from the enduring legacy of those who stood up in the face of injustice, often risking or sacrificing their very lives. Their example invites all of us to wake up to systematic injustice, income inequality, and the immense suffering that flows from them, usually only fleetingly reported or entirely disregarded in the mainstream press and history books. Yet herein lies the transformative power of awakened social movements.

Equally important and transformative, if less dramatic—each of us, in any and every moment, can, if we remember to do so, cultivate insight into deep inequalities and injustices, especially around race and gender. Awareness is capable of holding all of this in a given moment, and seeing things as they are, including the presence of bias or disregard, however gross or however subtle or unintentional. Seeing things as they are is a form of knowing before acting. It is inherently wise. In taking in what is unfolding, we radically accept the entirety of it in the moment, even as we discern the injustice, harm, delusion, oppression, and structural forces that sustain all of it.

However, acceptance does not mean passive resignation. Nor does it mean turning away. Quite the opposite. It invites a turning *toward* these forms of ignorance in ourselves and the violence and suffering that ensue from them. It invites and encourages holding them in awareness with some degree of kindness and compassion, however difficult, and then acting out of a greater wisdom and compassion, including for oneself. In this way, we can *respond* moment by moment, as appropriate, rather than merely reacting. We can work toward naming and righting inequities, institutionalized injustices, and intrinsic biases, because if we do not, then we are de facto complicit by omission.

Indeed, such engagement is what social activism has always been about. In this illuminating, timely, and frankly, intentionally challenging book, Rhonda gently guides us through the sometimes frightening, sometimes painful, but in the end, illuminating and freeing process of bringing awareness to our blind spots and our strongly socially conditioned habits of racializing and degrading others, and in the process, ourselves. To bring such patterns into awareness and to do something about them is indeed the work of both personal and societal liberation. This "inner work" illuminates the very heart of social justice and how it might be approached and nurtured through mindfulness practices in community and through the discernment and new degrees of freedom these practices entrain.

In the end, it is a radical act of love and sanity to cultivate mindfulness in these ways through regular embodied practice. It can also be a courageous political act in support of truly equal justice for all. Rhonda shows us why such work is so necessary and how it can be so profoundly healing for ourselves and for our world.

Jon Kabat-Zinn
May 22, 2019
Northampton, Massachusetts

INTRODUCTION

❦

It's 6 a.m. on a cold morning in San Francisco, and I've been standing on the curb for a few minutes more than I'd like. The Uber I had called to get me to the airport for a short flight to Southern California is late. I've got a day of challenging conversations ahead of me, and I am feeling both exhausted and more than a little nervous. Waiting for the Uber is not putting me at ease.

For days, I have been preparing to present a speech on contemporary barriers to inclusion, and to facilitate a conversation about building community, on a college campus roiled by recent racist incidents. This could turn out to be a fiasco, and there is only one way that I know to complete my preparations for the work ahead.

I take a deep, slow breath in and a long breath out. I feel the ground beneath my feet and begin to regain a sense that the resources I draw on are not merely in my head. They are in my bones; they are who I am. In those few moments, I've come back home. Within minutes, I am in the Uber. As I settle in, I am feeling supported by the knowledge that whatever the day brings, I can drop anchor and tap into this inner ground, this deeper well within, through mindfulness meditation.

People often ask me how I came to the practice of mindfulness—which, at its simplest, is paying attention to life as it unfolds, grounded in the body and breath, and allowing that awareness to settle the mind, increase presence and consciousness of interconnectedness with others. I came to meditation for one reason: I needed deep healing.

I was born in 1967 in the small city of Kinston, North Carolina—an increasingly segregated town thirty miles and a wide cultural gulf from the coast, where tobacco farming, furniture making, and a quiet strain of white supremacy had long framed the way of life. The main road through the black part of town has since been renamed Martin Luther King Boulevard, but those seeking to use this street to leave the city were met, at least for a period of time, with an almost literal dead end. In an effort to keep tourists from venturing into the neighborhood deemed least camera-ready, the city had simply decided to wall it off. And even when the physical barriers were eventually removed, other barriers to residents moving on to greater opportunities remained very much in place.

My childhood home still sits in the heart of Kinston, on the other side of the wall that once existed. It is part of a racially segregated subsidized housing community called Simon Bright. To me, it had been an apartment, but to others, it was "the Projects." My mother had made our home pretty as best she could—with white vinyl pillows, a black vinyl couch and chair, and a carpet woven in red and black. After the little rental on Desmond Street where we lived before the divorce, this was home.

Despite being born into a family traumatized by many things—including the legacies and ongoing dynamics of racial and economic subordination, my father's military service during the Vietnam War, and his subsequent alcoholism and tendency toward domestic violence—I knew from a very young age that there was something more to life. Even as my family struggled to get enough food to eat each week and put up with the tacit assumptions of others that we would always be members of a servant class, I knew that this was not who we were. And even when my mother's second marriage left me vulnerable to my stepfather's repeated molestations and abuse, I held on to the belief that I would one day be free.

Indeed, as I grew into adulthood, I somehow knew my worth was not measured by the gaze of white people, or those who had internalized prejudices against people like me. And I knew that, despite the history that met me at every turn, life was meant to be lived joyfully. Seeing the realities of my family's situation fully might have been cause for bitterness, but for me, it was not. I saw how my grandmother's religious commitments steeped her in a larger, more hopeful view of herself and of the world, even as her life options were mostly limited to the sort of labor—tobacco picking, housekeeping—that would have been hers in a slave society. I saw how my mother, despite the many disappointments and abuses she had experienced across a lifetime of similarly restricted options for livelihood—shirt factory worker, nurse's aide—tended to lead with optimism and to give people the benefit of the doubt. And I loved the black experiences into which I had been born and all that they had given to the world—especially the many models of people struggling against injustice for ourselves and for beloved communities everywhere, all the while maintaining loving, praising hearts.

These things, together with the unexpected gift of mindfulness meditation teachings and practices originally from Asia, have helped me to tame and clarify my own often-troubled mind. And notably, they have also opened me to the possibility that we can transform the world.

My meditation practice began in fits and starts supported mostly by books, without producing any signs of great promise at first. I would sit down in my apartment alone, close my eyes, take a few deep breaths, and try to keep my attention on the flow of my breath, in and out. Immediately, my mind would wander or I'd feel bored. Sometimes, I would feel a bit defeated and stop trying for a while. I would remind myself that each instance of "failure"—each moment in which I realized my mind had wandered and intentionally tried to bring it back—was a moment of the very mindfulness that I'd been seeking. And so I'd begin again. And again I would find it hard to do! Indeed, in those early days, I would often find myself just sitting there for a few minutes, mostly lost in my usual repetitive and unhelpful thoughts.

Even though I definitely was not a natural at it, I usually did feel a bit clearer after trying to practice mindfulness. So I kept trying—not every day at first, but often enough that I began to see some differences in my overall outlook and in how I handled life's challenges. Still, the fact is that I had mixed feelings about committing to a regular practice. None of the people who seemed confident that meditation could help make me saner looked like me or came from a background like mine. After many years of struggling to develop a practice on my own, I was invited to join a group of lawyers who regularly met and meditated under the guidance of Norman Fischer, a former presiding monk at the San Francisco Zen Center. This helped settle me into a regular practice and an appreciation for a community of support for doing so.

By this point, I had quit my job practicing insurance law at a corporate law firm in order to teach law, a move that I had long dreamed of making. I taught Torts (personal injury law), as well as courses on race in American legal history, and contemporary issues in race and law. My work required me to keep turning again and again toward suffering around racism—what we call, somewhat antiseptically, "discrimination." Many evenings, I went home feeling sad and dissatisfied. As my years in the classroom stacked one upon the other, I found myself tilting toward depression. I was also frustrated by the extent to which my students seemed to suffer as they studied in traditional ways—reading, researching, arguing, writing, and delivering formal presentations about some of the most difficult issues of our time. I knew that the work was worthwhile. But it sure seemed to be hard on all of us.

During my darkest hours, I thought of those in my family who had not had my chances for success. I thought of my Grandma Nan—whom we called GranNan—and the way that she had centered her life in spiritual practice and a deep sense of purpose—the very thing I most wanted for myself and, if possible, for my students. Yet since I had never encountered a professor who explicitly strove to blend inner work—mindfulness, awareness, and compassion practices—with the subject matter that he or she taught, I felt somewhat despondent.

By grace, I found a good therapist. She said something that would change my life's course forever: "You can always leave your job as a tenured professor at a university in a city that many people would kill to live in. That option is there for you at any time. But what if, before doing that, you really explored how you might bring all of yourself, including your commitment to inner work and deepening awareness, into your work in law?"

And so, with the support of my meditating lawyers group, I began to do just that. Eventually, I met Jon Kabat-Zinn and learned more about his Mindfulness-Based Stress Reduction course. Hearing in him a language that I knew would work in law, I deepened my commitment to bringing mindfulness more fully into every aspect of my life. I saw that if I was going to continue to walk the path I'd begun—building bridges between communities traditionally seen as different—I would have to find a way to deal with regular indignities without going crazy or suffering further damage to myself and others. We were all suffering, after all. Even those who acted out the most extreme forms of violence, I sensed, had themselves suffered in some way. How could this not be so if they could so easily harm others? And so I deepened my commitment to sticking with myself and with others through the challenges of being vulnerable and opening my heart.

It had taken years for me to settle into a set of daily mindfulness practices, an array of supports that suited my needs. But as I practiced, again and again, I found a measure of peace. My heartbeat slowed, and my nervous system calmed me, breath after breath, as I developed the capacity to hold suffering more effectively. Meditation became a steadfast support for the everyday work of wading into the often murky and treacherous waters of having conversations about race with people I did not know well, and the sometimes murkier waters arising in such conversations with people I knew like family.

I came to see how these practices were crucial to the work of creating spaces in which people from a wide variety of backgrounds could sit together and talk about histories that we often do not discuss. For one, the practices help in the delicate work of tending to wounds that have not yet healed. In my classes, we would sit in reflection on the pain caused by racism, by one group after another against one group after another. Over time, we could see how fear, greed, miseducation, and the desire to be seen and appreciated were important drivers of all of this pain. We could see this and not become embittered, and we were not repeating the pattern. With the support of the practices, we were becoming whole.

It became clear to me that we could do a better job of working through race issues with the support of awareness and compassion practices. In all of this, something my GranNan used to tell me reverberated in my mind and felt more poignantly true each time I sat with others in their pain and vulnerability, listening with compassion: we are all one family who have forgotten who we are.

Through personal mindfulness practices, we can begin to ground, heal, and ultimately transform our sense of self, no longer clinging too tightly to a narrow and isolated sense of "I," "me," "my wounds," and the collective pain-stories of "my people." We can begin to be able to infuse our experience of ourselves in culture, community, and context with a sense of the valid, often painful experiences of others. And as we take in more of the whole, we grow.

The practices in this book can help us to process the pain and confusion that arise when we push ourselves or are pushed by others outside of our racial-identity comfort zones. These practices build the resilience we need to stay in the conversations and to deepen community when the going gets tough. In this book, I tell stories about people from a range of backgrounds who have used these practices to think differently about race and racism, and to work for "justice," a word that I define here as "love in action for the alleviation of suffering." Justice begins with our awareness of the present moment, extends through caring for ourselves, and shows up in the love we bring to our interactions with others and our responses to the social challenges of our time.

This book is composed of five parts. In "Part One: Grounding," we examine how race and racism shape our life chances, relationships, and points of view. We also explore the core mindfulness practices that ground us in awareness, insight, and resilience. "Part Two: Seeing" spotlights in more vivid detail how contemporary racism lives in us, in our relationships, and in our communities. We expand our awareness of racism by considering its personal, interpersonal, and systemic dimensions, and we practice deepening awareness through mindfulness. In "Part Three: Being," we allow ourselves to be with the difficult thoughts, emotions, and sensations that arise when we become more aware of racism. Through the practices of mindfulness and compassion, we soften the sense of a separate self and create the capacity for healing. Eventually we notice and begin practicing being with the ease and even the joy that arise as we re-create integrated communities together. In "Part Four: Doing," we consider what it takes to deepen racial justice work. This requires not only engaging in mindfulness practice, but also studying our histories and exploring concepts like "white fragility," while working with our communities to engage in transformative social change. Because conflicts will inevitably arise, we also examine skills for sustaining racial justice work and developing resilient relationships and organizations. Finally, in "Part Five: Liberating," we examine the fruits of our mindfulness practice as we experience social change and transformed lives.

Because there are so many rivers of pain joining and forming the ocean of racial suffering in our times, personal awareness practices are essential for racial justice work. In order for real change to occur, we must be able to examine our own experiences, discover the "situated" nature of our perspectives, and understand the ways in which race and racism are mere cultural constructions. It may be helpful for you to read this book alongside others so you can share different points of view and support one another in the meditation practices. As you'll see from my story and those of others you'll meet here, healing takes place in community. By experiencing new ways of looking at race, we can grow in our capacity to be with one another in ways that promote healing and make real our common humanity and radical interconnectedness. And this will set us on the path toward acting with others for justice—in solidarity with those suffering the most—with humility, kindness, and the capacity to keep growing and rowing on.

I hope that in this book, you will find support for living with your eyes wide open to the role of race in your life and in the lives of others. I hope that you will find guidance for working toward justice for all, through grounded, public-facing, radical compassion—the kind that touches everyone and all things, leaving no one and nothing out. May we form a vast ocean of healing to meet the suffering, one that refuses no river and renews us all. When things get hard along the way—as they will—may the practices, stories, and insights in this book be a reliable and lifelong source of support.

PART ONE

Grounding

Deep mindfulness arises from a view of our radical interconnectedness, that which links us each and all in our particular pain and possibility to earth, fire, wind, water, and space.

Be like the ocean

that refuses no river.

—BABA MANDAZA KANDEMWA

CHAPTER ONE

PAUSING AND RECKONING

I have a dream that my four little children will one day live in a nation where they will not be judged by the color of their skin but by the content of their character.

—REVEREND DR. MARTIN LUTHER KING, JR.[1]

But race is the child of racism, not the father.

—TA-NEHISI COATES[2]

The Weight of Our Racial Experience

In June 1984—twenty-one years after Dr. King bellowed the above words across the National Mall in Washington, D.C., and dropped his hope-drenched dream into our collective consciousness—I was perhaps *the* most hopeful sixteen-year-old girl in all of Hampton, Virginia.

Because despite a childhood that had often been a painful one, I had reached that moment when the dreams that had gotten me through it were actually starting to come true.

College—my passport to freedom—was just around the corner. And for the very first time, I was in love. His name was Jake. Yes, at that moment, there was more right than wrong in my world.

Which is why what Jake told me just days before I was to leave Hampton for a summer university course hit me so hard.

"My dad just kicked me out of the house," Jake told me over the phone.

"He did *what*? *Why?!*" I said this, knowing what would come next.

"You know *why.* . . . I told you how he is. It's because of *us.* He said no son of his is going be dating some *black* girl. . . ."

Oh, did I fail to mention that Jake and I had been raised in a world in which he was considered "white," and I, "black"?

(Micro reflection: Had you already made assumptions about Jake's race? Was the question forming in your mind? Either way, congratulate yourself: you've just brought awareness to some of the ways that your brain "does race"—i.e., the way that you make race-based assumptions and fill in the blanks as you go when reading stories, names, résumés, and so on).[3]

Jake had used the word *black* when he might have used some other. I knew that his father's way was something he was actively resisting. We were on the same side in this, and that meant everything.

But even with Jake's support, I still remember the pain that gripped me that afternoon, on hearing that my *race*—this category created by others that did not and could not capture much of who I really was—had made me unacceptable to my true love's family.

My race had made me the Other.

I had known that this might happen when we started dating, of course. But that did not make it any less devastating.

And I remember learning something more—that my being "a black girl" had not only made me unacceptable to Jake's working-class Virginia family, but had made me so unacceptable that they were willing to throw their own, reportedly beloved son out of their home and onto the streets like garbage.

It hit me hard that this notion that they had about me—or more accurately, about people supposedly *like* me, as they had never actually met *me*—had made me so unacceptable that they were willing to hurt their own son, and thereby themselves, and all to teach him, me, and anyone around us a multifaceted lesson.

It was a lesson about what must never come of his having been the first generation in his family to attend a racially integrated school in the South: as a white man, Jake must not come to see black people as equally deserving of dignity, inclusion, and love.

It was a lesson about who *they*—Jake's parents—took themselves to be: people profoundly and pervasively "white" in the American South in the twentieth century. They may not have had college educations, or achieved greatness in the eyes of the world beyond their hometown. But what they had *inherited*—the cultural, sometimes economic, and psychic value of *whiteness*—meant something and was in a way defined by their willingness to reject me, to reject this thing called *blackness*. Whiteness was more valuable than the safety of their own flesh and blood.

Despite my being an A student, a model leader who would soon be named Teenager of the Year in our town, I was not good enough to be associated with them. This hurt me badly. Yet I was clearly not the only one suffering. To this day, I cannot imagine how Jake must have felt to learn the limits of his father's love. The pain we both experienced in those moments has faded over the many years. But for me, its clarifying lessons remain. What happened to me and Jake taught me a lot about racism.

Racism is a complex of behavior and explanatory stories that enable some human beings to assert power over other human beings. Though it can seem natural or simply biological, it is not. Racism depends on the social construction of what sociologists have come to refer to as "racialized" bodies, which is to say, the idea and practice of people being assigned racial labels that, as we have been trained to understand, sit in a relative hierarchy of worth in relationship to other racial labels. We often refer to people as white, black, or some other race, without thinking twice about it, as if race is a part of the natural order of things. But race is a matter of *social imagination and construction,* of *perceptions* shaped by a given context. Someone who might be considered "too white" in the Caribbean might be considered unequivocally "black" in the United States. Throughout this book, I will use the same shorthand (black, white,

Asian, Latino, and so on), but what I really mean is how a person has been racialized in the place and time in which he/she exists. Racism operates in obvious and nonobvious ways that render the target of the behavior vulnerable, by degrees, to disrespect, disadvantage, harm, or even death. Racism, in my view, is not limited to individual bad actions based on intent to harm others, nor is it limited to those individuals who consciously endorse beliefs about the inferiority of others (although such actions and beliefs would certainly fall under the definition I use here). Racism encompasses both explicit and implicit beliefs and acts that justify the assertion of power—individually, collectively, or systemically—against racially maligned people and their white allies, so as to minimize their freedom, access to resources, and sense of value in the world.

So how does the definition of racism provided above apply to the conduct of Jake's father? The behavior was the act of throwing Jake out of the house. The explanatory story was this: because no son of his was going to be dating some black girl. The power was that possessed by Jake's father—a white man who had complete control over Jake's access to safe lodging, and denied Jake that access and safety as a punishment. And because this left both Jake and me vulnerable to heartbreak and physical distress, Jake's father had asserted his power over both of us. Thus, Jake's father's reaction was an act of racism.

In witnessing and reflecting on the actions of Jake's father, I learned a hard but important lesson about race and racism in America: despite all of our own triumphant experiences in finally desegregating Virginia's public schools in the late 1970s and early '80s, white supremacy—the dominant culture's deep-seated belief that white is above black in the hierarchy of all things—had not gone away.

We had not sung it away in the "integrated" basement of the Bethel Free Will Baptist Church, whose buses entered our neighborhood every summer Sunday morning, picked up brown-skinned kids by twos and threes, and hauled us across town to a pristine sanctuary where we sat alongside white kids and sang, as loudly as we could, *"Jesus loves the little* children, all the children of the world. Red and yellow, black and white, they are precious in his sight, Jesus loves the little children of the world!"—before being bused right back across town to our very separate and unequal homes.

No, white supremacy and racism were alive and well in hearts and minds, behind neatly trimmed yards and around the cul-de-sacs of city and suburb alike. They had not gone away, as we were given to believe, simply because the adults around us—especially the white adults, the ones in charge at our "integrated" schools—had stopped talking about them in public. And they had not gone away simply because we had been taught, under a twisted interpretation of Dr. King's inspiring words, to be "color-blind"—i.e., never to acknowledge, discuss, or respond to racism's continued existence and vitality, and instead, to pretend that none of us even "see" race.

What I learned was that the centuries-long war to end the policies and practices of white supremacy, to encourage a realignment of our allegiances in favor of *common ground* rather than our racialized identities and so-called affinity groups, had not ended. The battle over the degree to which black people and other nonwhites should be included in, or excluded from, the so-called American body politic had not been won by the civil rights movement after all.

As I came to see, we had only settled into an uneasy truce.

All it would take to inspire a new skirmish in this war would be what my romance with Jake represented: evidence that two people who had been racialized differently had, in fact, judged each other by character and not color, and for a moment, at least, found one another worthy of love.

And, as I would learn much later, all it would take to rekindle the full-out war would be the unexpected rise, through this quietly smoldering landscape, of the walking embodiment of the threat to white supremacy posed by the gains of the civil rights movement: a president of mixed racial and cultural heritage named Barack Hussein Obama.

In 2019, there are people who are surprised to see evidence of this ongoing war of inclusion/exclusion. They are shocked by its especially antiblack character and its virulently anti-immigrant themes. They are incredulous that the legal, political, and cultural changes that have taken place since the mid-twentieth century to shift the United States toward inclusive democracy have also engendered deep resentment among those racialized white.

But I am not surprised. I lived through the clarifying summer of 1984, and have been awake to the slippery yet ever-present nature of racism ever since. I have seen how readily it can be put into service to deem certain people unlovable, to raise questions about our common humanity, and even to cut ties with one's own kith and kin.

What I learned that summer inspired in me a desire truly to understand race and racism in our everyday lives and to see them for what they are: deep and pervasive cultural conditioning for grouping others into categories and placing them at enough distance to render their suffering less visible, for obscuring our intertwined destinies, and for turning us *against* one another rather than *toward* one another when we suffer *in common*.

In short, what I learned that summer inspired my life's work: dissolving the lies that racism whispers about who we really are, and doing whatever I can to reduce the terrible harm it causes us all.

Practicing "The Pause"

You have just read a reflection on an experience of race in American life, an example of what I call a "Race Story."

For just a moment now, let us stop.

Take a moment to check in with yourself. What was it like for you to read these words? What thoughts are coming up for you? What do you feel in your body now? What emotions do you feel as you consider what you just read? And again: Where in your body are you feeling these emotions, sensing the thoughts, questions, and other reactions you're noticing now?

Throughout this book, you will be asked to stop and reflect like this. This is an embodied practice that I call "The Pause."

The Pause is an aspect of the *practice* of mindfulness meditation that can lead you to the *experience* of body-based mindfulness. What is mindfulness? It is simply paying attention, on purpose, with the attitude of friendly, open, nonjudgmental curiosity, and a willingness to accept (at least for now!) what arises.

Over the course of this book, you will be exploring and deepening the practice of mindfulness, which can be hugely important for understanding our experiences around race and identity. Mindfulness is essential to developing the capacity to *respond*, rather than simply *react* as if on autopilot, to what we experience.

To practice The Pause, you simply stop what you are doing and intentionally bring your awareness to the experience of the present moment. This is the first step in engaging in mindfulness practice.

Pausing and intentionally directing attention to particular focal points in your experience help you more routinely to focus your attention at will, clarify the mind, de-stress, and minimize any trauma-based reactions in the body.

Just for a minute, turn your attention to the sensations of breathing in and out and rest here. As you do so, notice: What thoughts are in your mind right now? See if you can release those thoughts. Practice letting them be for the moment, just as they are. It may help to imagine them as leaves falling gently from a tree, or as clouds crossing a blue sky. It may help to think of the out-breath—here and throughout the practices described in this book—as a micro practice of letting go, of coming home to the resources of peace within you.

As you bring your attention back to the sensations of breathing, what do you notice? Settle into the experience of breathing and sitting, noticing your feet on the floor, your buttocks in the chair. Feel the support that exists for you in the body and the breath at this very moment.

Now allow yourself to explore any emotions or other bodily sensations arising—the sense of "I like this," or "I *don't* like this." Open up to what your body is telling you in this moment. Try not to judge your feelings and sensations. Be as specific as you can about what you notice. Most important: as much as possible, be kind to yourself.

Later, we will look at research suggesting the value of such mindful reflection—particularly as a means of developing the embodied emotional intelligence, self-regulation, and overall resilience required to work through the challenges of examining racism in our lives. But for now, see if you can just allow yourself to get to know what is arising in you in this very moment. As you bring this Pause to a close, sense the ground beneath you as you breathe in and out. Settle into the support of *this* breath, this connection with the earth, this deepening grounding in awareness.

Finally, if you can, take a few minutes to write about what has come up for you during your Pause. This is especially important if you experienced strong emotions, or if some of your own memories or Race Stories emerged from their buried places. In my own experience, and as research has shown, even short periods of writing about emotionally difficult events in our past can assist us in deep healing.[4]

As you continue reading, engage in the loving awareness practice of The Pause whenever you need additional support.

CHAPTER TWO

SITTING WITH COMPASSIONATE RACIAL AWARENESS

Biologically speaking, we are programmed toward being tribal as a
means of survival. We literally have to transcend an aspect
of our own biology.

—REVEREND ANGEL KYODO WILLIAMS[1]

Population geneticists agree that all of us are literally one human family.
What would our world be like if everyone acted on this truth?

—SHARON SALZBERG[2]

Mindfulness of the Racialized Self

What we call the self is shaped by the cultures in which we live. And because race is a cultural feature of societies built on racism, notions of self
include notions of race. The racialized self is produced by and helps re-
produce racism in our cultures. Mindfulness helps us understand and
expand our notions of self. And yet, talking about race and racism and
examining these through the lens of mindfulness is uncommon. This is
not to say that it is not being done at all. But many practitioners of mindfulness have been taught, whether explicitly or implicitly, that looking at
racism and exploring efforts to address it—or to otherwise engage in talk

of "justice" or "politics"—go against the core commitments of mindfulness. This may be a consequence of two factors.

The first has to do with the social locations of those who have brought mindfulness into the mainstream. Many of the teachers from Asia, to whom we owe most Western mindfulness practices, lived in cultures where *racial* difference has not been the dominant mode of oppression. And on top of that, most of the Western teachers of mindfulness are white in white-dominated cultures. As a result, they have had to work harder to see their own race and racism in the world, and to break the cultural norms against doing so.

The second has to do with the fact that Western notions of social justice are not reflected in contemplative traditions, at least not in the same manner or to the same degree.

Contemplating Racial Justice

So let's pause together and reflect: What is racial justice?

The heart of what I mean by racial justice is guided, first, by Dr. King's notion of justice—"power correcting everything which stands against love." Racial justice, then, is about taking actions against racism and in favor of liberation, inspired by love of all humanity, including actions at the personal, interpersonal, and collective levels.

Why might it be appropriate to consider engaging in racial justice as an aspect of living mindfully?

The short and simple answer is that racial justice, like compassion, is just one form of an ethically grounded, mindful response to suffering in our lives. Moreover, mindful racial justice seeks to alleviate not merely isolated incidents of racial suffering, but *all* suffering caused by racism—including suffering that is very hard to see. This necessarily presents a profound invitation to a lifelong practice of awakening that seeks greater liberation and justice for us all. Racial justice cannot exist apart from the effort to alleviate the socially constructed, unevenly distributed suffering of all marginalized people, or what I would call "social justice." And social justice cannot exist apart from racial justice.

Grounding in Racial Justice

We live in a world especially polarized by race and racism. Experts in peacemaking have noted that we must find ways to talk with one another across these lines of constructed differences, if we are to have any hope of resolving and dissolving those differences. And we must keep talking about these issues.

But just *talking* about race, even among people we know and love, seems so dicey and so fraught with potential for conflict and confusion that we need support.

We need support in the cultivation of the ability to sit compassionately with and talk about our own particular experiences with race, race-related injury, and alienation. We need help developing the capacity to be able to listen to the very different stories of others with compassion; to have conversations across lines of real and perceived difference that help and heal, rather than hamper and hurt; and to exercise the will to come back for more, with increasing capacity for empathy and a deepening desire for others to heal and thrive in the world.

This book is here to help you do just that.

The Differing Roles and Faces of Race

While we all need support in doing the work of racial justice, the specifics of that work will differ for each of us. The very nature of race—a concept, an idea created to implement and justify the hierarchy resulting from white supremacy—is that its impact can differ dramatically from one person's life to the next.

Some of us have to deal with race on a daily basis, because our bodies stand out alongside the more apparently similar bodies of others and we thus are repeatedly reminded—through the actions, words, and assumptions of others—exactly how we have been racialized in the minds of others. Some of us have experienced racism in deeply personal ways, to the point that race and racism feel like constant, haunting presences in every moment of our lives. Some of us have experienced subtle or overt institutional racism, such as bias in the systems of education, housing, health care, or employment in our communities, and know it has affected our life chances.

For others, race and racism impact life significantly, but under a completely different banner. The people who have become known as Puerto Rican, for example, have been given what amounts to second-class U.S. citizenship—without statehood, the right to full representation, or even the right to proper disaster relief from the U.S. government when a catastrophe such as a hurricane strikes. The people of Hawaii had to struggle mightily for the right to statehood, due to concerns on the mainland about the "racial diversity" of the islands. The people of Guam, American Samoa, the U.S. Virgin Islands—all of them, too, can attest to a long list of indignities suffered at the hands of the U.S. government.

The force animating these mistreatments, of course, is the same one that lies behind race and racism: white supremacy and related ideas of European cultural supremacy. It is no accident that all of the people mentioned have—or are perceived as having—darker skin tones relative to whites. It is also not surprising that there is no similarly degraded U.S. island, territory, or former colony where the inhabitants are people who have been racialized as white. Yet, those who hail from these places may describe their struggle as one against the ongoing legacies of colonialism, including cultural oppression and resource appropriation; they may not typically use the language of race and racism at all. Nevertheless, for present purposes, we recognize the unity of these issues under the umbrella of the term *racism*.

Still others, for different reasons, have not thought much about race as a factor in our own lives at all. This has often been true of white people owing to their status among the majority of the racialized groups in the West. Yet the recent rise in visibility of the contemporary white nationalist movement has perhaps brought issues of race to the fore for people racialized as white, engendering a range of different responses. Some have rejected that movement outright and are looking for ways to forge alliances with people of color. Others may wonder whether their suffering in a time of rising diversity is actually some new form of racism against which they should be mobilizing, even perhaps through acts of violence. Still others are experiencing loneliness, feeling that there is nobody with whom to discuss these issues other than those who might try to encourage their fears and capacity for bias.

And there are those, typically racialized as Asian, who have been drawn to or have identified with the "model minority" myth, the idea that some racial or cultural groups are inherently superior to others. These individuals may find themselves a part of a larger narrative that seeks to blame those who fail to succeed, and tries to dismiss racism as a false justification for failure. Those who subscribe to such views may not be convinced otherwise by this book, but it is written with the hope of opening up your mind, too.

Still others of us find ourselves on the margins when we hear the word *race,* because the conversations tend to be centered on the experience of specific racialized groups—black, white, Asian, Latinx—and we do not fit neatly into any one of them. And people for whom the term *multiracial* resonates may have a unique set of questions, challenges, and anxieties around the issues of race and racism.

For a variety of reasons, some of us would prefer not to think about race too much at all. We have been taught, as Supreme Court Justice John Roberts suggested, that "the way to get beyond race is to get beyond race"[3]—the mantra of color blindness. And given that we are for the most part poorly trained to discuss what feels like a difficult, weighty, and risky subject, it seems easier just to ignore the issue and try to "move past" it. But for all of us, our racialized identities shape much more than we realize. They influence who we end up gravitating toward or away from in our social lives, and the resources, experiences, and opportunities by which our lives are shaped.

Your experiences around race may place you squarely into one or more of the groups described above, or you may find that you occupy a very different place on the spectrum. Whatever your experience may be, this book, and the awareness-raising work it calls forth for us all—is for you.

ColorInsight

As explained above and as we all as know, our experiences of race and racism differ radically from person to person. In order to assist my students and others in seeing these aspects of our lives more fully, I have developed an approach that combines mindfulness and compassion practices with engagement with individuals from diverse groups. I call this approach, and the set of skills that support it, "ColorInsight." I believe that it can serve to lessen and perhaps even release the grip of race and racism on our sense of ourselves and one another.

The work of developing ColorInsight is multidimensional. First, we ground our efforts in the desire, the will, and the courage to turn toward, rather than away from, race and racism to examine its role in all our lives. Second, we work to develop a deeper and more nuanced capacity to perceive and to understand how race and racism operate in our own lives and in those of others. Third, we deepen our ability to be with others as they reflect on these aspects of their experiences—to listen without judgment and with compassion, and to work together with them toward mutually healing personal and interpersonal transformation. And finally, we commit to looking for ways to act in favor of liberation that touches on the collective and the systemic, thereby opening the door for transformation that benefits us all.

Mindfulness is essential to developing ColorInsight. Over the course of more than twenty years as a law professor practicing mindfulness and ten years teaching mindfulness to others as a support for understanding race, racism, and justice, I have found that incorporating mindfulness into hearing others' painful Race Stories—like my story of heartbreak in chapter one—has multiple positive effects. For one, it often starts the process of healing for the speaker. Equally important, however, it serves to soften and encourage the listener to respond by sharing his or her own stories, a process that ultimately leads to healing in the broader community. And once each of us has gotten our own healing under way, it can strengthen the inner justice advocate in us as well.

To read the following Race Story mindfully, Pause and take a cleansing breath. Release the thoughts and questions gathering in your mind for the present moment, imagining them, if you will, falling onto the ground below. Reminding yourself of your intentions, practice remaining lovingly in touch with your own embodied experience by noting reactive thoughts, emotions, and sensations in your body and responding to what arises with extreme self-care.

A "Race Class"

This is Seth's story.

Seth joined one of my Race and Law classes with a level of enthusiasm that surprised me.

Looking at him, most would identify him as white.

But in his own mind, his background was different. He shared with me that he was part Jewish and part Cuban. He had grown up in a neighborhood in Oakland, California, filled with people from a wide range of backgrounds, including a large percentage of black people. He identified with the views of those he had grown up with, but he didn't look like them. He therefore struggled to fit in.

I liked Seth immediately, because he was earnest and willing to be vulnerable about the things he needed to better understand. He met with me early on in the course, and shared with me his deep desire to learn how racism made people of color more vulnerable to oppression and harm and how best to respond. He cared about doing his part to help make things right.

While I appreciated his concern, I could see that he might gain even more from a closer look at *his own experience* of race. If he could explore and recognize the role of race in his own life, he might be able to develop insights about race that others might find more compelling.

"What about coming at it from your own lived experience?" I asked.

"My *what*?" He was surprised and skeptical.

"Your own experience. What has your own life experience taught you about how race matters?"

"Well, that's just it," he said. "I don't know. I am not sure what race I am." He shared that while people would most often think of him as white, his background left him feeling otherwise.

"And what does 'looking white' mean? How does it impact your interactions in the world? What does it mean to you, really, to be racialized white? How might it benefit you and the world if you understood this better?"

"I don't know," Seth said. He sat in silence for a moment. "But I like that you're asking me this. No one ever has. I'm excited to be thinking about this."

Seth and I spent many a Friday afternoon that semester pondering questions like this. By the end of the course, he told me something that moved me to deepen my commitment to this work. He said that while he had learned a lot about race and law, he had learned even more about himself.

"A class like this should be required for law students!" he said. "And really, it should be available to everyone."

Creating Space for Racial Justice Work

For those who are new to this work, we may have to create space for learning about something that we thought we already knew. It may take a while to get comfortable thinking and talking about race in new ways, to feel a sense of what multicultural educator Robin DiAngelo calls "racial literacy."[4]

Racial literacy requires emotional awareness. If you are like most people, you will feel strong emotions in reaction to what others share about race—and you will also feel emotional when you reflect deeply on your own experiences. Sometimes there will be tears. You should give yourself permission to feel your feelings, and to know what you know in your body. You may sense sharp judgments or the fuzziness of feeling "some kind of way," or you may feel exhausted or even bored. And you will sometimes feel elated, as you connect with others and their experiences in more meaningful ways. These and other emotion-laden reactions are important to notice. If you are not comfortable speaking about emotions, a big part of the work of ColorInsight will be about becoming more emotionally intelligent—that is, emotionally aware, articulate, and capable of acting in alignment with the insight that arises from all of this.

Painful, perhaps even previously suppressed, memories may come rushing into your mind, including reactions tied to unhealed wounds as they rise to the surface. And as a black woman, I realize that this work is often particularly painful for me and other people who have suffered from racism and identity-based bias. "Nonwhite" people may feel uneasy or even angry when engaging in this work, for many reasons. It may be because we are openly acknowledging—perhaps for the first time—that the pain of racism falls disproportionately on us, or it may be due to the common experience of having to deal with these issues in ways that seem designed to serve the interests of culturally dominant whites instead of ourselves. And all of us may feel the frustration or anxiety that comes with the thought that nothing will ever really change. Whatever their source and shape, the "bad" feelings that often come with addressing these issues may make it hard to embrace the mindfulness practices, to enter into conversations about race and racism, and to stay engaged.

Because we are mostly trained to turn away from looking at race (especially in the company of differently racialized people), uncomfortable feelings are quite normal as we seek to learn more about one another's experiences and prepare to do the work of racial justice together. Yet we need to be able to sit with these feelings and experience that discomfort in order to learn and to grow together. So a big part of racial justice work is about becoming more comfortable with being uncomfortable. Especially within cultures and institutions where a premium is placed on "being nice" or "getting along"—which is certainly true of most Western cultures—simply shifting the expectation to one in which we can stay in our discomfort long enough to deepen insight, but without getting stuck there, is an important part of the process of healing and transformation.

It is also very common to encounter a variety of *reactions to the reactions*—for example, clinging even more tightly to old ways of thinking and being. Denial and avoidance are not effective ways to deal with racism in the long term, but they often seem tremendously appealing in the short run. Resisting uncomfortable feelings and reactions and remaining addicted to unskillful responses are easy to do, but they are precisely what keep us from dealing with racial issues when they arise around us.

As we set out to look deeply into racism with mindfulness, we need to maintain a commitment to meet whatever arises—including our own and others' emotions—with an uncommon level of kindness and love, and with a genuine wish for healing. We need to develop and embody radical compassion and the will to be a space within which racial truth can be spoken and heard.

A Pause for Human Kindness

Having explored the value of a self-reflective pause in deepening our capacity for racial awareness and justice work, take a moment now to explore a micro practice I call the Pause for Compassion.

We begin, again, by noticing a moment of racial discomfort. We pause. We take a deep and grounding breath. What are the sensations in the body that make this discomfort known to you now? Consider placing one or both hands on the area where you feel discomfort.

Inwardly recite these phrases: "This is a moment of racial discomfort. Such moments are common in a world shaped by racism. I deserve kindness in this moment. And I offer kindness to others impacted by this moment as well."

Now bring kindness to an often underappreciated part of your body. Take a look at your hands, the palms, the outer skin. Notice any reactions you have to the color of your skin. Then, think of all the ways you have put your hands to work, the ways they have supported others, enabled you to feel connected to others along the way. As you breathe in and out, appreciate this part of your body as an immeasurable gift. And offer it love and appreciation. Extend the sense of appreciation from your hands to your arms, chest, heart, neck, head, and back down through your midsection to feel the ground. Breathe in and out with a sense of appreciation, of love for the gift of the body—the earth that walks, the physical manifestation of your unique journey through time, space, and cultures untold—for getting you to this place.

CHAPTER THREE

HONORING AND REMEMBERING

We take our stand on the solidarity, the oneness of life, and the unnaturalness and injustice of all special favoritisms, whether of sex, race, country or condition.

—ANNA JULIA COOPER[1]

Honoring Our Roots

The awareness that we explore here, the capacity for being more present to the relationships in our lives, is basic to human experience. Whatever our background, as humans, we share the ability to be more engaged, and to wake up more fully to the moments of our lives.

Many of the original teachings that form the basis of mindfulness meditation and related practices come to us from the recorded history of the Buddha, who was reportedly born into a life of great privilege. Upon learning that all humans suffer, however, the Buddha embarked on a quest to find the end of suffering. He explored the workings of his own mind and embodied experience, through meditation and other practices. He came to many profound understandings, including the biases of his time as reflected in the caste system and in the treatment of women. And he rejected the notions, deeply ingrained in his culture, that noble birth determined one's character, and that only men were suited for monastic life. The Buddha also taught that the body is inherently impermanent and unworthy of undue cherishing or conceit.

We owe much of what we presently know about mindfulness practices to a diverse set of Asian heritages that kept the Buddha's teachings and practices alive and spread them throughout the world. These practices are not religious; they do not require any belief system at all. Rather, they help us know our own minds and develop capacities for self-healing and embodied insight.

To do this, we will need more than a passing participation in looking at ourselves and our communities. We need deep commitments to working with others to minimize everyday oppression, whether it be through over-policing and the excessive use of force, immigration policies that separate children from their parents, or some other form of harm. We need the will to repair the many separations that characterize the sense we have of ourselves as individuals apart from one another, and distinct from the air we breathe and the earth to which we will all one day return. For this work, then, we will each need strong foundations.

Foundations for Racial Justice Work

Through mindfulness and deep compassion, any one of us, whatever our heritage, may become clearer about our relationship to racism and how we relate to others in ways that actually, though unintentionally, contribute to it. How do we develop this uncommon level of awareness and deepening sense of compassion? Over the years, I have come to see that certain fundamental attitudes or traits evolve as a result of these practices, supporting this and related inner work.[2] Perhaps the most important foundational attitude is an openness to explore without judgment. This one is so difficult for those who care about suffering that I often refer to this as being "as nonjudgmental as possible" in a given moment. We are each a sort of work in progress, after all, with heavily conditioned and easily engaged minds. We will judge. But an important distinction mindfulness asks us to make is between automatic judgment and the more considered, deliberative evaluation that we might describe as *discernment*. This distinction is essential to the work of learning how to alleviate others' suffering, or of "practicing justice."

A second important foundational trait is what many mindfulness traditions call *lovingkindness*. This is the feeling of care and concern for the well-being of oneself and others. While there are specific practices for developing this sense of caring for those we do not know, the essence of lovingkindness may already exist in your heart. It is the warmth and softening of heart that arises when we experience love and empathy.

The third most important foundation is *compassion*. I define compassion as the will to act to alleviate the suffering of others. It is distinct from pity, the way we may sometimes feel sorry for the suffering of those whose lives and circumstances we see as distinct from, and often somehow less than, our own. Compassion is close to but also distinct from empathy, even though feeling with and being able to take the perspective of another is essential for effective compassionate action. Compassion is the will, the wherewithal, and the motivation to actually do something to assist in alleviating suffering, whether it's our own or others'. We need compassion that embraces our own suffering—self-compassion. And we need compassion that embraces the suffering of others—other-regarding compassion.

The fourth important foundational attitude in support of the journey to live mindfully with the desire for social justice is *patience*. The fact is that the best answers to the most profound questions of our lives are not given to us at once, fully formed. Indeed, they may not even arrive in our lifetimes. The problems we experience in our relationships with others and in our efforts to live free of racial bias were not created in the span of one lifetime. Therefore, expecting to solve them in short order is a recipe for frustration. So as we deepen our capacity to work with racial injustice, an important trait to develop as we go is our capacity to be patient with ourselves and with others.

A fifth foundational attitude for ColorInsight is what mindfulness teachers sometimes call the *"don't know" mind*. This refers to our ability to accept our own ongoing need to learn, and to live with inevitable uncertainty. We resist seeking overly simplified answers to the most complex questions of our lives. We realize that we experience and form the answers to our most profound questions as we go about *holding the questions* with compassionate awareness. One of the foundational traits of living mindful justice, then, is being able to be humble and open to learning more, to live with ambiguity, to stay present and engaged even as the answers we seek, the outcomes we pursue, elude us.

A sixth foundational trait is *steadfastness*, the capacity to stay in the struggle. It is the will and the ability to turn toward the difficult, to go with the flow of our lives, even when it involves uncertainty, tension, and conflict. Contrary to what has been long and widely advertised, living mindfully is not living without discomfort. It is living with awareness that discomfort, like joy, is a part of a life well and deeply lived. It is living in a way that allows us to take each of the things we wish we could change, the things that cause us discomfort and even pain, and accept them *for the moment* as simply the way things are, however ugly or unpleasant. And yet it is doing so without feeling reduced or diminished as human beings, without cutting ourselves off from others.

Finally, we turn to that trait without which none of the others can be adhered to with consistency when the going gets tough. The seventh foundational trait is the *courage to seek and act for justice*. Healing social wounds requires that we engage in public acts of acknowledgment of harm done (whether intentionally or through oversight or neglect), offer apologies where appropriate, and take action seeking to make amends to those injured or harmed—to make things right as best we can.

It is sometimes said that we do this in the spirit of restoring the community to the state of well-being it knew before the harm; however, given that our country was actually founded on racial *in*equality and forms of exclusion, we need a vision not of restoration, but of *real* change. We need to understand why and how justice in action may lead to healing and redemption for ourselves and for the generations to come.

While these traits may come naturally to us, they also can be further strengthened through practice. And when we can see that racial injuries are just one of many causes of deep wounding, we need to step up to the great challenge of our time—that of creating something that has never truly existed before: a world in which *everyone* truly belongs and is supported in thriving alongside diverse groups of others.

Each of these foundations of mindful racial justice work are crucial. The good news is that we can develop each of them along the way, through our regular engagement with mindfulness and compassion practices.

This work will be difficult. It will challenge us to examine the subtle ways we participate in, and in some ways benefit from, the patterns of racial suffering we see. In this book I distill teachings and curated practices from a range of traditions that support us in this work, as well as research in social psychology, sociology, and neuroscience, and the invocations of some of the most eminent peacemakers of our time.

My core personal practice—and the one at the heart of this book—is the formal mindfulness meditation practice. As you'll see in these pages, mindfulness meditation may take a variety of forms. One of the practices, Awareness of Breathing Meditation, involves focusing your attention on the sensations of sitting and breathing—each in-breath and out-breath—with an attitude of friendly openness to your experience and with the intention of becoming more aware of the fullness of life in the moment. It's a practice that can help make you more present to your experiences, so you can see the choices you have when it comes to relating to them.

Most of the time, we almost forget that we are breathing throughout the day; we breathe without even needing to be aware of it. And yet, the moment we suffer from breathing difficulties of one sort or another, we see that we are dependent upon the miraculous respiratory system for our easeful existence.

When our breathing body works, simply and as it should, we are infinitely blessed. The moment that we are aware of our body breathing while we sit is a moment to appreciate the infinite miracle of our simply being alive. Regardless of the pain of the moment—whether physical, emotional, or psychological—there is much more to the moment.

Sadly, however, if we are not careful, we can go months or more without fully appreciating the simple truth of this. With attention and kindness, focusing on the sensations of breathing may give rise to a sense of our blessedness in being alive, and a deep source of gratitude for who we are—whatever our background or race; our state of illness, disability, or ability; our monetary wealth or lack thereof.

For these reasons alone, committing to a regular mindfulness practice would likely be a good thing to do. A growing body of research also confirms a range of physical health benefits—from lowering blood pressure to improving your immune system and beyond. More to the point, the body's capacity to recover from stressful situations appears to be enhanced by regular mindfulness practice.

The mindfulness and compassion practices in this book assist you, then, in becoming more skillful dealing, in real time, with difficult emotions and reactions that arise when working directly with race and racism. Taken together, they may be considered basic operating instructions for managing the uncertainties and challenges that are inherent to the human condition—including "race problems."

Our ability to skillfully handle difficulties deepens over time as we practice mindfulness. These exercises have been shown to literally rebuild our biological capacities for well-being—the central nervous system that helps us downshift from stress-induced arousal, the part of our brain capable of experiencing compassion for others. They have even been shown to have the effect of slowing the aging process, which may otherwise occur more rapidly as a result of the stress of racism.[3] For those raising children exposed to racism and other distresses, the practices of mindfulness and compassion—both for themselves and for their children—may set the next generation on a path for greater health, well-being, and resilience over the course of their lifetimes.

Even more profoundly, simple mindfulness shows that the air that we breathe depends on the actions not only of ourselves, but of those around us, and of the natural world. Knowing this, our hardened sense of ourselves as separate (and too often, alone) begins to soften. We see that everyone and everything is connected, and we learn to better respond to the interpersonal and environmental conditions, policies, and structures that cause distress and suffering. We can change the way we act in the world to minimize the suffering of others.

The benefits I have described so far are especially important to those of us who, as a result of various factors—our inherent life circumstances, the activist work we do, the diverse relationships we choose to maintain—see, encounter, and engage with racism or other forms of social injustice on a regular basis.

Deepening Awareness Through Mindfulness

In mindfulness meditation, we set aside time and space to become more aware of our experience. In this way, we slowly develop more of our inborn capacity for meeting each new moment with fresh aliveness.

Often immediately, and certainly for many over time, these practices assist us in calming our minds and bodies, in seeing more clearly and comprehensively, in lessening our reactivity, and in becoming more wise about our responses to the stimuli of life. We can begin to see, then, how mindfulness meditation might help give us something to draw on in the midst of a difficult moment or conversation.

When anger arises suddenly, for example, we may find ourselves reacting in kind. Yet if we are able to notice the sensations that accompany anger and examine them, we may be able to learn something. We can slow down the reactive habit long enough to see what there is to see about our habits, our conditionings, our patterns of emotional reaction. And we can choose a better way to respond.

When we are able to engage our awareness to *choose* how to respond, we wake up to a new power for navigating the world. We can allow for the fierce and enlivening energy of strong emotions like anger to help us gauge when we should take action to address injustice. And we can decide to act on that energy in a way that lessens anger's raw, destructive potential.

When we come to know more about our own mind and when we learn about its conditionings, habits, and tendencies, we are better able to regulate responses in ways that maximize our effectiveness in the world.

The following core mindfulness meditation practices—Awareness of Breathing, Body Scan, Moving Meditations, and Mindful Reflections—provide the basis for developing, deepening, or maintaining your own daily mindfulness practice as you read this book. Although additional practices will be introduced as we go, you should use one or more of these core practices for grounding in awareness every day.

AN "AWARENESS OF BREATHING"
MEDITATION PRACTICE FOR EVERY DAY

Practicing mindfulness meditation on a daily basis will help you develop the capacity to stay with the challenges of racism as it arises in the world and strengthen your ability to work against it. As we deepen our ability to stay present and to notice and regulate our emotions, we will increase our emotional and mental flexibility, so we can process the events that cause us distress—including the thoughts, emotions, and bodily sensations that come with them—in new ways.

To start, consciously establish a posture for your practice. Decide whether you will practice in a seated position on the floor or in a chair, or if you would prefer to stand or use some other posture—you must trust your own instincts for how best to support yourself here and throughout this program.

Now, as you consciously settle in, increase your focus on the position of the body in this moment. If you are using a cushion on the floor, experiment with sitting on the cushion until you are able to sense solid support from the floor up. Hold your spine erect but not rigid. You may prefer to have your eyes closed or open. Either is fine, but if you choose to keep your eyes open, select a point on the floor, a few feet away, and keep your eyes focused there as best you can to avoid distractions.

If you are seated in a chair, sit so that your feet can reach the floor, and place them flat and flush with the ground beneath you. If necessary, use a pillow or other surface to raise your feet so that they are flatly supported.

With this version of mindfulness meditation, we turn to a point of focus, some point in the body where we can rest our minds and soak in awareness of the experience of the moment. Because the experience of breathing is at the very center of our body's natural ability to manage stress and emotion, most teachings recommend beginning meditation practice with a focus on awareness of breathing in the body, moment to moment. (If focusing on breathing is simply too difficult for you, skip to the next practice, the Body Scan.)

Now simply take a few deep and focusing breaths, gradually increasing your capacity to maintain light but clear attention to the sensations of the entire flow of the in-breath and the out-breath as they alternate. Allow your breathing to settle into an easeful, comfortable rhythm and pattern, and bring your attention even more fully if you can to the experience of breathing. If it helps, locate a particular position in the body where you can feel the sensations of breath flowing in and flowing out, such as the outer nostrils, where you may feel a slight change in temperature with each breath in and out; or in the region of the belly, just below the navel, where you can feel a deep breath as the diaphragm expands into the region and displaces the organs, causing the sensation of rising and falling. Place one hand in the region for even further support and focus.

Whatever you select as the point of the body on which you will place your attention as you breathe, continue the practice, focusing on the sensations of breathing in and breathing out. If and when your mind wanders, simply and gently bring your attention back, with kindness and with as little judgment as possible. Begin again with the next focused in-breath and continue following along.

Start with practicing for 2 minutes, then for 5 minutes, and increase your awareness of breathing practice to 15–20 minutes per day. If it helps—when you first start practicing or on any given day that you need extra support—you might consider counting inwardly just beneath the breath. Gradually, extend your practice periods up to 30 minutes per session, once or twice a day.

A "BODY SCAN" PRACTICE FOR GROUNDING IN AWARENESS

Given that examining bias and racism in ourselves and in others takes an emotional and mental toll, it's important to practice becoming more aware of emotions and sensations of distress as they arise in our bodies. We need to become more aware of the subtle ways that we carry race and racism in our bodies, including how we carry wounds and trauma that need to be seen and lovingly acknowledged in order for them to be healed. We need to deepen awareness of how we tend to react to emotions and other sensations of distress in the moment that we first sense them as tightness in the neck, as turnings of the stomach, as flashes of apprehension or fear in the heart region. The Body Scan Meditation is one of the best tools for getting to know our bodies in ways that help us work with race issues because it increases our sense of connection with our bodies in the world.

As with any of the meditations that I guide here, please be kind to yourself as you engage. The body has most likely experienced any of a wide array of traumas, and hence we need to be especially aware of how some of these practices may challenge your sense of being safe. Here as elsewhere, be your own best guide as to how you engage in this practice, and if it proves too challenging, consider shifting to a movement-based practice (see page 41) or back to Awareness of Breathing.

So let's begin by consciously taking a position for your Body Scan Meditation practice. You can practice in any position, but traditionally, this practice is done lying on the back, with the hands resting at the sides on the floor.

If you're sitting in a chair, adjust your posture so you feel the support of the ground beneath you, place your feet flat on the floor, and sit with your spine upright but not rigid and with your head resting in alignment. If you're standing, bring your attention to your feet on the floor, about shoulder-width apart, and settle into a sense of grounded support. And if you are lying in the traditional position, allow yourself to feel the weight of the body sinking into the supportive ground below, holding you in a sense of belonging to this place at this time.

When you are ready to begin the body scan, direct your attention to the sensations, the life energy in your left foot, starting at the large toe and allowing your attention to move gently from one toe to the next. Then, bring your attention up to the top of the foot and the bones, muscles, tendons, and systems within it. What can you sense as you attend to the feeling in your foot? Moving up, rest your awareness on the sensations in the ankle, the shin, the knee, the hip. Then, switch to the right foot, and repeat. Once you've scanned both legs, bring your attention (as your comfort level allows) up through the buttocks, the groin, and into the abdomen. Notice the sensations in each area of your body.

If any thoughts or emotions arise, simply notice them, allowing them to be present as you breathe in and out. From the lower abdomen on up through the diaphragm, lungs, and chest, scan up through your midsection, feeling, as best you can, the aliveness in each of these important regions of your body. As you move through the region of the heart, sense how you feel there. Is there tightness? Is there openness? Are you able to feel the strength of your own beating heart, its spacious capacity to give and to receive?

Breathing and releasing focus on the heart, gently scan up through the chest and shoulders, and then down each arm, hand, and finger. Return to the upper body and scan up the throat, into the face, and up to the crown of the head. Now take a moment to direct your attention to the skin. Reflect on your skin as the largest organ of your body. Be kind with yourself as you allow any thoughts, sensations, or feelings to surface. What do your skin and skin tone mean to you? How have you been wounded or how have you benefited as a result of the particular skin that you live in?

Gently let go of all that has arisen for you as you've explored being in your body in this way. As you come back to the sensations of breathing, allow a sense of your full being to expand and flow down, from crown to toes and back up again.

Sit in awareness of the sensations in the body as a whole, allowing that which is good and well within you to be known, felt, and appreciated.

Movement-Based Meditations

Having explored meditation while staying relatively still, we are now more ready to explore meditation while in movement. There are many kinds of movement-based meditations, including tai chi, qigong, yoga, and some of the trauma-releasing practices that I explore in small part below. All of them assume some degree of capacity on your part to move your body at will, which may or may not be possible for you. Moreover, some positions may be more triggering or desirable for you than others, depending on your past experiences. So please engage in the following only to the degree that you feel comfortable, and be encouraged to adapt these practices to suit your particular body and physical needs.

We will explore two different types of moving meditations: Basic Moving or Walking Meditation, and Gentle Yoga.

BASIC MOVING OR WALKING MEDITATION

To begin, come into the position you would typically inhabit to move your body across a room. For most of us (unless you're in a wheelchair), this means coming to a standing position.

In this position, place both feet flat on the floor. As much as possible, bring your awareness to your feet, to the feeling of being in contact with the floor, and through the floor, with the earth.

Select a path for your moving meditation. It need not be very long. Ten feet or so would be plenty. More would also work.

Standing (or sitting) comfortably, feel the length between your feet and the crown of your head, your height. Stand erect but not rigid, and breathe deeply in and out, feeling the flow of energy and awareness through your body with each in-breath and out-breath.

Now, we'll begin to practice mindfully moving forward. If walking, notice the impulse to lift one foot. Feel the shift of weight into the stable leg, and feel the movement through the lifting leg as it rises and prepares to meet the earth, heel first, then ball and toes. Notice the feeling of the foot as it moves and lands, and notice the rise of the alternate foot. With each step, notice the feeling of connectedness between the body and the earth.

If you're using a chair or walker, notice the motion in the hands, feet, or other parts of the body as you move forward, keeping your awareness in the body as best you can.

Take a few paces, keeping your attention on the body in motion. When you come to the end of your path, pause and prepare to turn around and begin moving back toward your original position. Notice the body turning to one side or the other, completing the turn with awareness of what it feels like to shift perspective. When you are ready, mindfully move forward, one step or push or lift at a time.

Through regular practice of this form of meditation, traditionally known as Walking Meditation, you may become familiar with what it means to feel the body in motion throughout your daily activities. Slowly we become used to maintaining awareness of the body even as we go through our busy daily lives, and to living in more grounded support as we go.

GENTLE YOGA

The most well-known movement-based meditation is yoga, the ancient tradition aimed at deepening the sense of union between awareness and the body.

There are many forms of yoga. For our purposes, we embrace a simple set of standing movement practices to provide a taste of what it means to bring the mind to rest in the sensations of the body being stretched a bit and kindly testing its limits.

We'll start simply, by coming to a standing posture with your arms dangling comfortably at your sides, your hands alongside your hips. Again, please modify and begin in whatever position is comfortable for you if you are unable to stand. Seated yoga is equally beneficial for our purposes here.

Take a few deep breaths. On an in-breath, raise both of your arms slowly away from your sides, extending upward as far as you comfortably can. Keep your attention focused on the sensations of raising the arms, allowing attention to remain in the upper arms, the lower arms, the hands, bringing your hands closer and closer together. If possible, bring them parallel to one another above your head.

Hold this position for about 20 seconds, keeping your attention on the sensations in your body.

Now allow your arms to gently float back down to your sides, keeping your awareness in the body, until the arms and hands rest once again at your sides.

What is the energy level like in your body now?

Now let's practice neck half-circles. Begin by lowering your chin to your chest, and then, at an easy pace, gently roll your neck to the right, left, center, right, and center again. Repeat this 8 times.

Next, explore some shoulder circles, beginning by bringing your shoulders together over the heart, then rolling them back and expanding your shoulders out, bringing your shoulder blades together at the center of your back. Repeat for 8 cycles, then reverse direction, beginning by rolling your shoulders back and continuing for

8 cycles. Keep your attention on the body in motion, and on the breath as you breathe in and out in rhythm with these movements.

Now place your legs hip-width apart, place your hands on your hips and, starting to your right, make a circle with your hips as best you can. Again, be careful with your back and don't push beyond what is only lightly out of your comfort zone. Reverse direction, repeat, and come to center.

Finally, bring your legs together, bend slightly forward, and place your hands on your knees. With a little dip motion toward the ground, swing your knees around in a circle for 8 cycles. Reverse direction and repeat.

What is the level of energy in your body now? As you pause, check in and see what sort of movement your body most wants to feel. You may wish to gently fall forward at the waist, allowing the hands to drop to the ankles or, if you're flexible enough, the toes. You may wish to explore a balancing posture, shifting your weight to one foot and then lifting the other. You may, if space permits, wish to explore lying down practices. Or you may simply want to shake it off. Be gentle! The various body-based postures are endless.

As you explore these practices, you may decide to work with an experienced teacher to get the greatest benefit from embodied mindfulness. But for now, see if you can begin to bring greater awareness to the sensations of life, of movement and stillness, within your body as you move throughout your day.

Trauma-Releasing Practices

As trauma experts like Peter Levine, David Treleaven, and others are helping us understand, the body holds on to trauma—events that cause deep distress and leave us feeling helpless, frightened, overwhelmed, or unsafe. The severity of trauma varies along a vast spectrum, from stress to post-traumatic stress disorder (PTSD). Traditional sitting mindfulness practice, alone, will likely not be enough to help us release the trauma that we carry, individually and in various collectives, around race and racism. Indeed, if not engaged in with care, meditation can in some cases exacerbate trauma and cause further harm.[4]

Mindfulness can help you become both more trauma-sensitive and more trauma-resilient. It may help you recognize when you or others are touching upon or reacting to latent trauma, and help you respond with appropriate acts of care and compassion. So when you begin to feel the pain of your own race-related wounds, or if through the application of mindfulness you become aware of tension, unnecessary fear, or other unusual body sensations when in the presence of a racial Other or when recalling memories of such encounters, make it a practice to gently and compassionately explore ways of noticing more fully and working on releasing your embodied trauma.

While the full work of releasing racial trauma is beyond the scope of this book, I include a few suggestions here (and in chapter nine) for the foundational work of honoring the messages of your body and tending to your own needs through practices that have been proven beneficial. Set aside time to support your body in ways that may allow you to release the particular pain you carry. Gentle, trauma-releasing body movements may include yawning, stomping, coughing, sighing, humming, and singing.[5] Writing, drawing and coloring, storytelling and mindful speaking, and listening can also help. For our purposes here, simply notice when you are feeling the signs that for you indicate an unhealed wound, and find a private space where you can choose to move your body or otherwise do what might help you experience some relief. If you feel the need to shake, growl, dance, yell, or otherwise enact a physical release, give yourself deep permission to do so. Don't worry about looking silly. Give yourself the freedom to heal.

Many of us know that dancing, singing, and holding hands with caring others seem naturally to support us in healing and coming back to our sense of well-being. Other practices, combining movement with visualization, may also help. One such practice is what I call the "spiral of healing." Begin in a standing position or while seated on the ground.

Touch into the part of you that suffers from a race-related or other wound. Breathing in and out, offer kindness and the wish for healing to that part of you. Now imagine a spiraling movement extending from that place in your body, and see if you can move in a way that allows a spiral of healing energy to move from that place outward through you. Start small and increase the size of your spirals as you go. Allow yourself to shake and release as you move in whatever way you'd like. Try giving yourself 5 to 10 minutes in the practice. If it helps, listen to music that you find nurturing and inspiring. As you spiral the wound energy outward, also allow the reverse—and spiral inward the energy of loving healing. There is no one right or wrong way to do this; recall that your body is mostly water and is built to allow energy and information to move through, release, and be transformed in the direction of your greater good.

You deserve to heal. We all do. A trauma-releasing movement practice may be just the thing to assist you in deepening your process. And your own deep, embodied healing is an essential part of the process of bringing justice into the world.

AN OCEAN OF LOVINGKINDNESS MEDITATION

This practice is about opening the heart to feelings of kindness and wishing well-being for yourself and others.

First, think about a person who has made you feel loved, cared for, or nurtured. Extend a wish for well-being toward this person, either by imagining your love expanding like a light from your chest reaching out to them, or by inwardly repeating phrases such as the following:

May you be happy.

May you be at ease.

May you be free from suffering.

Now offer those same wishes or phrases toward yourself. This may be challenging, but do release any judgments or criticism, taking a deep breath, and offering these phrases to yourself. If it helps, select an image of yourself at a point in your life when you particularly needed a loving response, such as a moment of a race-related injury. See yourself at the age, time, and place where you were then, and extend the wish of loving awareness and healing support.

Continue repeating these phrases or expanding the light of your love to cover yourself for several minutes. Traditionally, such practices might be expanded into increasingly widening categories of people—from particular friends or loved ones to people you know casually but not well, to someone with whom you may be having some difficulty, and finally to all those in your community or nation, and beyond. As you experiment with this meditation, see how far you may be able to expand the circle of your own kind concern.

Finally, as you prepare to transition out of this awareness, as best you can, let yourself feel your own being as part of an ocean of love.

And when you are ready to complete this practice, simply sit in the expanded awareness of the love that you feel in your heart for yourself and for others.

Mindful Journal Reflections

For each of these practices, take a few moments to jot down some reflections about your experience.

Notice any thoughts, emotions, or sensations in the body. How are you feeling now, compared to the way you felt before the meditation practice?

How has your practice impacted your state of mind? Your sense of yourself?

Pay attention to the area of your heart. How does it feel, following the meditation practice?

Note to yourself any ways that you feel different as a result of your mindfulness practice. Include any insights or questions that arose; it may be important to inquire more deeply about your experience and to explore answers to these questions as you continue to practice.

Meditative practices like these, adapted from some of the greatest teachings of the world, are at the deep heart of the embodied awareness method developed in this book. Regularly engaging in them will support and nurture you. And they just might transform your community, and the world.

These practices may increase awareness of the obvious and nonobvious ways that racial identity has shaped much of our life experience. When we are ready and open to what they reveal, they will assist us in seeing more of race's and racism's subtle manifestations in our lives—in our own thoughts and in our interactions with others. They help us sit with what we see long enough to learn more skillful means of working with what we see. They are an important component of how we can heal from the wounds of racism and deepen our sense of ourselves as a vital part of a human family in need of more public lovingkindness.

Sticking with the readings, with the practices, and with yourself, you will find that new insights arise over time. In this chapter, you've begun reckoning with racism with the support of mindfulness. As we do the outward-facing work of racial justice, we must do the inner work of healing from our own experiences with racism and developing the mental and emotional capacity to handle daily challenges. Embodied mindfulness practices open us up to the deeper ground on which we stand. They not only support us in developing the resilience we'll need to grow, but they help prepare us for the real challenges of living in more just and equitable ways with others.

CHAPTER FOUR

MINDFULNESS PRACTICE AS COLORINSIGHT PRACTICE

᠗

This work is something we all have to do. We all have to examine the
shadow we all carry as part of this society before we can heal our
unintended racism.

—RALPH M. STEELE[1]

We Begin with Ourselves

If we want to be a part of the ongoing awakening, if we want to stem the
rising tide of division in our time (of which racism is just one part, albeit
a central one), we have some choices to make. The choices are of great
consequence. We can go through our lives holding on to notions of race
that we were taught or adopted at some point in the past, and we can pas-
sively receive the messages about race and racism that pervade our
culture—that it's just the way it is, or part of the biological, natural way of
human life in a world of scarce resources. We can seek to be "color-blind,"
perhaps believing that we have transcended the need to be a part of race
conversations. But beware: the temptation to feel we are somehow so
evolved that we don't need to examine race in our lives—a form of what
Buddhist teacher and psychotherapist John Welwood called "spiritual
bypassing"—is just one of the many ways that we avoid the pain and personal challenge of dealing with the racism that we know exists.

The work of ColorInsight, however, calls you to do something different. It supports you in looking at race and racism as perhaps you have never done before, whatever your background or experience. It supports you in rejecting the temptation to normalize racism, or to bypass it. Instead, it helps you find ways to stay in the complex struggle for multiracial, democratic justice—in courageous fellowship with others. The practices and reflections in this book will keep showing you how. Together we will look at race in our lives with an ongoing, personal commitment to dissolving racism and its spirit-killing material consequences, when and where it arises, in all its forms. To do so, you will be challenged to really *examine* your beliefs, conditionings, and behavior. You will think and act differently in ways that will actually lessen racism's many impacts on you and on others.

By introducing teachings and practices focused on increasing your understanding of your own deep, subtle experiences with race in your life—and helping you develop the capacity to stay with the complexities they present—this book helps you deepen your ability to create and to maintain deep, rich, and diverse communities.

It's Not Personal

When we explore the original teachings on mindfulness deeply, we see that the awareness it supports has personal, interpersonal, and communal systemic implications. It's an awareness that supports you in waking up to the many facets of your life in the world.

Indeed, as the historical Buddha reportedly taught, mindful friendship, staying in relationship and good fellowship with practitioners in human community, was not "half of the holy life." It was all of it.

Actions aimed at alleviating suffering—working to distribute resources in the direction of fairness and increasing well-being for all—help heal the world. Taking such action is another form of justice itself. Thus, if we really hope to gain the true benefit of mindfulness practice, we must start by seeing it as a very personal practice whose benefits we realize in how we relate to and engage with others—including those we are tempted to view as less worthy because of the deep teachings of racism. Mindfulness practices help us to deconstruct the racialized identities we have constructed, and the racism that these identities were created to uphold. Awareness helps us to live in the freedom that comes with experiencing the possibilities inherent in our common humanity.

As by now you have no doubt come to see, this work is not for the faint of heart. We are working to heal ourselves, yes. At the same time we are working to disrupt, deconstruct, and break open patterns that make normal and "okay" the suffering of people at the margins of our lives. And we are working to build a new world—one that actually inclines toward the liberation of all, rather than toward our greater but more subtle enslavement. Because all that we do is subject to change and is impermanent, we are seeking to develop the capacity to do what we can with a lightness and joy that keep us from taking ourselves too seriously and, at the same time, illuminate the dire necessity of continuing to do our loving best even in the face of some defeat. Let's get to work.

Waking Up to Racism and Its Temptations

In the United States, there has been a resurgence of *explicit* bias and racism strong enough to make our concerns with understanding and ferreting out *implicit* bias look positively naïve. Racism and colorism, in forms both implicit and explicit, along with additional forms of Othering and disrespecting people who are "not our kind," exist in many parts, if not virtually every part, of the world.

And so we Pause. What if this difficult time, this moment in which we seem more racially and culturally divided than ever, signifies not the beginning of the end but a profound opportunity for a new beginning? What if, through the pain of seeing the way things are, we now have a new chance to get it right? What if this time in which we can all see more clearly than ever how easily we can be divided by appeals to racism is just what we need to help us work for racial healing in ways that we never have before?

We can no longer deny that race matters. We can no longer believe that racism is a thing of the past. Given this, if we want a just world, we have to engage in efforts to lessen the harms of racism occurring in our workplaces and communities every day of our lives. What can we do? How can we work with others toward truly inclusive, racially just democracy?

Once we have recognized that, indeed, racism is a problem in our midst, we can turn toward the work of looking deeply at its roots. We can see what wisdom teaches us about how to solve at least some aspects of the problem, those rooted in our own minds and ways of being with others. And we can set ourselves on a lifelong journey toward working to re-create structures, redress wrongs, and begin real healing—starting with ourselves and extending to others.

The journey of racial justice is multidimensional. One dimension of that journey may be thought of as an *outward* one. We consider and reflect on how race and racism operate today, noting its similarities and differences from the past. We look at how notions of race have shaped virtually all aspects of the contemporary world—our brains, our perceptions, our thoughts, our interactions, and our communities—and we work with these notions through teachings and practices. We grapple with the legacies of race-making in our culture, including the structural and institutional racism that we have inherited over time. We adopt practices and policies that have been shown to decrease bias in our lives and communities. We take this outward journey into the world with a commitment to understanding race and racism as never before, and to helping to redeem the wrongs of the past through our healing actions today.

The outward journey is essential. To work on ending racism for good, we must see and come to terms with how deeply racism is embedded in our culture and in the social practices that make up how we live and work.

And we must see how our own experiences and our responsibility to make the world a better place are tied to the experiences of the generations that have come before and set us on the road to redeeming the future for our children and theirs. Thus, to end racism, we must change. And from that place, we must change the world around us.

To paraphrase the novelist William Faulkner, the past is not dead. Indeed, it's not even past.[2] Somewhat similarly, James Baldwin reminded us that to change absolutely anything, we must first have the courage to face it.[3] We must face the fact that racism is essential to the culture we have inherited and are subtly re-creating each day. It has shaped our communities and life opportunities in ways that we can no longer ignore. We have to face these facts if we ever hope to change them. We must commit to doing the ongoing work of learning about, repairing, and redeeming the wounds still festering from our histories and the harms we have collectively done to those marked as racial or ethnic Others.

Doing so requires that we commit to truly understanding those harms. Yes, we must work to repair and heal from them ourselves. And we must pass what we know on to our children. We must commit to projects of racial justice that change the structures by which racism maintains its footprint in the world. The specific work of the outward journey will look different for each of us, based on our own particular life experiences and positions within social structures. But we each have work to do.

To do this work involves a second dimension of practice, learning, and growth—an *inward* journey or commitment to ongoing personal awakening. We must awaken to the ways that race and racism have shaped our own brains, our ways of being in the world, and our hopes for the work we might do together.

Much in the contemporary world re-creates and sustains racism. It does so by teaching us to look out for ourselves and "our own kind" first, last, and always; to think little of the injustice and pain that others face; and to think mostly of (but not *be* in) the present and perhaps the future, but little of the past. We are given to believe that we are all lacking much and live in a world of great scarcity. We must do more, dominant culture tells us, to earn more; and, to fight for more of our share of a shrinking pie. In short, we live in a culture in which we have lost touch with the unfathomable richness of our true human inheritance and with the imperative that we honor it, share it, and pass it on.

Through the Doorway of Shared Human Inheritance

Take a few moments to reflect on what you view as some of the many positive aspects of our shared human inheritance. Consider anything from language, to the capacity to cultivate and share the foods we eat, to music, and to the various ways we have learned to thrive.

What are some of the things that the broad family of human beings have passed down through the ages that you value most?

What have you been given as a result?

What more are you willing to give back?

Now allow this inquiry to dissolve, and as you do so, let your awareness expand. Drop into the silence and let go, as best you can, of the sense of yourself, of your efforts and needs as apart from others. Allow your sense of self to soften. As you breathe in and out, imagine your human life story as a river, flowing into the ocean of humanity, all a part of the more than human world. Rest in the ocean of awareness, and all of its powerful possibilities from here.

Now allow yourself to return to the feeling of yourself in this body, in this place, in this very moment. Gather and center the sense of yourself as a body and being with lived experience that matters, in a world of others. Allow yourself to feel strong in your being and gifts, even as you interconnect with the experiences and heritages of others. Separate individuality and common humanity may come together in your awareness now. Gently allow yourself to feel the "both/and" of your own deep identity.

CHAPTER FIVE

TRUE INHERITANCE

My practice of gratitude involves remembering my ancestors. We all have a family history that makes up a great part of who we are, whether we agree with what our ancestors did or not. We suffer when we cannot see a part of ourselves or when we disown a part of our history. Whether our history was born out of oppression or privilege, violence or compassion, courage or defeat, grief or joy, remembering it uncovers suffering and moves us to grace and a possible future.

—MICHELE BENZAMIN-MIKI[1]

What Race Am I? Or "Where Are You *From*?"

Thinking about race made Shela anxious. She had been raised in Southern California by parents who were originally from Syria. She had a head full of thick, brown hair, and her skin tone was fair with just a hint of brown. I knew that she was enjoying the Race class immensely and, by her own measure, was learning a great deal.

But one thing troubled her. So much so that she found herself in my cool and softly shaded office on an overcast morning when she could easily have been elsewhere. After sharing a bit of small talk, she got right to the point.

"What race am I?" she asked. The earnestness in her large eyes reminded me of that in so many students I've met who feel the same sense of marginalization in conversations about race, the same urgent desire to fit in somewhere, to know what most others so clearly seemed to know about themselves—and more often than not, about "us."

"Well, Shela, as we've been discussing in class, race has no meaning other than what we give to it in a given culture, time, and place."

Her inquisitive gaze was unchanged.

"How have you been treated in terms of race?" I asked her.

"Well, that's just it. Most of the time, people seem to look at me as if they are searching my face for some indication one way or the other. Eventually they may get around to asking me something like, 'Where are you from?' When I tell them Los Angeles, they are not satisfied. They try again: 'I mean, where are you *from* from?' When I say that my parents are from Syria, they sometimes ask, 'Are you white?' And I don't know what to tell them. Sometimes they don't ask, but look at me as if they suddenly just know—or maybe decide—that I am not. I've asked my parents, and they don't know. So I don't really know how to answer the question. Am I?"

Looking at Shela, I could see that this question had brought her real distress. I knew that I could talk with her about how the Supreme Court dealt with the question of whether people from Syria were white in ways that were, at best, inconsistent.[2] As anyone who has studied this area of the law knows, the answers to questions like hers were not to be found in the courts. And as fewer people still to this day know, they are even less likely to be found in genetic "science."

"How do you feel when people ask you questions about your race?" I asked.

"I don't know what to feel," she said. "I mostly just feel like I don't belong anywhere."

"My dear, you belong," I said. "You belong everywhere."

Hearing that, Shela exhaled. And something inside her lit up. She was shining a bit brighter as she sat across from me. I continued on.

"Shela, what that question means when it is asked of you probably varies with the specific context. In a social setting, people may be trying to put you in a category for acceptance or marginalization. In an institutional setting, you may be asked as part of an effort to track how the institution is doing with regard to their objectives, such as, perhaps, promoting some notion of diversity. Once you understand more about what such a question may mean in one context or another, you may feel more comfortable deciding how to respond. Your answer may, in the end, differ depending on the circumstances."

The young woman's brow furrowed as if she were confused. My heart softened with a sense of understanding.

I took a deep breath and continued. "How other people see you through this notion of race does not determine who you are. Because the concept of race is not a scientific one, people may apply it to you differently. You will be considered white by some people. And you will be considered nonwhite by some others. This is because there is no inherent meaning in this notion of whiteness. People tend to look at one another and decide whether someone is white or not based on features like skin tone, eye color, hair type, nose and eyelid shape, and the like. Because your features do not clearly signal one type or the other according to the rules of identity common in our culture today, people who ask you that question are trying to slot you into a set of categories that fit their own understanding. And they are doing so for reasons that have more to do with their own needs than yours."

I paused and took another deep breath.

"The point is this: your *true* identity, who you *really* are, may have little to do with the way that race attaches to you in the world. And your cultural inheritance as a member of the human family with particular ties to the part of the world we call the Middle East is rich beyond belief."

We smiled at each other. In that moment, at least, the questions no longer mattered. The struggles she would face in a time of increasing anti-immigrant rhetoric and Islamophobia remained. But from this place, she could feel a bit of space around the stories about "people like her," space in which some of the wounds caused by such stories could dissipate. She would continue to work for a more just world for those like her. But she would be mindful of doing so in ways that lessened the risk of repeating the patterns of Othering's endless cycles of injury and revenge.

As Shela's story shows, examining your experience with race can, if you are willing, enrich your life. It can provide a pathway to connection and to a sense of purpose each day, for the rest of your life. And because healing changes your brain, body, and genes by helping you loosen the grip of your personal stories of grievance and clarifying who you really are, your work can provide a corrective bridge between your life and the lives of those who will live on in the generations to come—a bridge leading to collective healing and redemption.

So far, we've begun to look at what we may learn and become when we explore our experiences with race, especially with the support of practices like personal meditation and reflection. We have begun to understand how these practices can deepen our effectiveness in grappling with race and all that travels with it, personally and politically, whether alone or with others. They will help you come to terms with the often unconscious ways that we all participate in becoming psychologically and socially attached to ideas and ways of living that serve to make and remake race, avoiding or pushing away ideas and practices that unmake race, and remaining confused by race in our own lives and in others'. We are turning to the ways that we create suffering by accommodating, minimizing, or otherwise being comfortable with race and racism without mindful awareness. And we are experiencing our capacity to let go of these notions in an instant and to connect with the heart of another human being in a way that really can change everything.

By engaging in the reflections here so far, you may have already begun to see more of how you actually relate to race and racism. Think of the buried ideas or stories about race that have arisen in your own mind. Think of the stories you now see that you have received as true without the benefit of much evidence. Consider the family histories that have been shared, the aspects that have been lost, and the pressure to forget what connects you with so-called others. You may be starting to recognize your own miseducation, your own habits and patterns of reactivity when it comes to race and racism. Do you tend to avoid, attach, or remain confused and unaware? When are you more likely to do one than another and why?

As you begin to notice more about how you "do" race and racism and how it has been done to you, and as you learn new ways to respond, you start to see more clearly the patterns of thought and behavior in your communities that influence your own ways of thinking. Doing so, you may understand more fully identity-based suffering and the practices—both social *and* mindfulness-based—that may bring it to an end.

Sitting and breathing, separately and together, we begin to realize just how we have been molded by circumstance, culture, law, politics, and so much else. When you are open to doing so, you may begin to understand more fully the connections between patterns and social practices in our so-called history and the realities of the present. From this place, you may experience, as I have, a kind of softening of your socially produced identity or sense of self, without losing the sense that you are a part of a community to which you belong and in which you can feel truly alive. We are better able to feel our interconnectedness with others, to learn from them, and to appreciate them more fully. And we are willing and able to make a new tribe—to join the community of those who understand, embrace, and are awakening to our fundamental interconnectedness and too-often-forgotten but very real common humanity.

"FROM PLACE TO GROUND" PRACTICE

Taking a position for a meditation practice, whether seated, standing, or lying down, bring your awareness to the position of the body in this moment. Feel the connection between the body and the ground. Take a few moments to ground yourself intentionally in the here and now. With a few very deep breaths, imagine the flow of the breath extending through the height of your body, from head to toe, and through the width of your body, from side to side.

On an in-breath, begin deepening awareness of who you really are. Call to mind your connection to your parents, and through them, as best you can, your grandparents, and the great-grandparents whose names you know or do not know. And so on.

What do you know about your own ancestral heritage? What do you not know?

Recognizing that you may not be aware of many details, invite yourself to reflect on the following:

What do you know about the places that your ancestors called home?

What do you know about the languages that they spoke?

What do you know about how your family came to the place that you call home?

What parts of the story are fuzzy, unknown?

What parts have been hidden, denied, buried, or left out?

Breathe in, examining what you know and do not know about these aspects of your place in the social world. Allow yourself to feel what comes up for you as you engage in this reflection. Name and note the emotions, and let them go. Name and note the sensations, and simply let them go.

Now consider the actual community in which you live. For now, think of this as one aspect of your "place" in the world. Consider the fact that every person in that community is a member of a broad, rich lineage within human history. And see how those differences pale in comparison to the things the communities' members share in common.

Take a moment to consider the ways that different histories reflect common experience as human beings.

Think of the peace and cooperation that silently exist in your community, to whatever degree they exist, and the ways in which your life has benefited from thousands of moments of participating in a community that practices "getting along."

Now breathe in and out, feeling the deeper ground of your existence, and that which you share with us, with the rest of the world. Allow the awareness of your common humanity to infuse your sense of your place in the world in this very moment.

On the next in-breath, call to mind what you know about some one particular aspect of your lineage. And on the next out-breath, release what you know, and sense into the common experience of breathing that all human beings share.

Continue this cycle, breathing and alternately considering aspects of your place in the world and the deeper ground of your human existence, all held by the ocean of awareness.

When you're ready, gently bring yourself back into simply sitting and breathing. Transition out of the meditation with gentle kindness.

MINDFUL JOURNAL REFLECTIONS

Take a few minutes to describe in your journal the bodily sensations, thoughts, and emotions that arose in you as a result of this practice.

In part one, you've begun to explore the ground of awareness from which insight may arise, including mindfulness-based ColorInsight.

Move on to the next part when you are ready to look even more closely at what there is to be seen.

PART TWO

Seeing

Mindfulness is about recognizing what is, seeing more clearly and fully what there is to see.

These and thousands of other such things have brought me to see the whole caste system of the South, the whole complex net of its senseless cruelties and cripplings, as no mere accidental grotesquerie of history, but rather as that most hideous of errors, that *prima materia* of tragedy, the failure to recognize kinship . . .

My dream is simply that sight will one day clear and that each of the participants will recognize the other.

—CHARLES L. BLACK, JR., CONSTITUTIONAL LAW SCHOLAR[1]

CHAPTER SIX

LOOKING AT THE REALITY OF RACISM

There are people, no matter what ethnic group they belong to,
whose way of thinking is full of understanding and humanity,
whose way of speaking is full of hope and confidence,
and whose way of acting is full of compassion.

People can see the nobility in them.

—THICH NHAT HANH[1]

Contemplating Race and Racism

Mindfulness is a form of contemplative practice, a form of contemplation. But what is contemplation? How would you define it?

One definition of contemplation that I learned many years ago at the Jesuit university where I teach is simply this: a long, loving look at the real.[2]

If we are to end racism and its suffering, or even do effective work toward that end, we need to really see what we are up against. To contemplate it.

We need to take a long (lifelong), loving (heartful and compassionate) look at the reality of racism, and its underpinning, justifying idea: race.

Race: A Remarkably Persistent Imaginary Idea

Shela's experience, as discussed in the last chapter, helps us see a very important fact: the tendency to categorize and rank-order human beings—based on real and perceived differences—is pervasive across social groups and societies. Sociologists tell us that a countervailing tendency is also pervasive: the impulse to minimize differences and seek equality and fair treatment across our common humanity.

These two tendencies compete for dominance in any given place and time. The tendency to rank and order humanity reached a pernicious extreme in the Holocaust during the 1940s. And as a response, the Holocaust gave rise to the highest expression of a countervailing view of common humanity through the establishment of the United Nations (which took place in my current hometown of San Francisco in October 1945) and the Universal Declaration of Human Rights, adopted by that body in 1948.

In reality, each of us actually influences the direction our society takes—whether that be in favor of more hierarchy and domination, or of egalitarianism and human-dignity-based justice for all. Because remaining "neutral" or keeping silent favors the status quo, we must come to see that as we live, choose, and act, we are actually engaging in projects either of equality *or* oppression. Always.

Shela's story also helps us see that the notion of race is one of the most devastatingly effective constructs that we have created, used, and maintained to separate groups and build a sense of "natural" hierarchy in our societies. Over the course of Western history, since the period that gave rise to the transatlantic slave trade, race has served as an ever-ready channel for fear and threat—for justifying privileging some over others, for making some vulnerable for the benefit of the privileged.

Consider what it means to understand race as an imagined idea rather than a biological fact. Anthropologists tell us this. Geneticists tell us this. A U.S. Public Broadcasting Service documentary sought to clarify the matter in prime time: race is an illusion.[3]

The trouble is that the illusion of race is a very powerful, very seductive one. Although race is a biological myth, we have nevertheless created a vast lore of "race-making," by which we have identified others and ourselves.[4] Shela's pain came from realizing that this was happening to her, and that whatever the rules were, they were being made up variously as she went along. But what may have been less easy for Shela to see is how she participates in the making of race—both her own and others'.

We all do. We attach notions of race in ad hoc, culturally, and regionally defined ways to places, as well as bodies. In our minds, neighborhoods, states, and even continents are often implicitly or explicitly racially identified. And we perform and act in ways that reveal our investment in maintaining these notions of race and racial difference.

Racial identities, like other social identities, have been created in various cultures from the numerous ways that we categorize and group subsets of people within our populations. When we say that race is a *social construction*, we mean that race (like gender) is created and re-created, day to day, through social habits, trainings, and conditionings that range from personal performance to institutional policies, and are most often so subtle as to evade our conscious awareness.

Not one of us can escape from engaging in ongoing, often subtle practices of racialization or race-making—the personal, interpersonal, and ultimately systemic processes by which races and their social implications are made and remade daily, monthly, yearly, in each generation.[5] Through the subtle, often unintentional, social practices of racialization, we give political, legal, and social meaning and value to racial identities.

And yet, as we experience race and racialization today, these practices are neither as simple nor as uniform as they were in the past. For example, research over the past generation has helped us to see that the firmness with which we construct race is actually different for each racial group. In addition, the lived experience of members within so-called racial groups may vary widely with the intersections of other identities, such as class or sexual orientation.

When we look more closely at this thing called "race," then, we see a more complex picture than first meets the eye. It is so complex and so pervasive, in fact, that its inherent emptiness is often very hard to see. At the same time, if we can see its emptiness, we may be tempted to try to ignore race altogether. What we must become adept at doing is seeing race in more nuanced and sometimes contradictory ways. We must see how it is real and not real, at once. And we must at the same time resist investing it with the stories and meaning about it that we have inherited from previous generations. We need perceptive flexibility and the capacity to let go. Mindfulness can help us build those.

The Phantom of Race Arises in the Breach

As Shela's story helps make clear, racism often shows up in others' reactions when we appear to challenge or to violate our culture's conventional rules regarding race. These rules may be unspoken, or merely hinted at. They may vary greatly from place to place, from culture to culture. They may convey subtle understandings about which people we are expected to value or not, to respect or not, to love or not.

Taking the time to look at some of the ways that race is constructed in context—that is, in particular places and social eras—to see how the meanings we attach to similarly or differently hued bodies may vary across cultures, or even within a single culture, helps us see just how illusory the notion of biological race really is.

Consider a person growing up in Barbados, Trinidad, or the Dominican Republic, with skin color in the warm brown range. While he would not necessarily consider himself black in his home country, upon arrival in America, he would very soon be so categorized. The rules are not as rigid today as they were a century ago, but terms like "Afro-Latina" still give way to more confusion than understanding.

Pop star Rihanna was not the first immigrant to the United States to learn that she would be considered "black" under the rules of racialization still in effect here and in Europe. Yet as a child, she had been bullied for being "too white" in her native country.[6]

So, if we stop and take a closer look at the racial category we call "black," we may begin to see that blackness in the United States is not necessarily what it is in other countries. That's because the made-up rules that determine what constitutes "blackness," "whiteness," and other racial identities vary across societies, often in ways that reflect the somewhat different functions and uses of *racism* across those societies.

As a result of the centuries-long development of the law, practices, and social policies of enslavement, by which "black" and "white" were formed as polar opposites in a hierarchy of human worth, the white/black divide has traditionally dominated the American imagination when it comes to racial justice. So much so that when we talk about race in this country, we almost automatically think we are talking about black people. Or, to be more specific and in line with the typical narrative, about blacks in relationship to whites. This is so common an approach that it gave rise to a criticism of the oversimplification of how race works in the United States as "the black/white paradigm."

But of course, the story of race in America is *a lot* more varied than that. We know that racialization or "race-making" practices in our culture have resulted in a handful of commonly identifiable "racial groups" that extend beyond "blacks" and "whites," including Asian, Latino, American Indian, and "other." We have inherited systems that slot us into race-based categories even before we are born. Each nonwhite group has suffered greatly over the course of our history and, in that sense, has been subtly used to construct the often difficult-to-see privileges associated with whiteness.

And yet, we can see great diversity within the so-called Asian-American race, consisting of vastly different ethnicities such as Chinese, Filipino, Japanese, Korean, Pacific Islander, and sometimes East Indian. The centuries-old rules determining "blackness" and "whiteness" tend to make the same absurd collapsing of difference into sameness difficult to see. Segregating these groups into various communities and distributing opportunities along racialized lines only reinforces these often subtle thoughts and beliefs.

Meanwhile, genetic scientists have found more variation within so-called racial groups than across them.[7] In short, if we look closely at any of our racial groups, we can see clearly that these notions are social, cultural constructions that continue to impact the world.

Race Varies Across Racialized Groups

How we do race—that is, how we and the broader society participate in constructing it from one group to the next—often varies quite significantly from one group to the next. For example, in a well-regarded study of racial experiences and self-identification in the mid-2000s, researchers examined self-identification data from the 2000 census and interviewed multiracial individuals with Asian, Latino, and black backgrounds. Their analysis supported the conclusion that "the social construction of race is more rigid for blacks than for Asians and Latinos."[8]

Moreover, a recent study revealed important class-based differences among differently racialized groups in the United States.[9] Household income inequality varied across different groups, with Asian Americans generally out-earning all others in the United States, and Latinos earning the least. But it is worth noting that reported household income figures are typically not disaggregated to show how many adults' incomes have been added together to get to the total. This may mask the fact that some racial groups have to combine more incomes to get to the same level as a single wage-earner of another racial group. Also interesting is the fact that income inequality within these groups varied widely, with the gap being greatest *within* the Asian-American group when compared to others.

These variations suggest we must exercise caution lest we make too much of the similarity within each of these groups individually, to say nothing about broader amalgamations like "people of color."

Bringing mindfulness to bear on this information helps us to hold the complexity of racism in mind. Because our thoughts about race are often more impressionistic than factual, we should be open to being wrong. And because race-based impressions impact our lives, we should be open to listening and learning what we can. Our mindfulness practices support us in being willing to see and to see through: mindfulness helps us to hold our gaze long enough to see the paradoxes of race, to see through the construct of race and to see how it can be both real *and* fictional at once—and to see the way that it can be both debilitating and surmountable in some cases at the same time. And with mindfulness, we are able to hold what we see lightly, to look at it without turning away or minimizing what we see, and let go when we need to let go.

The complexity and contradictory nature of race does not justify ignoring it. We are willing to admit that despite knowing that race is less real than we sometimes think, most of us remain committed to applying the rules of race to ourselves, to our loved ones, and to others in ways that make a material difference. And others are conditioned to apply them to us and to those with whom we live and work. In other words, despite the fact that scientists consider race to be a social construct, we continue to define ourselves by these notions and often believe that they are more biologically based than science suggests. Just because race is not real does not make race and the privileges and disadvantages attached to it any less real in their profound consequences in each of our everyday lives.

RACIAL EMOTIONAL AWARENESS PRACTICE

Take your seat. Take a few very deep breaths, and then allow your mind to rest on the sensations of breathing in and out.

What thoughts, emotions, and sensations come up when you are asked to turn toward the topic of racial disparities when you are alone? What comes up for you in mixed company?

What are some of the stories you tell yourself to explain these disparate outcomes in the world? To what extent are these based on actual facts?

What insights on race are you aware of now that you may not have been aware of before beginning these practices?

Now release the thoughts, emotions, and sensations that arose as you looked at this issue.

AWARENESS OF THE EMBODIED SELF: LOVINGKINDNESS FOR THE YOU THE WORLD SEES

Take a few minutes to bring your attention to your body in this moment. Gently focus on your experience of this very moment. Get granular: notice the subtle sensations of breathing in and out, including the points of contact between your body and the ground beneath you. Rest in the strength of these grounding sensations.

Now call to mind one aspect of your outward identity that other people notice by sight or sound alone when they encounter you. This might be your gender, your age, or what you may think of as your ethnicity—aspects of language and culture that are part of how you identify yourself in the world.

As best you can, settle your attention on this aspect of your social identity, this way that you have been met according to the largely unspoken social and cultural rules of your time. Home in on this aspect of who you *appear* to be, which a person might notice or surmise *without* having had a conversation with you. Consider the impact of this in contexts in which you are known by others. Now consider the impact of this in contexts where you are not known—how this affects how you are received, what opportunities may be available to you, whether you are given the benefit of the doubt when those in power exercise discretion.

Pause and notice what thoughts, emotions, or sensations are arising in you right now. Look for any signs of denial or resistance. These may feel like sensations such as warmth, fuzziness, light-headedness, even sleepiness. You might be feeling bored or suddenly restless. See if you can slow down your processing; notice the thoughts behind these sensations.

Then, practice letting your thoughts (judgments, stories) go. Imagine each as a cloud floating across a blue sky, and return to the sensations of the body and the breath.

Now drop into the sensations of your body in this moment. Feel your connection with the ground beneath you. Breathe in and out, lengthening the out-breath as desired to assist in enhancing the sense of calm peacefulness within you. Allow your breathing to return to an easy, effortless rhythm.

Now, from this place of nonjudgmental awareness, gently, and with as much will to alleviate any suffering that arises in you as possible (self-compassion), turn toward the particular sensations of reactivity you notice in this moment. What does this feel like in your body?

What were you taught to believe about bodies like yours? About differently racialized bodies?

How might this aspect of your social identity have shaped your experience in the world? Have you spent more time in places where you were in a significant minority or majority based on your race or gender?

Are there ways that this identity has been a source of comfort to you? A source of advantage to you?

Are there ways that this identity has been a source of discomfort to you? A source of disadvantage to you?

Pause and reflect for a few minutes, again, with as much kind gentleness as possible. Notice the sensations, emotions, thoughts, and reactions that arise within you, especially any tendency to move away from what you know. As you bring this meditation to a close, offer appreciation, love, and kindness to the part of you that brought you to this willingness to know and to grow.

CHAPTER SEVEN

DEEPENING INSIGHT THROUGH COMPASSION

⌖

> But race is the child of racism, not the father. And the process of
> naming "the people" has never been a matter of genealogy and
> physiognomy so much as one of hierarchy. Difference in hue and hair is
> old. But the belief in the preeminence of hue and hair, the notion that
> these factors can correctly organize a society and that they signify
> deeper attributes, which are indelible—this is the new idea at the heart
> of these new people who have been brought up hopelessly, tragically,
> deceitfully, to believe that they are white.
>
> —TA-NEHISI COATES[1]

If Race Is a Fiction, Why Do We See It Everywhere?

For most generations in America, race was primarily created and reinforced by law, especially around enslavement and immigration. To better
understand how we got here, we have to consider just how and why race has
been constructed historically, particularly the making of blackness—and
conversely, whiteness and nonblack "Otherness"—in the United States.

During the country's first century, for the all-important purpose of
defining by law who could be held in lifelong captivity as a slave, compared
to those who would be eligible for freedom and citizenship, the "one-drop"
rule was developed: a person with even one drop of black blood was considered black in most parts of the colonies. They would be subject to

enslavement, and later, their descendants would be subject to race-based segregation—and would be vulnerable to all of the physical and psychological violence by which these systems were *really* made and maintained.

People not known to have so-called black blood were eligible for social and legal status as white. But citizenship law (or to be more specific, "naturalization" law) was created to further define whiteness and to render its demands for cultural assimilation invisible. The original federal law governing who could become a U.S. citizen, passed in 1790 (just three years after the Constitution went into effect), made it abundantly clear that citizenship was open only to "free white" men.

Until 1952, being legally categorized as "white" meant being given preferential treatment under U.S. citizenship law. Because Eastern Europeans were subject to marginalization, even immigrants from Europe changed their names to make them sound more generically white, further distancing their descendants from heritages and cultures that predated their embrace of whiteness. Further, courts of law took it upon themselves to determine whether a representative of one immigrant group after another was "white." In cases dealing with a Japanese resident and graduate of the University of California at Berkeley, a South Asian Indian who was the first turbaned soldier to serve in the U.S. Army, and a host of other potential citizens, the courts grappled with the question of "Who gets to be white?" and the material benefits of whiteness (including freedom from post-slavery segregation and the threat of violence, access to land, and fair wages). In a series of landmark cases, the courts decided that virtually none of these people was white. Hence, they were denied the right to become full citizens.[2]

All of this took place against the backdrop of the physical conquest—the harassment, killing, and literal clearing or "removal"—of the original, indigenous inhabitants of the land that we call the United States and its "territories."

The racial categories made and reinforced by slavery, immigration, and other laws were supported by laws and policies dealing with housing, policing, due process, education, and so on. They created incentives for all of us to negotiate what came to be called "the color line"—the cultural line dividing "whites" from "nonwhites." This social-legal complex of culturally visible signifying acts worked: it deeply embedded the idea of race, the normality of a race-based ranking, and the wide array of practices necessary to create a social hierarchy into the foundations of our culture.

The system of politically derived, socially sanctioned, and largely economically motivated race laws—governing everything from who could be married to whom, to where one could live, go to school, sit on a bus—defined one's racial experience and reinforced the big lie: the pseudo-scientific notion of racial difference. Once created, the system had a self-reinforcing character that makes the "reality" of race hard to resist even to this day.

It should be no surprise, then, that in the 1980s, more than one hundred years after the abolition of slavery and a generation after the modern civil rights movement, my then-boyfriend Jake and his family had been racialized white, and I, black. It should be no surprise that a social rule that went along with explicit, antiblack racism—that whites do not date blacks—would have survived into our lifetimes. And it should be no surprise that we continue to be tempted to live our lives in ways that reinvest in and maintain the rules protecting the interests of whiteness and to create new ones to govern racial relations for generations to come.

Over the years, the daily reminders that I am judged by my race and have been made to pay more and earn less because of my race have been sources of suffering in my life. I have learned many times and in many ways that racism is real. And if racism would cause me to suffer, it would cause many others to suffer in ways great and small—from doubting whether we belong, to paying more for credit, cars, rent, and houses (where available), and to being subjected to over-policing, police brutality, and unnecessary death.

Not surprisingly, research shows that race-based bias is pervasive.[3] At the same time, unawareness of our own biases—the tendency to have what social psychologists sometimes call "blind spots"—is extremely pervasive as well. In other words, most of us are biased, and while we can see biases in others, we tend to have great difficulty seeing just how biased we are ourselves. What's more: most of us have internalized the messages of our culture that reward us for biases *against* brown and black people, and rewards us for biases *in favor of* whites.

SELF-COMPASSION PRACTICE: PRACTICING TO HEAL YOUR OWN RACIAL SUFFERING

In ancient teachings the world over, influenced by a range of practices from Christianity to Islam, we are called to understand suffering in the world, and to meet it with love.

The teachings of the Buddha present us with the idea that while some forms of suffering are common to us all, there are causes of suffering, and there is a path to ending our suffering through mindfulness. The suffering we experience often arises from three basic habits: clinging when we should let go, pushing away when we should embrace, and being content within the fog of ignorance.

For this practice, call to mind a time when you were discounted or disrespected because of some aspect of what you look like or how you are perceived. Allow yourself to feel and sense into the part of you that can meet your own suffering with kindness.

If most of your suffering involves witnessing, at some distance, the suffering of Others (and perhaps talking with Others about their suffering), note what this suggests about your own lack of race-based disadvantage. Consider how this kind of privileged position has affected you. Has it contributed to any conflicts? Disconnections? Denials? Numbness? Anger? Confusion? Shame?

To whatever degree you feel any kind of suffering in this moment, admit it. Feel it. Name whatever pain, discomfort, or other bodily sensations—nausea, fatigue, headache, tightening of muscles—come with admitting what your privilege has meant in your life, what it has protected you from, and how you have clung to it.

Then, say to yourself gently: *"In this moment I acknowledge racial suffering in my mind, body, and community. Racial suffering is part of the human experience in societies where race matters. I deserve some support and kindness during this moment of racial suffering."*

And now, take a deep breath and look closer. See if you can look into the heart of the part of this suffering that is about race. As before, see if you can meet this with kindness.

Repeat the following to yourself: *"In this moment I acknowledge racial suffering in my mind, body, and community. Racial suffering is part of the human experience in societies where race matters. I deserve some support and kindness during this moment of racial suffering."*

Now sense where this experience of racial suffering is showing up in your body. Is it in tightness in the chest, the sudden rush of warmth that signals anger? Again, as best you can, give it a word. Is it disrespect? Is it something like shame? Or denial? Notice it and simply acknowledge: "The suffering of [rage, everyday disrespect, shame, denial, or numbness] is present."

Breathe in and out, and, as best you can, allow yourself to take in what you are feeling. You are working on deepening your capacity to see what there is to see and to accept what you see and feel for the moment.

Then you become aware of the causes of suffering. Is there some way in which you are trying to hold on, to grasp what you need to release? Or are you pushing something away? Or are you feeling confused, stuck in a fog of ignorance, or denying what you know?

Take a deep breath. Allow yourself to feel what you are feeling. What words describe that feeling?

Now see if you can let yourself feel the measure of your own desire for well-being, for relief from this suffering. Sense into the way that all human beings have the same desire to be free, to be loved.

This kind of practice—this act of cultivating awareness, love, and self-compassion—is what I call "personal justice." Cultivating a sense of personal justice—love correcting that within ourselves that revolts against love—is the foundation for well-being. Self-compassion practice is one aspect of personal justice practice. We'll explore additional practices as we go. For now, see if you can identify some of the ways that this particular practice may be one of the pathways to your work in racial justice. Write a brief note in your journal to remember your insights.

If Racism Is Still Alive and Well, Does It Hurt All of Us . . . or Only Some?

Although a good part of my racial suffering has come from my experience being black, I also had a sense that people racialized differently were suffering from the politics and cultural rules of race, just as my boyfriend Jake had suffered when we dated each other "out of line."

We all learn the rules of race, the often subtle messages about who matters more and who matters less. Research and everyday experience confirm that even people of color have internalized the rules by discounting our own nonwhite bodies and being more prone to hurt or otherwise discount people who are not white.[4]

Racism costs all of us. But it does not cost all of us equally.

Law professor Patricia Williams put it this way: "To be visibly black in this culture is to feel race every day—one can't forget it entirely when walking down the street. You're fingered, inescapably tagged—boxed in not by the form but by collective presumptions and cultural prejudgments—about beauty, criminality, intelligence, manners, articulateness, merit, health and contagion. That's the larger meaning of a social construction, after all: it has walls."[5]

Professor Williams's emphasis on the black experience, and on the particular problem of antiblack racism in the world, may seem unremarkable. But if you look at it closely, you can see that it suggests that both racism *and* progress along racial lines can happen simultaneously. There has been progress over the years; there *are* black lawyers and law professors, after all. *And yet* racism remains. There are fewer black lawyers and law professors, for example, than would be predicted by our numbers in the general population. And disproportionately higher criminal convictions, sentences, and deaths by police.

Yes, antiblack/pro-white racism remains a particular and perhaps defining aspect of what racism feels, tastes, and smells like in the United States (and in many other parts of the world). A white president of the United States, surrounded by an almost all-white leadership team, has reportedly referred to black countries as "shitholes." So, we need to see that antiblack/pro-white racism is a particular problem shaping our culture at this time (even as we see that it is not the whole or the sole problem).

We need to see that the black/white divide was central to understanding race in our parents' generations. More deeply than we can imagine, it helped shape their views, values, and what they dedicated themselves to fight for and against. Because we cannot help but see the world through the eyes of the generations who have taught us, the legacy of that black/white paradigm remains important to our understanding of how race influences us all.

And yet, we need a much more complex understanding of race and racism today. We must see racism through the lens of people from a full range of backgrounds. And we need to understand that this complexity does not, alone, mean that racism is somehow less a problem today than it used to be.

In the United States, we are significantly more Latino and Asian today than we were a generation ago. The changing racial characteristics of the population resulted in part from immigration law and policy reforms in the 1960s, reforms aimed at reducing the lingering pro-white bias in the system. The immediate effect of the changes was an increase in a curated, highly educated strata of immigrants from Asia, Latin America, and the Caribbean. In the generations since, increases in rates and forms of immigration and intermarriage have given rise to new patterns of identity formation around race and national origin, including a rise in those who identify as multiracial.

None of these changes has eliminated racism. None has done away with its distinctively pernicious antiblack antipathy, and subtle, almost invisible pro-white themes. Yes, the questions today are often more nuanced and more complex. When we seek to see and understand racism today, we have to look closely, patiently, and with the capacity to see unconventionally.

We examine what we see and ask: Is it some version of the traditional white versus black paradigm? Or, is this a version of the broader white versus nonwhite (or "people of color") story? Has the plot thickened, such that we would be better off looking at the black versus nonblack divide, in which people of color generally are acceptable, but black people are less so to virtually everyone? Or are we witnessing something that resembles a three-way approach to understanding race and racism today—white, black, and variously ignored or manipulated "Others," depending on the needs of the moment? Or, something else?

And what is at stake for whiteness in all of this? Whatever whiteness is in our culture's imagination, and whatever is at stake, it isn't exactly what it was in the past. It is not what it was for Jake's parents. In a world in which race-based identity seems to be a gateway to political power, I am not surprised that in the absence of other ways of thinking about it, some whites will be drawn to a version of white identity that gives them a sense of revitalized political strength. The rise of white nationalism and related racism is understandable in this light.

We have all encountered whiteness and its dictates. If you have been racialized white, you may want to look very closely. How was this identity formed in your family? Was a name changed, its spelling anglicized? What neighborhoods or other structures defined your ancestors as white? These and other questions must become more commonplace if we are to advance. As a culture, then, we must be prepared for a long and courageous look at the nuances of whiteness. Fortunately, more and more of us are doing just that, with whiteness-sensitive racial justice organizations showing up across the country. But this work must not be episodic. It is not about going to one conference or retreat, listening to a presentation, attending a workshop now and again. Or even, much as I'd like it to be so, reading just one book.

This. Must. Be. Ongoing.

Because our unwillingness to look at the majority experience, at whiteness in particular, and to reflect in a fulsome way on the experience and functions of white identity, is a big part of what we are up against. But if we have the courage to examine whiteness, to see it more clearly, we might be able to ask *and answer* better questions together. And we just might be able to see how actually to do the work, together, of redeeming the history of white supremacy, of acknowledging it, actively rejecting it, and deconstructing it where it remains as a part of our culture. We might be able to envision a new story of America without leaving white people bereft of a sense of belonging in it today.

Yes, racism today is complicated. Considering whiteness more deeply is essential to contemporary antiracism work. For all of us. Because whiteness is like the air we breathe. We are all in it one way or another, and we need to bring awareness to it if we are to make a more just future.

The Costs of Racism

For people of color, the cost of racism is partly psychological—making it nearly impossible for some of us not to think about race as a factor in our experiences in the world. But the fundamental cost of it is material, creating and reinforcing walls that block access to necessary resources—including education, money, health care, and political power—rendering the vulnerable all the more so.

The legacy costs of racism differ, depending on the stereotypes and histories that our skin and features call to mind in social interactions with others and the structures of inequality in which we live and work. But it does cost *all* of us. And the costs of racism are truly immeasurable. They are not only economic or financial, but show up in every dimension of our lives, including the social and emotional, the personal and political. As one recent participant of a workshop reported from her vantage point as a black community organizer: "Race-based [antiblack] violence is *everywhere*." Which, to the extent true, means that the temptation to invest in cultural white supremacy as protection against that violence is everywhere, too.

Racism and structural inequality cost us relationships with those whom we are told not to care about. We lose a sense of peaceful, common community, and this costs more than peace of mind—research shows that people who live in societies with relatively less inequality enjoy healthier and longer lives.[6]

But what's even more is this: racism costs *lives*. Not merely through hate crimes and biased law enforcement, but through the soft deaths that inevitably result from structural discrimination embedded, sometimes unintentionally, within public policies—in areas ranging from health care to education to the environment. The fact that racism costs some of us more than others obstructs our ability to see it more clearly together and to do the work of disrupting the system of privileges it was built to maintain.

Understanding Privilege

The notion of privilege, and in particular, white privilege, has been a mainstay of discussions about racism in the United States and other countries around the world since the 1990s. Despite the relative simplicity of the idea—that with our country's massive historical investment in cultural white supremacy came social, cultural, and institutional practices of attachment to it that lead to innumerable unearned benefits tied to white skin and proximity to it—talk of privilege is often fraught.

What sensations come up for you when you hear the phrase "white privilege"? Notice the sensations in the body, the thoughts, and any emotions that come up for you.

Over the years, I have learned that many people find it difficult even to think about privilege, much less discuss it in mixed company. In fact, many who consider themselves engaged in antiracist education find it so unhelpful that they no longer use the phrase.

But let's look at it together.

White privilege is the structural, systemic means by which whiteness is preferred and white experience is considered both normal (i.e., what is most often the case) and normative (i.e., what should be the case) in a given place and time. It comprises the often subtle systems that normalize and give added value to white experience and perspectives.

Obviously, a biased point of view might often arise from the experience of white privilege. That biased point of view is a key aspect of the lived experience of being white, but it also rubs off on the rest of us. Whether consciously or not, most people in a racist society—not only those most privileged—come to believe, or at least to internalize, the typical explanations by which white privilege is justified. Moreover, they often come to believe that they lose less and gain more when they follow the rules of racism that disadvantage the racialized, nonwhite Other.

Research has shown that, over time, antiracist policies such as school integration raise the outcomes and performance measures for all.[7] And studies show that societies with less inequality experience greater health and well-being.[8] Rather than operating as a zero-sum game in which people of color benefit while whites lose, we all benefit from inclusive organizations, welcoming environments, and the lessening of inequality that leads to more just communities.

Privilege and the Benefits of Dismantling It Are Hard to See

The benefits of inclusion are not obvious. And reports of these benefits are often difficult to hear. Here again, research can help us understand why. Psychologists describe our tendency to resist such information and to prefer to focus on and overstate even minor losses to our positions as "availability bias"; we spend more time worrying about what's most available to remind us of how we have suffered in the past and what we still have to struggle against.[9] These reactions may further reveal what psychologists call "negativity bias"—our tendency to focus on the negative and downplay the positive aspects of experiences.[10]

It is important to note that systems and structures of privilege may be associated with our gender, age, immigration status, the language we speak, our sexual orientation, and our looks (including height, weight, and skin tone, especially our degree of "lightness" in white supremacist cultures). And all of these intersect with and may inform privileges or disadvantages associated with our perceived race. It is essential to take these intersections into account, to realize that our experiences are shaped by many things. It's critical to bring nuance to our discussions of the privileges associated with whiteness.

The challenging truth is that white privilege may move those advantaged by it—whether by being considered "white" or by mere proximity to whiteness—a bit more smoothly and beneficially through life in ways that can be genuinely hard to see. And it may be even harder to admit it to ourselves and to acknowledge it to others. Perhaps most challengingly, because it is not controlled by its holder, white privilege is almost impossible for any individual actually to dislodge. But there are ways to disrupt it, and admitting that you have white-skin privilege may be a first step.

How much privilege plays out in our lives depends on context—where we are, what we are doing and with whom, and the cultural stories that circulate around us and send racially coded messages about who belongs and who does not. I call this difficult-to-see racial context "racetext." It is our will to ask, "Who is in this room?" and, on looking around, to note that we are mostly, as I often hear from at least one courageous white person in response to this question, "a bunch of white people." Racetext is also there when we don't ask this question.

Silence around what we know about racetext is harmful. Our blind spots make it difficult to see that such silence actually biases our environments. It creates psychological comfort for those whose privileges are supported by the silence, and it creates vulnerability for those harmed by it. This is one of the subtle ways that our environments may be biased in ways that maintain white privilege. Our blind spots, combined with our penchant for individualism, make it hard to see how race-text shapes whether we are seen as—or feel like—one who belongs, or as an "Other."

The great difficulty many of us have in seeing racism, racially infused contexts, and other aspects of bias helps explain why both mindfulness and compassion can help us with antiracist work. Compassion—for ourselves and for others—helps make it possible to recognize that what we have been trained to see is simply not the whole picture. Self-compassion helps us to acknowledge the cognitive dissonance that arises when this is pointed out to us. It helps us to bear the pain of seeing our own biases and the work we need to do to minimize their harm.[11] Compassion for others—fueled by an ethical commitment to doing no harm—helps us maintain the will to keep working at it when it gets hard, as it inevitably will.

Cognitive bias both arises from and gives rise to racism. Over the course of my lifetime, I've seen shifts in the nature of racism in our culture—from explicit racism to the subtle racial insults known as *microaggressions*, and unfortunately, back to explicit racism again. Microaggressions can take the form of questions like, "Where are you *from?*" when one's race is ambiguous to the questioner. Or comments like, "You speak English so well!" from a white woman to an Asian American whose family's roots in the San Francisco Bay Area date to the Gold Rush.

The results are the same. They convey disrespect and leave in their wake a persistent sense of vulnerability to being discriminated against or worse—to being a victim of violence. Microaggressions are a subtle form of unconscious racism. And for a time not so long ago, most people thought that this was the only sort of race problem (if any!) that we had to deal with today.

As we have already seen, the truth has turned out to be otherwise. We are seeing a rise of old-fashioned conscious, explicit racism, and in some cases racist terrorism. Once again, the lesson is that racism is a more constant, slippery, and persistent feature of our culture than we often tend to think. The tendency for it to persist and arise again and again might even be permanent.

Seeing Is Awakening

I lived through the post-'60s fight for public, inclusive justice in the United States, the one shaped by the fickle policies and practices of integration and affirmative action. In 1977, when I was just ten years old, a brand-new school opened up within walking distance from our modest home. It was equipped with a planetarium rather than a pool, and it had spaces that could be adapted for all kinds of learning experiences. It was integrated and predominantly white, and yet I felt inspired and included enough as a student there to run for—and to win—the position of seventh grade president. The new school operated for just three years, before being placed into presumably better service as the headquarters of the city school board.[12]

Most kids in my neighborhood were reassigned to less-inspired schools. By luck, I ended up applying for and gaining entrance into a magnet school that brought together students across the socioeconomic spectrum. In this and many other ways, I bore witness to how the scant efforts at transformative justice in the 1970s gave way to so-called color-blind policies of the 1980s—those that taught us that "the way to get beyond race is to get beyond race"[13] and rewarded us for looking away as the structures of racial inequality reasserted themselves.

If we are willing to take a look, we will find that the data of our very own lives tell a story of differences in outcomes in terms of race. Whether we look at education rates, health outcomes and life expectancies, police brutality or "disproportionate police contact," we see evidence of continuing disparities in life chances and vulnerabilities correlated with race, with blacks performing worse than whites and others across most indicators. We must challenge the notion that, rather than reflecting injustice and discrimination, these outcomes reflect simply natural differences?

If we lived in a world without pervasive biases, especially antiblack biases, we might be able to justify the conclusion that differences are natural. But given the persistence of such biases, ignoring the connections between bias, racism, and outcomes in the world seems like willful blindness. Those willing to see will see.

And if we are committed to fairness, to a world in which race matters less and less in people's lives, then we need to do more than see. We need to take a stand. We need to be willing to look for evidence of ongoing bias against people who have been traditionally discriminated against. And we must be willing to share what we see. We have to be open to seeing contemporary racism in our everyday lives and beyond. From color-blind policies in a world in which everyone still sees race, to microaggressions, to false equivalencies between experiences of differently racialized people.

If we are willing to see, we might recognize just how we participate in the normalization of racial inequality. We might become aware of how we have been trained not to see inequality as "our" problem. If we are willing to see, we just might notice how it is that in our neutrality, we are in fact contributing to the ongoing injuries of racism.

The truth is that America—including our Constitution, institutions (legal, educational, religious, cultural, and so on), and founding doctrines— was built on and shaped to accommodate white supremacy. The legacies of that history have faded but have not gone away. The tracks that they carved into our dominant culture run deep. And this, in a nutshell, is why we "see" so much race and racism to this day. Although it is hard for some of us to hear and to reflect on this, the plain truth is clear from the historical record—seeing race and practicing racism are part of our country's DNA. Seeing the pervasive structures of white supremacy that run through dominant culture is its own moment of awakening. From there, mindfulness may help us determine how to relate to what we see.

The Civil Rights Movement Made Racism Harder to See and to Name, Not Less Prevalent

Multicultural democracy in the United States has been a dream of many across the generations here. And yet, it has always been more dream than reality. We are increasingly reminded of the threat of racially motivated violence, which has such deep roots in our culture that we should not be surprised when it arises from time to time. Here and now, we face the fact that the ugly underpinnings of our past, fanned by the fears that accompany rapid change, are increasingly resurgent today.

Although we don't always discuss it, racism is often, if not always, a theme in everyday politics. Politics is about power, the power to distribute collective resources. Given the way that whites were for so long the most favored racial group under citizenship law, were considered most normal and best suited for positions in leadership and pop culture stardom, and were deemed most deserving of wealth and status—the ideology and practices of white supremacy became fused with what it meant to be "American." It should be no surprise, then, that when many of us think of those most deserving of America's wealth and resources, many of us in some way think of whites. The presumption of entitlement to participate in our political community and to enjoy well-being within it is one example among many of the subtle privileges of whiteness.

Even when we see white privilege, however, it can be difficult to know what should be done about it. After reading a great deal about racism and its effects, a white male participant in a recent discussion said: "I don't know why we should be talking about reducing the privilege of whites. Why can't we simply *increase* the privilege of everyone else?" He seemed unable to see that the privileges of whiteness actually depend on, exist because of, the deprivation—the "keeping down"—of others. To feel racial privilege is to feel privilege *over* some other racialized group.

Because of its stature in American history, culture, and political discourse, racism seems more legitimate to many of us than we can easily admit. Disavowing it can seem like a rejection of the founding heroes of our society. And yet, to see racism and our role in limiting the harm that it causes, we have to confront this and decide how to take on this history in humanity-affirming ways today.

Many if not most people will admit to believing that there is at least some basis for racism's underpinning concept: race. Despite what science says, belief in biological race remains. And even if it isn't biological, many believe it is something real that is indelibly stamped on racialized cultures. If you believe that race is real, then the notion of differences in capacity and worth based on race may seem all the more difficult to resist. This, too, may get in the way of taking a firm stance against racism and in favor of relating to one another from the perspective of our common humanity.

Nevertheless, to move us forward and out of the endless cycle by which race continues to have an outsized impact on us all, we must take action to dissolve racism in our midst. Precisely because our history of white supremacy has deep and lasting legacies, we need to continually confront and disarm them. We have long needed to engage in a thorough uprooting of the ideology of racism and its legacies in all of our institutions and communities. The simple truth is that we have not done this. Even at what some see as the high point of the U.S. civil rights movement—when *Brown v. Board of Education* held that segregation of public schools was unconstitutional—we did not explicitly name white supremacy as a wrong that must be made right. We did not confront and then commit to *undoing* the ways of thinking that gave rise to segregation and other oppressions over the course of our history. To this day, we have not admitted the sins on which our fragile democracy rests, nor asked for forgiveness and sought true redemption. We have not done the work necessary to give birth to a political community in which all of our children truly belong and in which traditionally marginalized people receive equal respect.

Beyond the urgent work of addressing and, to the extent possible, healing wounds of trauma we've experienced—individually and as communities—we need to engage in the work of seeing and minimizing the effects of bias in our minds and social lives. Over the past quarter-century, there has been an explosion of research and development of tools to assist us in seeing the hidden workings of our own minds. If we are willing, we are more able today to understand and to develop ways of disrupting our habits of biased reactions to others than ever before. And we can help others do so as well.

Becoming aware of and grappling with the fact that our minds and bodies are biased in ways that support white supremacy, even though we consciously believe that they are not, can be difficult in and of itself. We need a commitment to meditating on this. And we need a great deal of self-compassion along the way. Self-compassion sustains us as we do the painful work of seeing ourselves and our circumstances rightly, and this is the first step in personal healing and societal transformation.

Collective Healing as the Foundation for a More Just World

Personal healing must precede the transformation of our communities. We already have every potential, every capacity that we need to do more to actually overcome the racism that has plagued our nation for so long. If we have the will to commit, to learn together, and to work on ourselves to help us remain awake and willing to grow, we can do this. If we are willing to engage in the practices that advance revelation and transformation, we are on our way. And if we understand that this work will be ongoing if it is to make real differences in our lifetimes, we can't be stopped.

We *can* bear the difficulty of exploring means of redressing racism— not merely personal or interpersonal acts of bias, but structural and broader systemic causes as well. And we truly *can* get to a place where being and working with others around these issues is a source of healing— a source *not* of painful re-wounding, but of daily and unceasing *joy*. We can begin to heal not merely the wounds of racism, but the disconnection from the abundance of our earth home.

If we are willing to continue to look at how race has operated in our own lives and in the lives of others, we can deepen our understanding of race and truly change how it operates in our lives and in the lives of others. We can overcome racism, sexism, and the variety of other ways that we act on habits, impulses, and conditionings to see people who are different from us as "Others."

We *all* need to notice, reflect on, and work against the habits we have of seeing others through the lenses of the clumsy categories of race and stereotypes. Every. Single. One. Of. Us. Research confirms the usefulness of taking steps to free ourselves from our tendency to internalize the judgments of others. We can take back our power, our agency. We can change how we perceive and relate to our experience, a shift that in itself may free the mind. From this place, we can be sources of deep change in the world.

Simply looking with patience and compassion at how we "do" identities in our own lives, and how identities have been and still are being "done" to us, deepens our ability to see more completely all that we have been trained not to see. By thinking about the makeup of the communities in which we've lived and worked, the schools we attended, and learning how they got that way, we begin to see how our own and others' experiences are shaped by much more than what we thought or intended. Our thoughts are shaped by our environments in ways that are essential to see more clearly.

MINDFUL REFLECTION

For now, take a moment to pause. Imagine the people in your social circle who are actively working to minimize social distances, bias, and racism. Think of those around the world working toward the same goals. Now expand your reflection to include the ancestors on whose shoulders we all stand. Imagine linking arms/hands with all of these people. You are not alone in your aspirations for a more just world in which we remember our common humanity. Allow the image of this circle to further support you through the challenges to come.

In this chapter, you've moved further along the path by beginning what I hope will be a lifelong practice of taking a long, compassionate look at race and racism. You've explored the harmful effects of racial suffering and reflected on some of the ways that race has been politically useful as a tool of division among people whose real interests are remarkably the same.

You've seen a bit more of how race has shaped your own experiences, interactions, and communities. And you may have noticed how seeing more fully can be both painful and heart-opening as well. The combination of learning and awareness and compassion practices that you have begun to settle into is not only healing, but will also generate new insight, new ways of understanding the life you live and the lives of others in ways that will touch and improve your connections with others.

Pause, with lovingkindness. Feel yourself breathing. Feeling the support for you on your journey, and appreciating the goodness in your own heart that got you here, take a moment to rest in that goodness before moving forward.

CHAPTER EIGHT

SEEING IMPLICIT BIAS

The great force of history comes from the fact that we carry it within us,
are unconsciously controlled by it in many ways, and history is literally
present in all that we do. It could scarcely be otherwise, since it is to
history that we owe our frames of reference, our identities,
our aspirations.

And it is with great pain and terror that one begins to realize this. In
great pain and terror one begins to assess the history which has placed
one where one is and formed one's point of view.

—JAMES BALDWIN[1]

This Is Your Brain on Bias

I am not Anita Hill.[2]

I do, however, share a few social identities with her. Two are visible
on sight: my race (black) and my gender (female)—along with all of the
meanings, assumptions, and stigmas associated with them. In America,
as in most other parts of the world, these two identities have been pushed
aside, downgraded, and placed at the bottom of social rank orders for
centuries.

The third social identity that I share with Anita Hill is not obvious
from my appearance alone. This identity—based on my profession, and on
the socially coded information it conveys—comes up in conversation

sometimes when I meet someone new. Because it is not usually associated in people's minds with black women, it seems to challenge the identity understandings that travel with the first two. Like Anita Hill, I am a lawyer.

The following story, my "Anita Hill" story, is just one example of how my identity as a lawyer challenges some people's assumptions about me. It is a story of everyday race-making.

It's October 1991, and I am spending my first Saturday night in the city of San Francisco. I am a law student in town for an interview, seeking a job at a law firm for the following summer.

I am standing in line at a café next door to a theater in the city's gritty downtown. It is intermission during a show I am attending, and I had followed the flow of people spilling out of the theater's dark seating area. The most important question in my mind at the moment is whether to get a gelato, cold as it is (it is summer in San Francisco!); I am encouraged by the fact that so many around me seem to be enjoying theirs.

I engage in a simple, flirtatious bit of small talk with a man in line next to me. By appearances, he is white and middle-aged. I am, as I have been for most of my life, open to talking to someone who does not look like me. Over the course of the chat, it comes out that I was not merely a young, petite, black woman, worthy of a flirty conversation. I am all of that *plus* a person who is studying to become *a lawyer.*

In that very instant, something seemed to shift in my conversation partner. For a split second, he seemed not to know where to "place" this information. Suddenly, he blurted out what remains in my mind to this day for its *Snap!*—its sudden revelation of something of the hidden racial context in which our interaction was being invisibly shaped, something of what social psychologists call "narrative scripts": the deep operating story systems running through our minds.

"Oh, you're a *law* student?" He stammered a little, as if somewhat taken aback. "Why, you might be the next *Anita Hill!*"

Ah, yes. "The next Anita Hill" is what I might become, and in that instance, I had already become—this notion of me and who I "might become"—derived from someone who by social identity characteristics alone, might be considered "just like me."

In its best light, this comment was likely meant to be a compliment. And yet, I could see in him a vague sense of awkwardness, of perhaps feigned admiration, and more than a hint of apprehension, trepidation, fear.

The meeting, like all meetings in the social worlds in which we all travel, was not gender blind. And yet, it was not merely between a man and a woman. There was more. There was race. And though we had not mentioned it, there was not a moment during our conversation in which we did not know that race was there, between us, running through us. His comment confirmed it. It confirmed that he was not (and could not have been) "color blind" in a chat with me.

Looking back, I can see that it was a meeting of what social scientists call our social "constructions," the conceptual inputs of the stories by which we make sense of the world. Allow me to offer a bit more context, which of necessity is only one-sided. I was not merely on a recruitment trip; I was on what was, at that point, the trip of my lifetime. In my second year of study as a law student, I'd been invited out by a law firm to interview for a position as a summer associate. From where I'd started, the odds of me getting to this place felt like that of winning a million-dollar lottery. High off the string of new life experiences unfolding for me, I was doing something new that would stand out in my memory, in case I never made it back to San Francisco again. And that's how I came to be standing in line at a café, next to a man I did not know, surrounded by a bunch of people I did not know, tumbleweeding along a part of the American cultural landscape that I did not know. As it happened, I was the only one who looked like me—a brown-skinned black woman. I moved through the strange, exciting streets with that open disposition associated with tourists from someplace else—in a city that, for all its reputation as progressive, is remarkably closed to less urbane, often liltingly accented, and pointlessly friendly people like the person I was on that day.

On my own for the night, I was delighted when this man struck up a conversation with me. When I dropped that I was a law student out on a recruitment interview for a job at a law firm downtown, his comment made clear to me something that I'd allowed myself to forget, or to believe might not be true *this* time—that my race and gender were inconsistent with my new-to-me identity as a lawyer. It apparently triggered a memory of perhaps the only other black woman lawyer that my white male conversation partner knew of—one who just happened, at that moment in time, to be all over the news in a not-altogether-positive way.

Because black women and white men often live very separate lives, we are, when we do meet, more vulnerable than we think to the incomplete, one-sided, white-sided stance of the typical media.

And so, back to that moment.

"You might be the next *Anita Hill*!"

I smiled and agreed, awkwardly. "Maybe!" I said, although I didn't quite understand what he meant.

It seemed that he had said this with a strange mix of "Congratulations!" "Oh, shit," and "Girl, 'bye!" Somehow I could feel that whatever he meant, this was most likely, ultimately, not a good thing.

I knew who Anita Hill was, of course. At the time, everyone did. Anita Hill had only recently accused the second black man ever to be nominated to the Supreme Court of sexual harassment.

Was this the only image in his mind through which he could make sense of me? Did he have so little experience of professional black women, of black women as lawyers, through which to make my existence otherwise possible?

Instantly, his willingness to chat turned to a businesslike focus on awaiting his turn to order refreshments. Instantly, there was a wall between us. Hadn't it, or the ghost of it, been there all along?

In the next few moments, the white man made his way to the register, ordered, paid, collected, and left the joint without further conversation. Of course the play was about to restart, so we both might have been inclined in any event to move along without the further delay of a final word or two. Still, the speed with which his demeanor changed, from friendly to distant, or defended, was striking to me.

Again, although I could see that he probably meant well—Anita Hill was, after all, a certain kind of success story—I was stunned by this remark.

And also, stung. I was not then and am not now Anita Hill. I'm Rhonda. And yet, in that moment, I had been prefigured, packaged, reduced to a facsimile of the one other figure whose name we both knew, whose characteristics seemed like mine from a squinty-eyed distance. The image put a tidy finish on a potential connection.

"The next *Anita Hill!*"

And so, that's the story. Just a small incident in the racialized, gendered life of one black female. Incidents like this occur again and again. If we are to "get" how race and gender affect our lives, we need to have the will and interest to reflect on such incidents in our own and others' lives.

The Roots of Our Implicit Biases

We've seen some of the many ways that our social identities are prone to reveal often unconscious but deep-seated notions that may lead us to put a foot in it. We will look more closely at how these identities are often not what they may appear to be. And we will practice ways of working with our identities that can lessen our dependence on traditional notions of them, and on the biases that they help us maintain.

Reflecting on such presumably minor incidents must push us to see the particular locations and contexts within which biases arise. We can look for patterns in what we see to deepen our understanding of our own experience and the role of our social environments in shaping our life outcomes. For example, the white man I encountered at the café likely had not had much more than passing experience with people like me. Data show that most communities across the country remain remarkably and persistently segregated, even if not legally required. Research and everyday life experience confirm that when we live in segregated communities, our limited ideas about one another, our notions of groups of "Others" who exist on the periphery, are remarkably durable. And the tendency to make *one example* the story of "all of them" is one of the oldest of human habits.

Thus it is more easily understandable that in the mind of a man who knew only that I was a black, female lawyer, I would trigger a connection to the only other black, female lawyer that he likely had ever really come to "see," even if only under the inevitably distorting lights of her testimony before Congress: Anita Hill. Psychologists say that we humans create categories and unthinkingly put our "roughly similar" experiences in them over time. They call these psychological shortcuts "schemas."[3] Schemas are unconscious, *sticky*, and essential for getting through the world—once we know the schema for a chair, we don't have to investigate, from the ground up, every four-legged object with a base at seat-height and a place for resting one's back. Obviously not all such associations are harmful, but when we do this to human beings, the harm is well known. Schemas shadow our conscious thought processing in ways that we cannot fully control and that, if we do not work to counteract them, persist over time. Social problems arise because we do not, indeed cannot, reserve our schemas for mechanical objects like chairs. It pains me to admit that while I have been known to give white men and people from all walks of life the benefit of the doubt, I've got identity-based schemas, too.

The process of becoming mindful can assist us in knowing ourselves, being more familiar with the habits of our minds and our own emotional reactivity—the anger, confusion, numbness, and outrage that arise when we see racism. It helps us become more self-compassionate and, thus, minimizes the drama of encountering racism.

Indeed, mindful awareness can help us figure out how to *respond*, rather than to *react*. We learn to see more clearly just what we might do, what more effective steps we might take. Sometimes, this means simply letting things go, but other times, it means resolving to make a difference—responding to our pain with understanding, with care for ourselves and others.

Attending to the sensations of pain with compassion is good for us. It is also essential practice for attending to the pain caused by racism. Whatever our intentions, we can do more harm than good if we are not able to bring kindness and compassion to it. And if we cannot bring kindness to ourselves, we will, in like measure, have difficulty bringing it to others.

Self-compassion helps us to bring mindfulness and deeper understanding to our pain. We bring it to bear as we ask questions like: What specific injury or pain have you seen in the world as a result of racism? What do you know or imagine the consequences of it have been? How has it hurt you personally? And what are some of the biases that you still carry as a result? How might mindfulness practice help?

PRACTICING MINDFULNESS OF INTENTIONS
FOR DOING RACIAL JUSTICE WORK

Take a few minutes to settle into the body in this moment and space. Feel the ground beneath you. Rest in the sensations of being alive.

Breathe in and out and reflect on the following question, Why am I reading this book?

Note what answer arises. Then, release that answer completely. Allow the feelings and thoughts, images or stories that have come up to fall away.

Breathe in and out for several cycles, settling into this moment.

Now, ask yourself again: What feelings or thoughts brought me to reading this book?

Take a few minutes with this inquiry.

Allow whatever insight might arise to simply be present.

Ask yourself: Where am I seeing racism up close?

How am I living notions tied to my own "race"?

What racial (or other identity-based) slurs am I using or hearing in my interactions with others?

What stereotypes am I coming up against or noticing about: Black women? White men? Asian women? Asian men? Mexicans? Latinas? Latinos? Filipinos? Haitians? Puerto Ricans?

As you reflect on the demographics of your own environment, bring to mind racial groups and the associations you carry with them.

What ideas about race did you pick up from your family or neighborhood? How are they affected by information you are receiving now (through media or otherwise)?

Now allow these thoughts, sensations, and emotions to drift away, to fall into the earth. Let them go.

And this is, perhaps, the most important aspect of the practice: see if you can just be present to any pain or distress that remains.

Now come back gently to a reflection on your intentions.

What *really* draws you to this work? If you are seeking something, see if you can name what that is. Allow yourself to simply accept what arises, without judgment. Do you want a sense of peace? Greater understanding?

Take a deep breath. Breathe in a sense of acceptance of what is here, with as little judgment as possible.

Is there any part of you that is wanting to feel better, more evolved, more "awake" than others? To prove that you are already a good enough person and don't really have to work on this too much more?

Which of these intentions would you most like to carry forward in the work ahead?

Be gentle with yourself as you let these many layers come into clearer focus.

If you can, take a few minutes to make some mindful reflections in your journal about what has come up. What might be behind your motivations?

Close with a reflection on the intentions you will bring to this work going forward.

Developing in ourselves the ability to understand race today requires the cultivation of the intention to see and to stay present with what we see in a way that allows us to actually get it. The intention-setting, awareness-raising practice I just detailed is an important step along the way. As you reflect on why this work matters to you, and on what you know about the difficulties we all face, you will find a deeper ground on which to rest when the going gets tough.

We will inevitably, at some point or another, feel misunderstood, or find ourselves on the receiving end of some strong feelings. Sometimes these feelings are leftovers that a person carries and drops on us from a prior experience for reasons that may or may not be clear to us. Sometimes they are perfectly justified by your own less-than-skillful behavior. Sometimes we offend or hurt others, even when we do not mean to do so.

While bringing mindfulness and intentionality to racial justice work is really important, it is in no way a means of avoiding responsibility when we mess up. We will have to figure out how to meet the part of us that is learning and growing and trying our best with kindness, and to meet the people we inadvertently hurt with the same. Our good intentions serve as both a ground and a solace, but never function as a justification for bypassing being present with racial justice work.

CHAPTER NINE

RAINing RACISM:
RECOGNIZING, ACCEPTING,
AND INVESTIGATING RACISM WITH
NON-IDENTIFICATION

> Through intense meditation practice . . . I came to uncover how I had
> internalized negative racist and sexist opinions and also came to see
> more clearly the truth of those experiences in my social and
> professional interactions.
>
> —BONNIE DURAN[1]

This Is Your Brain on Mindfulness

So far, we've been weaving together the mutually reinforcing disciplines of practice and, for lack of a better phrase, book learning, which are essential to developing insight into racism and racialization in our times. By sharing some of my own stories, my hope is that you will inquire into your own.

The contemplative practices of mindfulness and compassion are foundational to seeing racial dynamics at play and to moving with some ease through difficult terrain. Mindfulness teacher Michele McDonald distills the inquiry dimension of mindfulness practice into four key processes using the acronym RAIN: Recognize, Accept, Investigate, and Non-Identify. It is through this practice of inquiring beneath the surface of our experience that we wake up, see more clearly, and develop insight into the true nature of things. I rely on this practice just about every day.

Let me break down the RAIN practice in a bit more detail. When we practice mindfulness, we are developing the ability to notice, or *Recognize*. We pause. We observe from all angles—the obvious ones and those less so. Even in simple Awareness of Breathing practice, we are holding in awareness what we observe. If we want to explore further, we engage all the senses, witnessing what we are experiencing in real time. *Recognizing* is about deepening our perception to more effectively see and understand the pain we seek to address in the world and the joy, beauty, and everything else.

The next step in the process is to *Accept* (or allow) what we see. For the moment, we release any tendency to reject, to deny, to change, or to be at war with reality. As the saying goes, it is what it is. *Accepting* for the moment does not mean that we accept forever. It means we pause long enough to really see something clearly, as a prelude to really looking into what we see and deepening our understanding. It is not passive resignation.

The third step, then, is to *Investigate* what is coming up. This is the heart of the RAIN practice. It is through our gentle, compassionate, and courageous investigations that we learn and grow in self-awareness, empathy, and wisdom. We move in close and look underneath the hood, so to speak. We ask ourselves: What is causing this physical sensation, emotion, or thought? What conditions or trainings underlie it? Here we have to be willing to go easy on ourselves. We are opening to what we know in our bodies, what is written on our bones. This slow-going effort to know and to better understand (even a little bit!) our reactive sensations—our feelings of sadness or numbness, our protective pulling away, our unique way of suffering—is so very worthy of our attention.

Importantly, we investigate with the self-care that we have been working to establish deep within ourselves. And because our commitment to doing no harm applies to ourselves, it is here that we need to be able to spot the signs of past trauma arising within us. Dan Siegel coined the phrase "window of tolerance" to describe the internal zone of support inside ourselves wherein we may tolerate a comfortable level of discomfort.[2] In order to be a source of support rather than of further harm, mindfulness practice invites us to be sensitive to the capacity for the practice itself to, in some cases, reveal unhealed trauma. It is important to notice, then, when we are edging outside of our window of tolerance and to bring ourselves back into it.

Although a complete discussion of trauma sensitivity and mindful research-informed responses to it is beyond the scope of this book, the following list of suggestions will help you recognize when you are moving outside of your window of tolerance and bring you back into it:

- Pay attention to the sensations of pleasantness and unpleasantness that come up as you practice—they can be early indicators as to how and when to give yourself extra support. You may wish to open your eyes during a sitting meditation practice, or to pause and stretch. Shorter rather than longer practice periods may also ease the discomfort that may arise. Even putting this book down after brief periods of reading and allowing yourself to take a walk, talk with a friend about it, or journal what's coming up for you may assist you in maximizing self-care as you go.

- Become familiar with the particular signs of arousal that indicate you're moving into distress, and as soon as you notice these, take a break from mindfulness practice. It can be helpful to anchor your attention in the body—to let your attention rest in your hands or feet, for example. This can promote a sense of grounding that can help bring you back into relative comfort.

- As a means of enhancing your overall resilience, be sure to make time to do the things that bring you joy and make you feel greater ease in your own body. In addition to eating well, drinking water, and getting enough sleep, make time for proven self-regulators like getting regular exercise, spending time in nature, and being with people close to you and with whom you feel safe.

- Finally, if you notice that what is coming up is really the deep pain or disorientation of traumatic experience and you are unable to self-regulate through practices such as those noted above, you may need the support of a friend or even a trained professional.[3] What precisely you need to heal is something only you can know. Honor this self-knowledge by acting on it and giving yourself extra support as you need it.

For less intense reactions, simply take a look at them more closely through your journaling practice or sitting in silence for a few moments. Over time, our gentle investigative work helps us not only in deepening healing, but also in developing insight into what harms us and others in the first place.

The final step in the RAIN process, *Non-Identification*, is about increasing our psychological flexibility. It is about learning to let go of tendencies to get stuck in or to identify with the thoughts and emotions we uncover in the RAIN process—in other words, being nonjudgmental, or nonattached. We pay attention to tunnel-visioning and the proclivity to fixate on one narrative (e.g., "I will never get over feeling sad about this"). And we sense into the spaciousness around our thoughts or emotions (e.g., "Actually, even now, I know that part of me is not defined by my sadness"). We use "non-identification" or "nonattachment" to describe this way of working with our minds to open to experiences of liberation from the pain of any given fleeting moment.

The RAIN process may in some ways represent mindfulness in a nutshell, but to reap its full benefit requires intention. Deep change— from mindlessness to mindfulness—begins with deep intention. This is as true of our efforts to transform society as it is to change ourselves. We must be willing to feel the pains of growth to change. Ultimately, this work calls us to step up to a view of ourselves as capable of becoming healthy, whole, free, and part of a community that includes the *whole* of the human family.

Recognizing the Subtle Dynamics of Race and Racism

This section, "Seeing," uses the "R" of the RAIN process as our ultimate guide throughout: "Recognize." The practices here open us up to seeing more fully the personal, relational, and systemic aspects of what race has meant and does mean in our lives. We are working to recognize just how we are impacted by race to see more clearly what we can do about it. Because racecraft—the shaping of our thinking around images, stories, accents, and messages we have been given about people—happens to and through all of us.

Sociologist Karen E. Fields and historian Barbara J. Fields coined the term "racecraft" to suggest the spellbinding similarities between racism and, well, witchcraft. They define it this way:

> [Racecraft is] the ability of pre- or non-scientific modes of thought to hijack the minds of the scientifically literate. . . . [It] originates not in nature but in human action and imagination . . . The action and imaging are collective yet individual, day-to-day yet historical, and consequential even though nested in mundane routine.[4]

This is not to say we all participate in racecraft in the same way or that it has equal effect on us all. It is not to say that the work that we must do is the same for each of us. Because our experiences differ radically, we must take the time to see where we're getting stuck. But the fact is that each one of our minds has been shaped by our environment, the people we have lived with and those we have not, the messages we receive about all of this along the way. We are all subject to the many spells of racecraft.

Accepting Race and Racism as Part of Our Relationships and Communities

In the communities where I grew up, people were racialized crudely. They were, for the most part, considered simply either white or black. There were very few Latinos or Asian-Americans in those Southern towns then, and we were taught very little about their experiences. I learned nothing then about their views on race or racism. Because Hampton, Virginia, was a military town in the post-Vietnam era, there were a number of multiracial military families, but there was no space for talking about what those connections and disconnections meant for us. Even today, our dominant culture lacks an adequate means for unpacking race and racism as it applies in the lives of those who are biracial or multiracial—which, in a real sense, means all of us.

Fortunately, as an adult, I came to know, live, and work closely with Asian-, Latin-, and a range of other "-" (hyphenated) Americans. This of course accelerated when I actually moved from Virginia to San Francisco in 1993, where I have lived since. Here and now, I live in a world in which identities are much more varied and contested. And yet, underneath the appearance of greater diversity, patterns of bias based on skin color, features, and culture remain. Here, too, our neighborhoods bear the stamps of historical racism and the laws and policies that supported it. They remain racialized as a result. And socially, whiteness, proximity to whiteness, and lightness continue to mean greater acceptance and value.

Still, as has been the case since the civil rights era, workplaces often bring people who live in racially separated communities together for meaningful engagement around shared goals. Thus it was that in San Francisco, at my first law firm job, I met my closest friend and life partner: a Michigan-born, first-generation U.S. citizen son of immigrants who came from India as part of a state-curated wave of skilled Asians allowed to immigrate to the United States during the 1960s. He grew up in the suburban ring just outside of Detroit, in the city of Troy. He came up through the public school system at a time when the U.S. Supreme Court was in the process of reversing the promise of *Brown v. Board* to end a centuries-long policy of segregation in schools there and elsewhere.[5] He did not have the benefit of a truly integrated school environment. His sense of the world was shaped by a predominantly white community and brown-skinned parents who, like many immigrants to the United States, ended up doing what they could to take care of themselves, make a good life for their children, and limit their exposure to the oppressions of white supremacy.[6]

And so, our coming together was a kind of miracle. Based on my up-bringing in the South, where he would have been considered nonwhite and subject to racism, I believed that he would be more likely aware of racism and willing to ally with other people of color, even though our experiences had likely been quite different. This initially turned out to be less true than I'd thought it would be.

In an early conversation about how his family might react to our dating, for example, he mentioned that his parents had come to terms with the fact that he might marry "an American," so they would be able to "come to terms with *this*." ("*Ain't I American?*" I couldn't help thinking . . . "and aren't *you*?")

After hours and hours spent sharing our experiences of race and racism, we could see that our positions in the pecking order of race were not the same. And yet we had enough in common to get past our differences, understand each other's lived experience, and find common ground in the work of fighting racism together. From that place, we built a relationship that helps sustain me to this day.

Here again, I saw that interracial dating, even where successful, can carry certain risks. We have all been raised in communities shaped by biases, so we encounter and process the world in ways shaped by those biases and carry them into our relationships with others, even those we care about deeply. In this sense, then, microaggressions can often begin at home. Seeing the pervasiveness of bias in our intimate relationships can be painful, but it can also be a doorway into compassion as we try to reduce the impact of racism in our lives and in the lives of others.

Investigating and Responding to Bias in Ourselves and Others

Recently, and despite years of effort to disrupt their patterned operations, I had an unpleasant reminder that my own fairly unconscious schemas continue to persist.

In one of my classes, of about fifty students, we were midway through the fourteen-week course. I had met individually with a student named Rosarita numerous times. When she raised her hand one day, I answered, "Yes, Maria?"

She stared at me. I looked right back at her. "*Yes*, Maria?" The whole class looked on.

"It's Rosarita," she said.

Snap!

There it was: a reminder that I, too, experience the operation of stereotypes. Obviously, I had a schema for "Latina" and my brain had called forth a name that revealed it for all to see. After all, I did not confuse her for "Michelle" or "Mary." Reaching for a name, my schema landed on one that seemed appropriate, a "Latina" name.

As is true for all of us, stereotypes cause me to embarrass myself and do harm to others. In this instance, Rosarita immediately told me that she was offended that I'd misremembered her name in that way.

That moment in class was truly, well, *not* comfortable. It was decidedly *not* stress-free. I could sense that not merely Rosarita's, but all of my students' eyes were on me, waiting to see what would happen next. For just a moment, I felt the floor beneath me completely disappear, the sense of being "all good" with the members of my class recede toward the horizon.

And to be certain, Rosarita did not let me off the hook. She looked at me with disappointment. The air seemed to evaporate from the room, and I felt the heat and aloneness of vulnerability. What to say in response? My reactive impulse shouted, "Defend yourself!" and for a split second I thought I might minimize what I'd said as a minor mistake. After all, I certainly didn't *mean* to offend her. I didn't intend to cause her any harm. And people confuse names all the time. Heck, people mix up the names of their own children! And with fifty students, how could I be expected to simply remember every one without fail? I was getting older every day.... There were all sorts of ways to avoid the dawning awareness that this was an example of racial stereotyping, plain and simple.

How best might I avoid acting from these immediate impulses, what neuroscientists and mindfulness teachers call *reactivity*, and instead, more effectively *respond* with clarity and intentionality?

I took a deep breath down into my belly. I felt the ground actually still there, beneath me. I consciously drew on the sense of strength, self-compassion, and clarity that I knew from my sitting meditation practice could come to me with a moment of mindfulness. In an instant, I knew what was called for, and I had the confidence that if what I chose did not work, I would discern another response that might better fit the situation.

What did I do? Then and there, in front of the whole class, I apologized. I told Rosarita that I was sorry for calling her by another name. As I opened up to my own feeling of shame little by little, I could feel its tempting grip and the defensive strategies it might suggest. I let my contact with the ground support me in just letting that be and staying present for the next moment with my class. Although it was incredibly awkward for more than a few moments, I managed to ask her for forgiveness.

As we bring mindfulness more completely into the difficult moments of our engagements with others, we grow in our capacity to accept that we, too, are a part of the problems we seek to solve. Whether it is realizing that we seemed less willing to welcome a stranger of a different race, or that we questioned whether he or she belonged, we catch ourselves in the act of doing this. We see it and we work to bring mindfulness right into the hard place of our reactions. We notice the ground disappearing beneath our feet or our bellies sinking, and from that place, we bring attention to our feet, feel the ground return, and breathe in ways that reduce the feelings of distress. We see that even the most awkward, even painful actions and hurtful comments are grounded in causes and conditions often beyond the control of the person causing harm. We check our deepest intentions and bring about a change in our actions, words, or feelings. And though we may struggle to get through to the other side, we arrive at a deeper capacity within us not only to stay in connection but to do so in a way that keeps us fully present and grounded in a broader view of the possible.

And here is the good news: from awareness just like this, we may begin to respond differently to bias when it impacts us. The notion of "calling out" microaggressions, for example, has given way to the idea of "calling in," bringing the offender into conversation about the harm that is being done, and to put it even more gently, as Canada-based therapist Tada Hozumi says, "calling to"—calling ourselves to attention to such experiences, in a way that can promote healing. Moments when we are reminded of ways we may have been insensitive to another can feel shameful or even humiliating. We can work with this, too, bringing our awareness in to support just accepting these feelings long enough to see that this, too, will pass. We know in our bodies that racism and bias are pervasive. Rather than being "shocked" when it shows up in our community, we are prepared to acknowledge it and deal with it. We are willing to work with nearly anyone, doing what we can to create a culture in which we can address biases forthrightly. We do not, through a zero-tolerance approach, force these realities underground. And from this place, we seek to create spaces for acknowledgment *and* accountability, for learning and growing together that include mutual humility and compassion.

We all have minds that instantly, unconsciously create schemas and stereotype others. These schemas make it difficult to take in information that challenges them. When faced with information that challenges our stereotypes, we have seen that we often experience what cognitive scientists call "cognitive dissonance," the discomfort or stress that comes from encountering information that differs from what we have come to "know" or believe. And what's more, this dissonance is often experienced not merely as stressful, but as threatening—so much so that we engage in what cognitive scientists call "motivated reasoning" aimed at pushing back and seeking to maintain our positions even against evidence to the contrary.[7]

The good news is that while such habits are pervasive, they need not be permanent. Our minds are not only capable of being remade, they are, in fact, being remade every day.

I've had a lifetime of experiences that have given me opportunities to reflect on what gets in the way of connecting, and how race plays a role in that. And I have been fortunate to have been born with a powerful will to learn, to grow, and to connect with others. Through daily mindfulness practice, I am able to stand up to the challenge of being vulnerable. I grow in my own ability to respond rather than react to the many ways I am challenged by interpersonal engagements with difference. I am also challenged by the call to examine how I live and participate in systems and practices that create, re-create, negotiate, and to a surprising degree maintain, generation after generation, socially prescribed roles.

Mindful engagement has shown me what research suggests: that the social habits by which race and racialization have been constructed may in fact be deconstructed. What sociologists and neuroscientists describe as the processes of race-making are pervasive. The perceptions that we have about race form the expectations by which we perceive others in the world. Traces of this show up in each of our encounters with others. With mindfulness, we can gradually come to see that the processes by which we can unmake race may become equally pervasive.

Building Your Skillfulness

Having expanded our capacity to stay with discomfort long enough to see it more clearly, we may now explore what is hidden in plain sight in our interactions with others, and deepen awareness of the many ways that our experiences are shaped by history and place. "It is to history that we owe our frames of reference, our identities, our aspirations," James Baldwin observed. "And it is with great pain and terror that one begins to realize this. In great pain and terror one begins to assess the history which has placed one where one is and formed one's point of view."

Living in the Long and Broad Now

Through mindfulness, we may begin to see things through a wider aperture. We can see and feel the legacies of racism in our midst. We can breathe in the palpable reality that the past is an integral part of the present.

We can see that even though people of color may outnumber whites in coming decades, whites remain, by far, the majority in the United States, making up 76.9 percent of the population in 2016. (Surprised? Given the rhetoric of fear posed by the "browning of America," many people believe the percentage of whites to be less.)

Moreover, as we have seen, we can reflect on the fact that, for example, people of color continue to bring home less income than whites in the United States. The black-white income gap is, indeed, slightly worse today than it was in 1963. In 2016, black families took home on average 60.7 percent of what white, non-Hispanic families did. And on average, black families have one-sixteenth the wealth of their white counterparts.

Part of the dominant narrative of our culture today is to blame those at the bottom of the socioeconomic ladder for their situation, to believe that these figures reflect failures on the part of blacks, Latinos, Native Americans, and so on ("They don't want to work" or "Their culture is to blame"). With mindfulness, we can inquire into whether and to what extent these outcomes are legacies of systemic barriers, or of the sort of biases we are hopefully becoming more able to see in ourselves and in others. Because while we need to regularly look up the available, verifiable, actual facts that help us to see a bit more of the way things *really* are, what we most need to learn to minimize our contributions to harm comes from examining how our minds think about race. This is where we exercise the intention to encounter the painful and terrifying realizations about which Baldwin wrote.[8] It is often painful to encounter the embedded racism, sexism, homophobia, and the like that are the legacies of our social worlds. And it can be terrifying to realize that no matter how hard we try to work to uproot these, the struggle will, in all likelihood, be ongoing.

The practices and approaches that I share in this book come directly out of my own reflections on history, current data, and my own experiences and those of others. They led to my own often painful, terrifying realizations about the everyday stuff of race-making, of racecraft, in my own life and in the lives of those around me.

Take a moment to reflect on some of the ways that your life experiences, opportunities, and circumstances have been shaped by your race and continue today to be affected by it.

Awareness practices help us investigate and explore the very rough waters of these aspects of life by noticing when we get caught, and coming back to an anchor in the ground beneath these realities, like a supportive safe harbor in the storms.

CHAPTER TEN

DEVELOPING MINDFUL RACIAL LITERACY AMID COMPLEXITY

It is crucial that we see the variety of lived experiences within oneness
in order to see who we really are as living beings. . . . We are all raced,
sexualized, classed and so on. This can be difficult to see.

—ZENJU EARTHLYN MANUEL[1]

Naming a woman's racial identity does not mean we have lost sight of the
fact that she is comprised of innumerable different identities and dimensions. Using concepts like "race," "black," or "white," does not mean
we do not see the ineffable whole, but that we see these projections as
socially relevant elements of the whole. Race factors into our interactions
with others, and so "reading" race—recognizing when it arises, resting
attention on it as it moves through an interaction, and investigating its
flow and functions—is an important skill. It is essential to the development of ColorInsight, as well as the capacity to talk about race with some
stamina rather than undue fragility.

Given the focus of my work, the opportunity to talk about race comes
up nearly every day of my life. Over the years, I have seen a number of
patterns. There are people who have a lot of experience thinking and
talking about race and, hence, are more comfortable doing so. Most often, they are people of color. And there are people who have very little

experience thinking and talking about race and feel uncomfortable doing so. This is very often the case for people racialized as white, but it may be so for any number of people who have not had much chance to reflect on and discuss this aspect of their own lives.

What good does it do to talk about race in mixed company, when our differences in experience will prime us to suffer in the process? Talking about what we know disrupts silent witnessing, avoidance, and other forms of resisting clear seeing in such moments. From there, we can all see what we are dealing with more clearly. Courageous awareness practices open up the possibility of questioning what we have been taught and the lessons we have unconsciously absorbed from the broader culture. As you read the stories shared here, consider whether you are feeling even more strength within and more courage to tell your own. Our experiences are not shaped solely by race, of course, but intersect with other social identities as well—forms of privilege and disadvantage that combine with and inform race in interesting ways. As we deepen our practices for staying with the racial character of what we experience, we become more familiar with these subtleties.

One factor that shaped my life was attending college at a well-resourced, deeply connected, predominantly and historically white male institution for higher learning—the University of Virginia. Founded by Thomas Jefferson, this university has historically educated, socialized, and credentialed a range of mostly white men and women, from Edgar Allan Poe to Robert F. Kennedy to Tina Fey.

Against the odds, I graduated from UVA "with Distinction" and continued my studies at its law school. Later, and against even longer odds, I became a law professor. Over the course of this trajectory, I was generally one of a few, and sometimes the only, African-American person around.

Along the way I developed what W. E. B. DuBois called "double consciousness"—the ability to see through the lens of the whites who trained, educated, and held the power to evaluate and credential me, as well as through the lens of my experience as "not-white." More than dual consciousness, I developed a sort of multifaceted prism of perception: a white-male-and-black-female-previously-lower-class (and more!) awareness capable of moving as I moved across a constantly shifting social world.

The fact that I "made it," that I traveled far and wide among communities so different from those in which I was born and raised, says a lot about the success of the civil rights movement and about the possibilities that exist for people in our society to become more than we expect of them, when given sustained structural support. I have done my part, but I did not "make it" here by my own work alone.

I have had the opportunity to see, meet, and help people of all backgrounds who would like to live in a world of greater fairness and justice. This has, indeed, heartened me and solidified my commitment to the ongoing work of desegregation and effective integration. My experience shows me that more is possible when we create pathways that enable people to learn, to grow, and to thrive. Because I have seen this, I am committed to living in a broad and diverse network, and to working to make such connections possible for everyone. In working through the challenges of talking about race, we deepen our connections with ourselves and with others. And without realizing it, we are embodying a skillfulness that is visible to others and helps create healthier and braver spaces for others struggling to recognize, accept, and name the racial barriers they are up against. In this way, we help develop the racial literacy of all those around us, creating the foundation for lasting change that embraces all.

The Costs of Seeing

And yet, my "making it" and developing a language for describing some of the racial dynamics I've encountered have come with costs. I have felt the strange sense of invisibility that occurs when so much of what is presented as valuable emerged from people whose experiences in the social world were not only unlike mine but steeped in the culture of white supremacy and black (and sometimes more broadly nonwhite) subordination. When I spoke out about this, I sometimes encountered yet another penalty—the cost of being one who sees what we are taught not to see and does not remain silent.

I learned that to remain in such environments, I often had to choose. I had to choose when to speak up and when to stay silent. Speak up too much, and the question of "fit"—as in, "Is she a good fit?"—arises and lingers. Speak up too little, and I risk being complicit in a situation I know to be unfair. As a consequence, I struggled to hold on to a sense of the importance of my own point of view. Sometimes I lost the battle. And I wasted a fair amount of time reframing and "shaking off" the many forms of bias that cropped up in integrated settings. Most of these biases were subtle—for example, not being invited to lunch with other students, lawyers, and professors; being expected to know the thinkers who had influenced those around me, even as thinkers who had influenced *me* (W. E. B. DuBois, Carter G. Woodson, Anna Julia Cooper) were unknown and unappreciated by professors and peers alike; and so on. But sometimes, for example when a colleague called black candidates for a position on the faculty "lazy," and when another reportedly described an Asian-American candidate as "not the only Sony on the shelf," they were not so subtle.

The microaggressions and worse that we have to navigate in public spaces every day to "make it" can cause real harm. Being present and bearing witness to these injuries is necessary to combat them and help create more just spaces for others. But if we are not also able to relate with these realities, to release the harm they cause, and to be transformed by the experience in ways necessary for our own healing, the costs of these injuries can do lasting damage to ourselves and the communities we seek to represent. This is where mindfulness as a practice and a way of life comes in.

The Struggle Continues

Despite the opportunities I've had, I could see how my social identity in majority white spaces was often, well, unexpected. To the judge who was surprised to see me representing an international insurance company in a multistate, multimillion-dollar dispute, my presence didn't fit with the biases he carried. To the black bailiff, who thought I must be there to represent criminal clients, my presence was unpredicted by the biases he carried. Since limiting ideas about my race and gender continued to show up in my life *every day*, and since the price of success often involved some form of invitation to be complicit in these ideas, I had a decision to make. I could leave such settings and join together with people more like me, or I could stay within the predominantly white spaces and try to make a difference from within.

I decided to remain. And I looked for ways to help myself with the struggles that I would encounter, the hard days that would be a part of the journey. I started paying attention to what I had learned about keeping myself strong and healthy in less than healthy circumstances. I realized more than ever the pain and frustration that came with keeping both my eyes and my heart open. I learned from everyday experience that bearing witness to discrimination of all types, again and again, was not easy to do. It's not merely uncomfortable; it's often deeply despairing, physically draining, sometimes debilitating, even terrifying. Because speaking out comes with a cost, we waste untold amounts of energy trying to figure out how to avoid revealing what we see, when so many around us seem *unaware*, or worse, downright *unwilling* to see. Staying in the struggle demanded sophisticated practices for recognizing the incoming artillery of racism, understanding it while moving through it to the ground of my wholeness. Doing so required a strong will to be present with what such spaces would reveal.

Strengthening the Will to See

A key part of the work of racial justice is developing the will to see how racism has been denied, avoided, silently bypassed, or otherwise made invisible, all of which constitute the infrastructure and practice of cultural white supremacy. If we are not willing to see what causes harm, or to have empathy for the suffering of others from it, the healing process is made that much more difficult.

As a black woman working and living in predominantly white environments, dealing with social identity bias, with racism and its links to sexism, homophobia, and so on, is not optional for me. It hurts every single day. And it is completely unnecessary to our existence. The unnecessary, socially constructed, surplus pain that daily compromises so many lives and threatens us all is something I cannot and will not ignore.

So some time ago I decided I would do what I could to strengthen my own ability to be present to race and racism, as a means of promoting my own and others' healing and of minimizing the damage. To my years-long regular journaling practice, I added a commitment to meditation. I added the practice of offering gratitude for the particulars of my life, eventually including the painful ones. I took up yoga, healthier eating, and then a practice of mindfully running through the streets and neighborhoods of this City by the Bay. Slowly I realized that in doing something for my own well-being every day, I was not being selfish. Instead, I was deepening my own capacity for continuing to learn, teach, and work with others here and now, to make a difference that I could feel in work with others.

Yes, We All Need to Examine Race and Racism Mindfully—Again and Again

Though I believe it is essential for each of us to share what we have seen and experienced in the world, I am aware that what I have seen is not the whole story. And that is where you come in. Because however beautiful and engaging our own stories are, they are only one small part of the big story of what it means to live as human beings together. I think that we have gotten to where we are—that we keep fighting the same battles—in no small part because we are too afraid to say to one another what we know about bias and racism in ourselves and in our world. If humankind is to survive and to thrive, I believe that this must change. Indeed, I believe that we each have a responsibility to reflect on our particular life stories and to assist others in becoming more real about race and racism, more committed to combating it, and more grounded in trustworthy community as a result.

Many of us have participated in workshops and read articles and books on how to talk about race more effectively. But we need more than helpful communication techniques. We need a more profound, a more nuanced understanding of our experiences around identity. We need an understanding that prepares us not only to talk about racism and other identity-based harms, but to do something with others to end them.

What we need is the capacity to hold nuance, complexity, and dissonance. We need to let go of "either/or" thinking, and develop ways of seeing both this and that at once. We need to be willing to be uncomfortable long enough for real understanding to emerge, and to work at it long enough for real change to happen. We need to be able to look long, lovingly, and closely enough to see the good and the bad in our most cherished "hand-me-down" beliefs. We need to be able to think critically about the new and often disguised forms of racism (like colorblindness) and white supremacy that have become so prevalent in the past few years. And we need the will to take actions that will help pave the way to new beliefs, understandings, connections across differences, and the outbreaks of justice that, more often than we acknowledge, do in fact result.

According to core teachings on mindfulness, we must also pay attention to aspects of the body itself, one of the four foundations of mindfulness.[2] This includes our unique physical appearance: skin color, hair type, the shape of our noses and eyelids, and so on. It may also include the way we speak, our accent, and the perceptions that others attach to our names. The body as an object of awareness includes all of the physical and more or less fixed aspects of our being, and the cues that they send to others. It includes our own perceptions of all of these aspects of our being. It is the raw material by which our "race" is made. As we become aware of the body, we might also begin to notice some of the ways that we have accommodated the "rules of race," some of the ways that we have been taught to perceive and understand race as it applies to ourselves, including what we may presume to be others' racial perceptions and understandings. We may become aware of the ways we feel we *have to* live, and among whom we must live, to be appreciated.

With mindfulness, we become more aware of the bodies in which we experience this world. We notice the subtle ways in which others react to us and assume things about us, based on our social identities. We notice the social signals we send and receive. We may reflect on the perceptions and feelings that we associate with our own race. If we are white, for example, we take a deep breath, and ask: What have I been taught or have I internalized as generalizations about white people? How was I taught these things? Where and by whom? What feelings come up as I think about this? We might then go further, examining questions like: What is it that I enjoy about being white? What would I gain or lose if I were only seen through the lens of the cultures of my ancestors? Whatever your racial background, take time to reflect on these questions, examining what we know about the messages we have internalized about "our own" race.

Eventually, our reflections will go beyond this to deepen our understanding of how we have been shaped by race, how our personal histories and life experiences have been shaped by race. We begin to see how our difficulties addressing race with one another stem not only from our lack of self-awareness, but also from the pervasive failure of our society—our schools, our churches, our families—to assist us in understanding how race plays into our social and political lives. And we accept this with whatever emotions come with it, being willing to feel the sting of shame, the tightness of anger for the moment, in service of learning and becoming more clear and able to work with it all.

Over the years, I came to see that mindful awareness of the experience of human suffering invited study of an endless range of the social structures that have been created to maintain it. Given my background in law, that has included reviewing the historical record of laws, practices, and policies that shaped our communities and social behaviors in the United States. I came to see reading and reflecting on the historical record of how we have shaped oppression through law and policy as an exercise in mindfulness.

Reading this history, even with the support of mindfulness, is difficult. So, we might start by building up our reflective resilience, our ability to look at our own thoughts, emotions, and biases around racist structures of oppression in our own experience.

To deepen understanding of these structures and develop the empathy needed to care about their effects, we need new ways of teaching and learning about race in community with others. We need to practice telling our own Race Stories, like the one with which I opened this book. Race Stories show some of what we have learned about race and racism. They can include moments when a joke or slur was made, when we observed a friend wearing blackface or speaking in a mock Asian accent and drawing her eyelids up in angles. These stories might include as much as we can recall of what we have witnessed, heard, and seen of how race and racism have shaped our communities, friends, and ourselves. But the key is to tell these stories with mindfulness and compassion. We are not telling these stories for the sake of hearing ourselves talk. We are not seeking to humiliate others, to make ourselves look good, or to appear as a victim. We tell them to practice admitting what is already in the room, and through this, to explore taking responsibility for choosing new stories and thereby further the process of setting one another free.

Some of us have more to lose in terms of the sense we hold of ourselves and of our innocence by admitting such stories. For people racialized white, for example, Race Stories may reveal more of what it means to be privileged, such as being stopped by police but not arrested, as these recent Twitter posts, using #LivingWhileWhite, begin to show:

> NYC cabbie here. Years ago, brought middle-aged black couple to Harlem. We had a delightful conversation on the way. Once there, conversation continued for a bit. Cop car with lights on pulled up to my window. Cop asked me, "Are these people bothering you?" #LivingWhileWhite

> Pulled over for doing 70 in a 40. "Miss, you should slow down and smell the roses." Pulled over another time with expired registration, speeding, missing passenger mirror. Verbal warning. Speeding, no license plate! Warning. I could go on. #LivingWhileWhite

> Several times, my husband or kids haven't had enough money to pay for something at a local business or restaurant and were told, "Just come back and pay when you can." #LivingWhileWhite

> My daughter 'fessed that she's been stopped 4 times for speeding in last 2 yrs (no argument from her) and got warnings. Indian boyfriend? One stop, 2 tickets. #LivingWhileWhite

When we resolve to look squarely at race in our lives, we are not trying to make ourselves the center of a new narrative about "the *real* victims" of racism. We are simply sourcing our first-person knowledge of what race and racism look like in the world today. We are becoming literate about how race operates, starting with where we are right now.

In so doing, we rely on mindfulness practices like those we have cultivated together throughout this book. We are learning to stay present to race and racism as it arises in real time. We are learning to observe the thoughts, feelings, and sensations running through our interactions with others. We deepen the core mindfulness practice of sitting and being with what arises by contemplative journaling—examining the thoughts, sensations, and emotions that lie beneath our Race Stories.

So I ask that as you engage in the practices to come, resolve to take a few minutes to write down what comes to you, with as little judgment as possible. Writing will be especially important as part of your healing process if you recall stories that bring on strong feelings of shame, anger, or sadness.

A lot of what we know about bias and racism shows up in very, very small details—the kind of details that we can very easily overlook if we are not committed to doing otherwise, and that we are often encouraged not to notice or are punished for remembering. Thus, we need a great deal of patience, time, and kindness as we resolve to look closely and to move more deeply, by degrees, into this work.

A MICRO MEDITATION ON RACE: TWITTER AND
THE PRACTICE OF SHARING A RACE STORY

Q: Using #LivingWhile*[fill in your race]:* What could you share in a tweet to describe what you have seen from the perspective of your own race? Keep it short: Twitter limits each tweet to 280 characters.

See if you can be present to the whole body as you reflect on the feelings, sensations, and images underlying whatever comes up for you in response to this prompt.

CHAPTER ELEVEN

MAKING THE INVISIBLE VISIBLE THROUGH MINDFULNESS

◯↝

All this comes from being willing to visit and hold our
own pain and suffering, as individuals, as a nation, and as a
species, with awareness, compassion, and some degree of
non-reactivity, letting them speak to us and reveal new dimensions
of interconnectedness that increase our understanding of those
root causes of suffering and compel us to extend our empathy out
beyond only those people we are closest to.

—JON KABAT-ZINN, *MINDFULNESS FOR ALL*[1]

Parts of a System

I claim membership in what I call the "Integration Generation": the sole
generation of children in the United States to experience the great political, economic, social, emotional, and intellectual benefits of intentional,
state-sponsored desegregation through the entirety of my public K-12
schooling, and the follow-on benefits of robust affirmative action in
higher education.

And while my life chances, and those of the broader political community of the United States, were forever altered for the better by those
experiences, I am also aware of the profound ways that I benefited from
having been born in the most impoverished part of black Kinston. Let
me explain. Despite its being structurally cut off from pathways to even

middle-class success, there was much of great meaning and beauty in the few blocks that formed the whole of my world in black Kinston before desegregation came.

One of my earliest memories is of my Grandma Nan emerging from her room in the early hours to the living room, where I often slept on homemade quilts (a "pallet") on the floor. GranNan would awaken before sunrise every morning. After thirty minutes or more alone in personal ritual of study and prayer, she would prepare a breakfast typically of eggs, sausage, bright-yellow margarine-topped toast and grits, get my sister and me off to Headstart or daycare, and get the other children off to school. Off she would go, then, to her work as a housekeeper for a family named the Outlaws. I eventually came to understand that on those mornings before joining us, she was centering herself on "something more" as a guide and ground for her day. And by her example, she served as my first spiritual teacher.

ColorInsight practice, the practice of becoming awake to our habits and conditionings around race and developing deeper insight into the complexities of the work of racial justice, is an invitation to do more than simply think and talk about our own racial experiences with mindfulness, although doing these things is important. To understand how race and racism may and often do get in the way of seeing our common humanity across perceived racial lines, we need to be willing and able to sit with how we have been formed by race and racism, and how, through these experiences, we may presently be shaping the racializing experiences of others. We can keep working to free our minds and actions from these habits, and take action to help free those around us.

This is not easy to do. It takes a special kind of effort for each of us to see more of what we have been trained not to see. But for those of us with the will to see and to pause with what we see long enough to understand, there will be much to support our waking up and understanding more deeply. Wherever we are, we can observe and better understand the structures of systemic racism in our own lives.

A Long, Loving Look at Racism in the Places Called Home Now

Even while living in one of the most liberal cities in the United States, I have ongoing work to do to upend the patterns of oppression in which I participate, patterns that get in the way of creating fairness and justice for all. The community in which I live now and the networks in which I move give me much on which to reflect. More and more, I can see the structures of privilege that keep some types of people down while lifting others up right in my own backyard.

San Francisco has always been rich in diversity and innovation. And since the Gold Rush era, it has always been a major site for the development, cultivation, and maintenance of white supremacy in America.

Californians pride themselves on being forward-thinking. We tend not to like to look deeply at our past. Hence, people here generally know even less about the early history of black migration to, and oppression in, San Francisco than the little they know about the decimation of the original indigenous American inhabitants. Children here often are not taught much about the virtual enslavement of Mexican Americans from whom the land was taken beginning with war in 1846, nor about the annihilation of the diverse Native American tribes. They are not taught much about the race war against immigrants from China and later Japan, leading to the exclusion acts and internment camps that provide a template for the Muslim ban and other anti-immigrant policies in vogue today. And they are not taught about the California law that, just like those in the Southern states, banned love across the races—the antimiscegenation law and policy in place until its highest court rejected it in the mid-twentieth century.[2]

If we take the time to teach ourselves about these histories (because they are still only very rarely taught in any other way), we learn that San Francisco—like most towns—has its own ugly and long-standing racist history that lingers across our picturesque landscape to this day.

Everyday Racism in Liberal Towns

Not having learned this history before arriving in the 1990s, I was a little surprised when I arrived to find San Francisco simmering a quiet brew of antiblack strife. A lawsuit by Chinese Americans had brought the city's famously successful desegregation plan to a halt, setting the place on the path to the resegregated public school system we have today. While some Chinese Americans organized to show their support for black life in the city, it was clear that the effort to build coalitions among groups of racialized communities here would be easier said than done.

And soon I came to experience more straightforward indicators of the bigotry that predictably follows segregation and the ideologies that support it. One day I was leaving my new office building on Market Street, wearing the suit and trench coat that was my "middle-class-signifying" uniform, when a young white man with almost no hair on his head said, just loud enough for me to hear it, "Go home, n——."

On another occasion, a real estate agent, herself an immigrant—but a blond one, from Europe—saw no irony in sharing with me and my then-husband, when I asked her about demographics in an area in which we were house-hunting, that "the Mexicans are *our treasure*."

When I eventually moved from practicing law to teaching it, I learned that even among my new, reputedly liberal fellow campus professionals, I was still vulnerable to painful slings and arrows in unregulated spaces. Some of those were meant as descriptive commentary about other groups—moments like one when walking to lunch with a white colleague (of Jewish heritage) who could not help saying, "This used to be a good neighborhood. Now it's all Asian."

Other racist commentary was directed at me. During a party held at the home of one of my colleagues, I was dressed in a sleeveless black dress and heels and probably enjoying a glass of champagne when another guest came over to me, wineglass in hand, leaned close to my ear outside of earshot of anyone else, and whispered, "I hope you won't take this the wrong way, but you look like a beautifully toned horse." (And yes, this was my sign to leave the party and to steer clear of this oft-smiling member of our community going forward.)

I didn't have words to describe these incidents well then. I am not sure I have the ideal words for them now. They felt like flashes of invisible racism—arising, wounding, and then disappearing without a trace to all but the target. So casual, so normal, so innocent. A slice here, a jab there, and then a quick move away as if nothing had ever happened at all.

But these things did happen. They happened frequently. And yet most of the white people I knew seemed completely oblivious to them. They seemed to have had no idea of the racial hostility that I encountered frequently on campus and in our City by the Bay. And the people who were not white seemed, in a whole host of diverse ways, to be trying to figure out, with little to guide us, how best to negotiate the strange terrain of liberal racism on which we find ourselves here.

As noted before, social psychologists call incidents like those I've just described as microaggressions—stunning, subtle insults or assaults that dismiss or degrade based on race or other identities.[3] Psychologist Chester M. Pierce, a black man whose clients tended to be black as well, coined this phrase in 1970 to describe the daily incidents of bias that his patients routinely reported.

Many people resist, or react with skepticism, to the idea of microaggressions. Critical of efforts taken to reduce their occurrence in our schools, workplaces, and other public spaces, people raise a number of objections. They claim that people are being too sensitive. The word itself is off-putting and aggressive, they say.

I have been told that being accused of a microaggression, like being asked to "check" one's white or male privilege, makes whites and men more likely to feel aggrieved and less likely to be sympathetic. I've witnessed whites retreating into safer, whiter spaces as a result. And more than one white person has shared with me that, when faced with such criticisms, they are more likely to take their own bruised feelings to those who are more sympathetic to them—advocates of white nationalism.

I have seen for myself the tendency some have simply to move away from or avoid dealing with race in mixed company when asked to examine subtle insults like these and help bring them to a halt. They carry stories of their own woundedness and feel defensive at the slightest effort to name the realities of racism in its subtle and not-so-subtle varieties. Fragility as it relates to race and racism, especially the inability of whites to bear even a small amount of the distress that comes with a racial challenge, is very, very real.

But ask those who suffer from microaggressions regularly if not daily, and they will say what research does: a lifetime of exposure to such slights and related discriminations takes a serious toll on psychological health and material well-being, with implications that extend far and wide.

So even as whites remain nearly 77 percent of the population, have sixteen times the wealth of the average black family, and have inherited a country built, for centuries, on systems (education, housing, legal, health care, and so on) in which they were privileged and Others were systematically held down, they are, in many cases, unwilling or unable to see their advantage and how twenty-first-century racism hurts people of color.

The broad differentials in outcomes across racial groups, but especially between whites and blacks, in many ways reflect the hierarchies established in the past. So much so that legal scholar Reva Siegel's phrase "preservation through transformation" seems apt.[4] Or, as our parents might have said more simply: "the more things change, the more they stay the same."

Whiteness—not as individual identity but as a generally invisible, virtually transparent way of describing the "normal," standard human experience and worldview—continues to hold unacknowledged sway in the systems of power that shape our life chances.

Even when we consciously believe otherwise, research has shown that implicit bias is pervasive. Most of us hold biases based on perceptions associated with racial identities. And because whiteness has been the dominant and most valued of racial identities, a majority of us hold biases favorable to white or lighter-skinned people (a dynamic that operates by degrees in what social scientists call "colorism").

Research also shows that there are even more pervasive ways that our biases show up—in our hidden tendencies to discriminate in favor of those we consider to be "more like us."[5] Such "positive discrimination" may seem less harmful. After all, how can favoring those like us be just as bad as actively working to "push down" those we see as different? But if you think about it, you can see that, in fact, it isn't all that different in terms of effect. The consequences for those who have traditionally held power and authority—and for those who traditionally have not—are much the same.

When stressed out, or when operating on automatic pilot, we often retreat into the ways in which we have been trained. We read cues that we have associated with race, cues that intersect race with gender, sexual orientation, and other forms of identification. In ways that range from unconscious to subtle to blatantly obvious, we all read and rely on such cues. It's worth noting that without these racial preconceptions, predictions, and ingrained ways of understanding our place in the world, some of us might feel our lives are, in some sense, *less* meaningful. This is so because many of us have learned to define ourselves, our heritage, and our sense of community by the concept of race (or ethnicity) as it has been given to us. Joining together with racial "familiars" is often a subtle part of how and why we feel safe in the world.

Hard as it is to fully understand, we all give meaning to race and its signifiers in our lives. Without our notions of race, we might feel that we'd have much more difficulty moving quickly through our daily lives. As uneasy as it may make us feel to admit it, social identities—and the shortcuts of our categories and stereotypes—help us make decisions. Relying on racial assumptions, in a certain sense, may simply seem efficient.

And yet: if we are not very careful, these racialized notions of who we are, these race-inflected assumptions about others, create barriers to realizing our inherent interconnectedness, and the fact that we are, essentially, one human family.

Often, we see ourselves as individuals, even as we lump others into racialized groups. And yet, if we see ourselves as separate, hard-bound, and apart from other humans in essential ways (as many people do), then the subtle but life-shaping trainings of race make our hyperindividualized identities seem all the more real. Ideas about race reinforce our tendency not only to see ourselves as separate from others in profound ways, but also to group others along the lines of demarcation that we have been taught to see. We are each and all engaged, to one degree or another, in race-making or "doing" race—the processes and practices by and through which racialization happens. In many and various ways, we each participate in the activities by which the idea of race remains strong, and the practices of racism remain rational. We do this in subtle, fleeting moments—in decisions such as where we will live, from whom we will learn, and so on—that set us on one road and all but foreclose others. Whether we are black, white, brown, yellow, or red, we are caught up in racecraft.

And yet, if we can see more clearly through the lenses of awareness, we recognize that while we are trained for division in so many ways, we are also inherently capable of experiencing connection with one another. Becoming more aware of our own racecraft, our own subtle racial predispositions and predictions, is a step toward increasing our capacity for doing just that. Noticing that we are sometimes guilty of microaggressions is another step in the right direction. Practicing mindful awareness of these aspects of our conditioning and habits of the mind helps us to know what we are up against *within ourselves* as we seek to make change in the world. The capacity to recognize and accept where we are and to investigate what must be changed to minimize the harm that our own views and blind spots cause others is essential to the work of racial justice. And the capacity to do all of this with as little attachment to and identification with the outcome as possible is essential to true liberation.

MINDFULNESS OF RACECRAFT IN YOUR LIFE TODAY

Pause.

Allow your attention to settle on the sensations of breathing.

Sense into the support of the ground beneath and within you.

Reflect on the following: Think of a time when you were interacting with someone of another race in the place where you live or work now, a time when the fact of racial difference became apparent to you somehow.

What were some of the thoughts running through your mind?

What notions of race do you recall being a part of this experience?

What sensations arise in your body as you recall this interaction?

What emotions come up for you now?

As best you can, describe these sensations, thoughts, and any accompanying emotions. Then ask: What was underneath these? Dig deeper. After your investigations, let all of these fall away and come back to the sensations of breathing and sitting.

MINDFUL JOURNAL REFLECTIONS

Take a few moments to jot down what insights arose for you during this reflective practice.

MINDFULNESS OF MICROAGGRESSIONS
AND INTERNALIZED BIAS

Pause.

Take a moment to focus on the sensations of breathing in and out.

Resolve to feel the support of the ground beneath you, the nurturance of what is well within the breath and body itself.

Now call to mind the term *microaggression*.

Breathe in and out. Allow the reactions (thoughts, emotions, bodily sensations) inside you to come to the surface.

What images, stories, flashes of feeling, or snapshots are coming up for you?

What feelings are arising in you?

How much of what is coming up seems to echo what you have been taught, or what you have witnessed or inherited from the culture? From your family? From your community?

Now let those thoughts go. Bring your awareness back to the sensations of breathing and sitting.

When you are ready, reflect on these questions:

When you hear about different outcomes by race, what are some of the thoughts, feelings, and sensations that arise?

What are some of the things you would say account for these differences? Allow as much as possible to arise and note the gist of your explanations.

What feelings come up for you when you reflect on these explanations?

Again, release what has come up and settle back into your sensations of breathing and sitting.

And now, reflect on these questions: *How have these explanations touched your own life and work? How have they left traces in personal thoughts and stories? How are they showing up now in your life today in your thoughts, sensations, and emotions?*

Finally, reflect on this: *How does race show up in your mind in ways that seem beyond or contrary to your own choosing?*

Again, now release the thoughts.

Notice whatever feelings are present. Allow the feelings that have arisen simply to be, without judgment, without (for the moment) trying to change them.

Sense into your appreciation for the part of you that has the motivation and the will to be with your experience in ways that make the world a safer, better place for all. As you breathe, sense into your interconnectedness with all that there is.

Take a few moments to jot down what sensations, feelings, thoughts, and insights arose for you during this reflective practice. Stay close to the body, resisting the pull to the brain-based way of processing your experience.

As we continue expanding our capacity to see race in our lives, both historically and up to today, we turn to the task of Being with these realities more effectively and practicing the way of awareness.

PART THREE

Being

Mindfulness asks us to experience being
with what arises, accepting—just for the
moment—what is in our lives, with
kindness.

Not everything that is faced can be changed

but nothing can be changed until it is faced.

—JAMES BALDWIN

CHAPTER TWELVE

MINDFUL SOCIAL CONNECTION

Where is your moment-to-moment practice of integrity in a world that wants us to compete primarily to benefit the gain of the privileged, the powerful, and the lucky few, instead of working for the equity and elevation of our human condition for the many?

—LARRY YANG[1]

At Home in a Racially Divided World

Over the past twenty years as a law professor and workshop leader, I've facilitated thousands of conversations with people about how race and its stand-ins (culture, background, color, accent, and the like) play out in the lives of everyday people. I've seen many of the ways that race and racecraft are factors in all our lives, and very often, painful ones. I've gotten to know thousands of people well enough to be trusted as a conversation partner in reflecting on these issues. I've listened to thousands of stories about people's lives and the moments that stand out for them as pivotal in teaching them something important about race. I have come to understand these conversations as foundational mindfulness practice. The connections they enable and the ways in which they shatter our former understanding of ourselves and the world are the essence of the path of waking up in the world, moment to moment.

Looking back on these moments, reflecting on how they remain with us and help guide our behavior when we come into contact with others, helps provide a starting point for developing awareness of how we participate in race-making and racist systems, and wise action to dissolve racism in our midst. When combined with a close examination of the systems within our society that play pervasive, albeit subtle, roles in shaping our thoughts, these stories from our own experience are important. They remind us of what we already deeply know but often keep buried below the level of acknowledgment. They provide fertile ground for the work of shifting our ways of being with others to create new bases for perceiving and understanding, for resolving conflict peacefully, and for the lived experience of freedom together.

Our personal Race Stories reflect forms of everyday social education. They capture moments shaped by the built environments and cultural communities in which we live and work. These geographic locations—the very places in which our long histories of racist external colonialism, through which we have meddled with the fates of less powerful, nonwhite nations; and internal colonialism, through which more powerful groups in our society have controlled the fates of the less powerful via racial segregation and hierarchy—are embedded in earth and stone, statues and monuments, blood and bone. They prefigure our interactions with one another, and they contribute to forming us as racialized human beings. As we have seen, our life stories and the physical locations in which we lived them have taught us a lot more about race than we usually admit. To live in ways that bring justice to life, we have to become aware of these subtle dynamics, the inputs of racism that move through us. We have to be willing to reckon with these in ways that disrupt the trainings of our past. We have to be willing to break what we have been holding in place and actually become something new.

For some of us, a moment of reckoning and the possibility for real change might come when we utter or hear a racial slur in the presence of people who are offended. Being forced by the critical reactions of others to reflect on what we carry deep within is one way of learning and sometimes growing, though it's often a painful one. But if we can reflect on these aspects of who we are without the pain and humiliation of the watchful eyes of the public, we might grow in ways that bring forth less widespread and reckless suffering.

For you, the moment of reckoning may have been like that which arose when a young Asian-American girl's mother advised her against playing with a black friend because, when it came to the friend's family, "they're not like us."

For you, it may be like a recovered memory of a Jewish-heritage grandfather, himself a respected leader in his community, teaching and insisting on having his beloved grandchild tell an antiblack racist joke, and then delighting in its effect on his adult friends.

For you, it may be like that moment when a young woman visiting the United States and working as an au pair learned that she was racialized as white, and the meaning of that to her host family, when the father of that family angrily demanded that she not date black men while living in his home.

Looking closely at these memories, these relational pain-points, we can learn a great deal. Feeling into what they created within us, we may notice the way such instances have shaped our movement through the world since. If we are willing to peel back the layers of conditionings that we have been bringing into the world since, we can learn even more. When we fail to do so, however, we create another barrier to connecting with ourselves and with others in ways that can change the world. When we resist looking at our own experience and trainings around race and racism and the suffering they have caused, we enter into conversations about race with less capability than we might otherwise have for making a real and lasting difference. Being with what we see is a choice toward living with integrity.

The Compassionate Path to Human Connection

In his first year of law school, Juan was assigned to a Personal Injury law class with me. The following semester, Juan signed up for another fourteen-week course with me, this time on race and law. Later, he signed up for a fourteen-week course on mindfulness and law. Slowly, over the course of three years, I got to know a little about Juan.

Like most people looking at him, I had noticed Juan's dark brown, loosely waved hair and the way that it had to be combed firmly away from his large eyes; his caramel-colored skin; his stocky build and preference for casual dress. I "read" the cultural cues that I had unconsciously associated with his name and silently guessed that he was Latino. Or "brown."

In class, I noted that Juan was one of the quiet ones. He was reluctant to raise his hand to volunteer his thoughts, but I could sense that he was intensely engaged. I later learned that Juan had been brought up to keep his true thoughts and feelings to himself. And yet, gradually, he came to feel more at ease talking with me about things he had long held deep within.

Juan's father had been an immigrant from a country below the southern U.S. border. It was a place where, at the time, violence was common. And he had taught Juan a few things about how to survive. The major lesson that had stuck with him through his young adulthood was, "Trust no one. Not even your family members." His father's sense of extreme vulnerability pervaded all that he was able to offer Juan, his young son.

Juan had received this inheritance with the measure of respect and appreciation it was due. He knew that it had come from the hard-won lessons of his father's own painful life experience, both in his country of origin and in his adopted country, the United States. Even more, Juan had seen the value of this lesson while growing up in Southern California. He had seen gang violence within his own predominantly Latino community. He had seen the prejudice and discrimination held by many Latinos against other minorities, including, in particular, African Americans. And he had felt discrimination and prejudice from many directions—including from black kids—against himself. All of this reinforced whatever innate tendencies he may have had to keep mostly to himself. He realized he had also learned to keep his heart closed and to hold on to his father's teachings as if his life depended on it, because he had come to believe that it did.

And yet, over the course of his three years as a law student, a shift had somehow taken place. One late afternoon, Juan sat with me behind a closed office door. He felt safe in that space and shared with me some of what he had come to see, deepening his capacity simply to be with it. Juan realized that his father's pain and suffering, his limited horizon, didn't have to be his own. Indeed, Juan found that the world had presented more opportunities for him to thrive than had been true for his father, his mother, or generations of people who had come before him.

Over the course of time, Juan came to see how the defenses that he had established to protect himself had a painful double edge: they kept him at a distance from those with whom he might otherwise be able to connect and feel the sense of belonging that his parents had not felt. He realized that belonging with others was just what his father had secretly craved for himself and what he had hoped to pass down to his children one day.

Juan said he arrived at these realizations through new life experiences, supported by the mindfulness and compassion practices he first encountered in the classes he'd taken with me. He grew in his capacity not only to see his life more clearly but also to feel his own feelings and to imagine those of others through the heart-opening practices that we shared together in our class on mindfulness and law. Juan experienced enough time in mindful, emotionally aware, connected community that he was beginning to feel that a new way of being in the world might be possible for him.

As we sat and talked it through together, he was able to find the words for what had shifted in him: he had learned the *value of being vulnerable* with others. He understood the strength that arises from caring for others and allowing others outside his family to care for him. Sitting with Juan as he spoke of his personal transformation was powerfully encouraging. But sharing this moment, as mutually affirming as it was, was not why he had come to see me.

Juan would soon be graduating. He knew he would be heading off into an uncertain future in a world in which identity-based conflict was common, and he had a question for me: "Will I be able to stay like this, to keep this . . . this openness even after the class ends and I leave this place?"

"I cannot guarantee you that," I told him. "But what I do know is that you can increase the likelihood of that by supporting yourself in being present and emotionally aware along the way. And you can do that by continuing to practice self-compassion and mindfulness, moment to moment and with love."

Exploring the Embeddedness of Awareness

Each of us comes to the work of developing self-awareness and empathy from a particular place, some situated experience that makes it easier—or not—to feel for others. We enter this work from a position in the social world that makes it more or less difficult to know about the suffering of others in the world, and from there, to broaden and deepen our consciousness. Depending on our social location and the social conditionings that accompany it, we will find it more or less difficult to see the links between our situation and that of others, and to practice new ways of being with ourselves and interacting with others.

The historical Buddha began his quest for liberation through what would become known as mindfulness catalyzed by an awakening to his own social position in the world. Born to the royal family in his village, he was sheltered from human suffering—including illness, aging, and death—during his formative years. As the story goes, one day the young prince traveled beyond the palace walls, and there, encountered a sick person, an elderly person, and a dying person. Seeing this suffering up close changed him—he began to wake up to the suffering all humans face and, from there, to his desire to understand suffering, its causes, and the means available to us to end it.

Unlike the kinds of suffering inherent to the human existence that the Buddha witnessed, the suffering that arises from racism is not inherent in being human. It is the unnecessary, unequally distributed suffering that results from the social conditions of our time. There are elements of this suffering that result from our tendencies to cling to things even when they are gone, to push away experience rather than to receive it, and to remain in a fog of confusion about what's going on. Awareness helps us minimize the pain of racial suffering, both by reducing our own excessive attachments, aversion, and delusion, and by grounding us in ways of being in the world that disrupt the unnecessary suffering of others and reset the possibilities of the future by transforming the present.

Hearing the Call

Once we heal ourselves sufficiently so that we can begin to see the landscape of suffering beyond our own front door, we see that the resources necessary for survival are not evenly distributed. We see that the right to control access to those resources is not evenly distributed, and that the advantages of some are directly tied to the disadvantages of others. When this is based on social characteristics such as race (and gender and so on), we are seeing identity-based social injustice.

When we recognize these things, we have choices to make. We can stick with the status quo, or we can take the risk of connecting with others, learning about the vulnerabilities they face, and compassionately acting to surrender our own privileged positions long enough to join together in the ongoing struggle for justice. If we are willing to see and to feel with one another, the ever-present dynamics of injustice move us to take action to minimize harm. Naturally, each of us will have different views on what compassionate responses look like. But the expanded awareness that results from mindfulness better enables us to answer the call to take compassionate action as best we can for now, surrendering some part of our attachment to the comforts afforded by systems that result in mal-distributed suffering, and to keep doing so with each new opportunity.

Answering the Call

As always, we begin with ourselves.

We continue the work of developing our emotional intelligence, the capacity to see and manage the fear, anxiety, and other emotional reactions that come with perceived threat. Even with some practice, most of us find it difficult to express at least some of our own emotions. And given that we may be emotionally reactive when talking about race, emotional intelligence is essential if we are to build the capacity to stay in honest connection with one another through our different experiences in the world.

Here is a hard truth to keep feeling our way into: even if we are not white, we have internalized biases against other people of color. We have been conditioned to compete with one another for attention in predominantly white spaces. Sometimes this makes us fearful and unable to rightly value one another, and sometimes it leads us to participate in systems that harm people of color. This is a sign of internalized racism that requires healing. And healing this will not be easy.

Whites are usually much less aware than people of color of the role of race and racism in their lives and in others' lives. But this is also true of some people of color, especially those whom some describe, with more than a hint of sarcasm, as having "honorary white status"—those acceptable enough to whites to be given a conditional degree of acceptance in traditionally white spaces, despite being a person of color. People of color who grew up in the homes of immigrant parents might also be unaware of race and racism. Whatever the cause, this lack of awareness may feel like a sort of groundlessness when the topic of racism comes up and may lead to silence, inarticulateness, or the tendency to avoid the conversation entirely.

It is tempting to judge such silence as naïveté or a willful blindness. And yet, so much of how we come into our awareness of race and racism is beyond our control. We are born into bodies we did not choose, bodies that signify group associations defined by the cultures in which we are raised. And we are born into families and communities that are not equally aware of or capable of teaching us about race and racism.

At the same time, since race is constantly being remade, and racism is constantly being reimagined and reinscribed, we each bear some responsibility for what we do to disrupt these patterns now. The mere fact that we did not learn about these matters as children or even in college—that we did not know about race riots in our region or about the laws prohibiting Asians from owning land in our state, for example— does not absolve us of responsibility for learning about them and working for collective redemption now.

So our present level of awareness, if we happen to know more than others, is nothing to hold with pride. And any lack of awareness is not our fault. Seeing this, we hear the call of the work of racial justice differently— with more humility and empathy, on the one hand, and more courage on the other. Mindfulness practice alone is not enough to support the work of racial justice. We also need to learn some of the untaught history that helps explain how we got where we are, especially in the places that we call home. We need the will to bring awareness to our ability to listen and to speak about what we are learning, seeing, and being with these realities in a way that is itself a mindfulness practice.

Deepening Body-Based ColorInsight

As I worked to support others in raising their awareness, I relied on what I knew about staying present in my own body. I practiced down-regulating my reactivity when I felt myself triggered and anxious. I relied on mindfulness as a form of holistic, body-based racial awareness. In paying attention, on purpose, with an attitude of friendly acceptance of what is arising, we may all get a fresh start.

As I hope you are beginning to sense for yourself, mindful awareness can help us wake up to and stay engaged in the work of creating deeper understanding and greater freedom around issues of race. And ultimately, it can help us to become resources in our communities, people capable of assisting others in doing the ongoing work of reconnecting to our common humanity through seeing, being with, and taking actions to let go of the illusions of race and to disrupt their harmful consequences.

Whatever my own ability to be in conversation with people who have work to do around these issues, I wasn't born with it. I was not always present and compassionate with others. It has taken me years to develop the ability, for example, to stand with a white man who believes that police brutality only happens because people of color behave in ways that provoke it, or to sit with a white man who believes that we should try to empathize with those who would prefer not to live in a community with me. My ability to do so has come, in large part, from my own commitment to regular awareness or mindfulness practice. As I have learned both from research findings and personal experience, what I practice—what I intentionally engage in on a regular basis—literally changes me. Like daily weight lifting, practicing mindfulness strengthens and sculpts the muscles of our mindfulness. By changing the brain and improving the neuropathways that support the functioning of crucial regions of our nervous systems, we strengthen our capacity for mindfulness and compassion in our daily lives. Many of the awareness practices presented in this book have been shown to change our brains in ways that not only support health and well-being, but also make it easier and easier over time to become grounded, mindful, and compassionate in the face of even the most stressful situations.

Because dealing with race on a regular basis—trying to understand how people came to be so *mis*understanding, and trying to keep our hearts open to trusting that a better way of being with others is possible—is not easy. In fact, in these days of heightened tension, miseducation, obfuscation, and confusion, it is often really, really hard. How can we live in ways that support our exploration of race and its implications in our lives, releasing its hold on our sense of identity, without becoming personally overwhelmed? And how can we keep finding the will to stay in these conversations, even when faced with others who would rather bypass the issues with some version of "Can't we all just get along?"

We do so by noticing when we feel ourselves drifting into distress and giving ourselves the care that we need. From there, we continue the work of building up our muscles for holding the space for complexity, for developing resilience and the steadfastness of commitment to do the work for justice within our communities. At the end of each day, we lay down our efforts and rest, allowing ourselves to be soothed by the currents of the ocean, not overcome by them. And we begin again on the next new day, grounding ourselves and then moving out in mindful engagement in the struggle. In this way, we make justice our life's work, one day, one action, one moment at a time.

At the heart of this work are deep questions facing each of us. The answers we seek require not merely rational conversation and analysis, but emotional literacy, social intelligence, and an ethical commitment to a vision of a more just world. When we develop those capacities and grapple with our questions together, we find answers, as well as the capacity to seek new answers when our old answers no longer serve.

We were born into communities and cultures that created the ways in which we have defined ourselves and others. We live out these conventional identities and even feel that we are choosing them, that we would not have it any other way. And yet, deep within, we may come to know that these conventional ways of defining ourselves are not all of who we are. At the level of deep mindfulness, there are no races, continents, or nations. And if we have the courage and the will, we take up the struggle to keep a clear-eyed view of our deeper being that is always, in an instant, capable of radical connection with our vast human family.

When we move outside of the circle of people who are familiar to us, conflicts arise seemingly out of nowhere. If this has happened once in our experience, we may walk on eggshells the next time we encounter someone who is "Other." We are tempted to respond to the struggles we face with shame, anger, denial, or a sense of frustration that leads to re-treating and staying with our own "kind" or "tribe." Despite our efforts to be kind, polite, and antiracist people, we are frustrated to find that the old, inherited patterns persist within us and within others and show up at inconvenient moments. We can be forgiven for wanting safe places to fall, and for sometimes settling for the illusion of safety in a more homo-geneous school, workplace, church, or community. But research has shown that there are more effective ways to approach these issues in our lives. Mindful awareness helps us see that we are all inherently vulner-able, but we need to enhance our ability to cooperate across lines of real and perceived difference in order to thrive. With the expanded capacity for empathy that compassion practice brings, we develop confidence to repair our relations with others when conflicts arise, and to build more robust pathways to deeper connection that can help us thrive.

Rotating the Center of Our Concern

Mindfulness is about seeing ourselves, our biases, our wounds, and the gifts that come from our relationships along the road we've traveled all more clearly; seeing our mutual relationships and interconnections more creatively and fully; and taking the risks necessary to find and create new ways of being with the conflicts and pains that race presents in our lives. It is about helping one another learn new ways of building spaces for working with the conflicts that arise when we come together across lines of difference, and for moving through the world with resilience in the face of these challenges, ready to meet them with awareness and compassion.

I've seen how my own moral and social imagination is stimulated by being with others who are doing the work of racial justice. I have seen how being with others who are working to see their own biases inspires me to see my own. I have seen how my own relative comfort and fear of vulnerability can be a barrier to helping alleviate others' suffering. I have seen how being together in community actually does lessen the sense that I am impassably different from those whose lives and identities are different from my own. Over time, I've experienced less fear and more joy in making resilient connections across difference.

And what's more, research is confirming what I have seen in my own experience and life as more than mere anecdote, selection bias, or good fortune. Awareness practices—mindfulness and compassion—have been shown to reduce bias and help make us more capable of dealing with the stresses of living and working in diverse community.

The ColorInsight approach emphasizes that we develop the habit of turning *toward*—not away from—aspects of our embodied experience that deal with race. We look at the psychological aspects of our experience— what our minds do with social identity cues. And we look at what the cultural aspects of our experience—the surroundings, context, and power dynamics in which we find ourselves—do to us and to our sense of our social identities. If we keep looking, we see how our sense of ourselves is constructed by our sense of the so-called Other, and the constructs that keep re-creating the sense of separation and impassable difference fall away.

Any effort to work toward increasing awareness of social harm, and of our mutual (though unique) roles in creating it, demands that we examine the intersections between race and other dimensions of experience— gender, class, sexual orientation, immigration status, religion, and so on—in specific moments in time in our everyday lives. We see how race-infused moments come and go across different contexts.

We come into the work with a view, then, that takes in as much as possible of the whole. It invites the full spectrum of our own experiences, and that of all humanity. From there, we might invite our communities into this work that leads to transformation and deeper caring in our relationships because the well-being of any one of us is bound up with the well-being of all of us.

ColorInsight practice explores that aspect of our awareness that John Paul Lederach calls "moral imagination"—the view that even in our greatest pain, "the welfare of my community is directly related to the welfare of your community."[2] To be human is to live with both inherent vulnerability and profound interconnectedness. *All* human beings suffer, desire the alleviation of suffering, and do so in the context of a world of suffering and vulnerable others. Because seeing this can be a catalyst for turning away, we have to work intentionally to break through barriers that make it hard for us to see that we belong, and everyone else does, too.

From the perspective born of these insights, we realize that the work of freedom, of creating inclusive, identity-safe spaces that support democratic liberation, is relational, moment-to-moment, location- and place-based work. It is work we can and must do wherever we find ourselves, prompting us to ask who is suffering here and whose voice we might bring from the margin to the center. And so, grounded in a deeper understanding that we each have work to do right here and now, we begin to ask questions like, "Who are among the *most* vulnerable in this community?"

According to law professor Mari Matsuda, starting with the perspective of those "at the bottom" is a core premise of social justice.[3] But mindfulness demands that we do not stop there. We then ask, "What can we do together to deepen our understanding of these hyper-vulnerabilities and assist in alleviating them? And how might our own desire for liberation and healing depend on our taking action now?" We do the work of listening to those who are most vulnerable and building bridges of support to increase their sense of belonging and our own. We work to build a sense of trust, knowing that we will make some mistakes along the way, but we are willing to take risks for the sake of improving our relationships with ourselves and with one another.

And we proceed by asking the next essential question: "How may we shift now to the work of addressing *other* vulnerabilities that are *also* present?" In doing so, we realize that our own vulnerabilities and identity-based suffering will not and cannot always take center stage. We develop the capacity and the will to *rotate the center* of our communities, to pivot around the concerns of differently situated people, ensuring that no one is left out and that the most acute suffering is addressed first. It is, as one teaching story goes, taking the arrow out of a wounded body before figuring out how it got there and who else might have been grazed along the way. Only then does it make sense to turn to the other suffering that the arrow may have caused. Turning toward people who are hurting more than we are helps strengthen us, deepening our ability then to turn to those who may be in some sense better off, but are still suffering. We move from addressing the deepest wounds and most pressing needs to creating space for those whose suffering may be less but is nonetheless important to acknowledge with kindness and compassion.

Through practices such as Mindful Communication and Rotating the Center, we create durable foundations within ourselves and within our communities to pivot from one set of concerns to the next, and yet never lose sight of the desire for everyone's well-being. This dynamic approach to paying attention to how identity-based difference creates vulnerability is at the core of equity and justice.

Compassion for the Wounded Racialized Self

As we engage in ColorInsight practice, in time we may sense even more of the ways in which we carry wounds associated with racism into our interactions with others. For some of us, the dominant culture has told us that our "minority" culture is somehow deficient in subtle ways—that our ability to feel, to dance, to be in our bodies, is somehow a measure of unworthiness. We have heard the dominant culture tell us that our bodies, the shape of our eyes, our hair, are somehow, inherently, not only not beautiful, but completely unacceptable. We learn this through questions we have been asked, even by people who claim to love us:

"Have you ever thought about getting your nose done?"

"Could you just stop bringing up the issue of race? Let go of your [Latin/ black/Asian/American Indian or Native American] complex?"

We have internalized racism in the messages from so-called friends and lovers, as we have taken into our souls and psyches trainings and conditionings from our own parents and grandparents, who said things like:

"Don't go outside without a hat on! You don't want to get too dark!"

"You can take the girl out of the ghetto, but you can't take the ghetto out of the girl."

"Don't date any darker-skinned black or Mexican person."

We have *all* internalized white supremacy to a greater degree than we realize.

And there is more. As people whose faces, skin tones, eyelid shapes trigger race fantasies and racecraft in ourselves and in others, we have endured the pain of the daily, silent erasures that come from people around us who have decided we are not deserving of full respect. Sometimes our wounds feel particularly fresh and we develop ways to keep ourselves safe from others who might hurt us. We decide that it is safer to stay "with our own kind." Or we choose to avoid addressing issues of race and racism altogether.

Whatever you bring to this call to turn toward painful experiences of race in your life, you must view yourself with compassion for the suffering you have endured. Healing ourselves is the first step of awakening, of accessing joy and connection despite the biases we all carry and from which some of us have suffered more than others. Regardless of whether others understand, we must learn to be with ourselves with a fierce love.

CHAPTER THIRTEEN

PERSONAL JUSTICE

෨

What do we need? "A curated, adapted set of awareness (mindfulness)
and compassion practices—experienced at the level of the personal, the
interpersonal, and the systemic—as central components of teaching and
learning about race."

—RHONDA V. MAGEE[1]

The Art of Practicing Self-Compassion

As you've already seen, actively engaging in self-reflection with kindness
and practicing self-compassion are essential to healing. If we have not
been fortunate enough to have been deeply loved by others in our lives, it
is all the more important for us to become capable of deeply loving ourselves.

Healing our own wounds is at the heart of ColorInsight. We can only
help others heal if we are able to heal ourselves. Thus, you must take the
time to really feel and sense how you have been harmed by racism and
white supremacy. Take the time to see and to know how you carry that
harm with you every day. And however much you may have already healed,
be open in this moment to the possibility that even deeper healing can
come to you, too.

Practicing self-care and self-compassion does more than help us
heal; it gives us the strength to stay in the difficulty of looking at ways
that we miss the mark of our own highest expectations, and stay in the

fire of conflicts that may arise with others. Dr. Kristin Neff of the University of Texas at Austin is a pioneer in researching the benefits of self-compassion as a means of expanding our capacity for engagement in the world. She and others have shown how simply pausing and noticing distress as it arises, and then inviting conscious reflection on this moment of suffering, allows us to see that we are wounded, and to work with what we see in ways essential to our own self-nurturing and healing. When we notice that we are suffering, we can meet that suffering with the recognition that all humans suffer in similar ways from time to time. We can step up and offer kindness to ourselves and to others in such moments. Thus, our suffering may become a conscious gateway into the experience of common humanity, which is at the heart of healing from the wounds of racism and additional forms of Othering, and of minimizing the likelihood that such wounds may turn into grievances that lead to the desire for revenge.

Finally, we must invite a kind response to our suffering. We recognize that we deserve support and nurturing, and we allow a sense of support to enter into our hearts. Self-compassion is a critically important foundation for working with bias. It allows us to bring kindness to our own suffering, which despite our best efforts, we carry with us when we have been hurt, thereby limiting our capacity to engage with others. It allows us to meet the suffering that naturally comes up for us when we become aware that we, too, sometimes engage with people in ways that do harm.

THE SKILLFULNESS OF COMPASSION FOR SELF AND OTHERS

Begin by taking your seat, by establishing your usual posture. Noticing your feet on the floor, drop into the present moment as you bring your attention to the sensations of breathing in and out. (Note: you can also engage in this practice while standing.)

Bring a particular focus for a moment on any memories that come up for you when you think about race and racism.

Notice any sensations in the body, focusing on where they are most noticeable in the body, in this moment.

What feelings are arising? Sadness? Anger? Pain?

Breathe in and sense more deeply into these feelings. Note where they arise in the body, and their characteristic sensations.

It may be challenging to name your feelings. Becoming emotionally aware is a core aspect of mindfulness practice. Bring kindness to yourself and to any reactivity you notice as you explore this practice.

Continue to reflect on your feelings. What do you feel? What are the sensations that come with each of these feelings? Tightness in the chest or heart area? A sense of emptiness? A knot in the pit of your stomach? Numbness? Tension in the region of the neck or face? Sense into whatever is arising, however subtle. If intense sensations arise, you may slow down or pause. You can always come back to this and any other exercise after you have given yourself additional time and support.

Breathe in and out as you allow greater awareness of these feelings.

Now sense into your compassion for yourself in this moment, your desire to be free of any feelings of *dis*-ease. Allow one hand to come to rest over your heart, and one hand to come to rest over your lower belly.

As you do so, breathe in and out and sense into the support that your own compassionate touch brings.

Now call to mind a person who has nurtured and offered loving support to you. It could even be a pet with whom you felt completely safe and loved. If you find it difficult to identify someone from your own life, think of a figure in your historical or spiritual lineage.

Although more than one person may surface, allow the first image that comes to mind to serve this simple purpose. This is a mindful visualization practice, and it will be easier for some than others to really bring this visualization to life. Whether it's easy or challenging for you, breathe in and out with openness, and try to make the image as vivid as possible. Sense into any feelings of warmth, ease, nurture, or love that arise as you bring this image to life.

Allow any thoughts, any sense of struggle or judgment that arises, to simply fall away. Settle into the sense of breathing in and out with compassion for yourself.

Continue to hold the image in mind for two to three minutes, making it as vivid in vision and feeling as possible. As you do so, sense into the quality of your heart. Notice any residual warmth from these good feelings, which may not have been there before. As much as you can, allow the sense of any positive residual effects to expand through your body, from head to toe.

Now see if you can imagine these good feelings expanding beyond the bounds of your physical body. Imagine them expanding to reach others around you, whether near or far.

If you are willing, imagine extending these feelings of warmth to others who experience the pain of racial wounding at this moment, and then extend it to those who are feeling any other sort of pain or suffering. Imagine extending the lovingkindness you feel in ways that might reach and help relieve the suffering of others.

When you are ready, allow the particular images that you have been holding to fall gently away, to dissolve.

Rest in awareness of simply sitting and breathing.

If you have not done so, bring your hands back to rest comfortably (on your knees if sitting, or if you are standing, by your sides).

MINDFUL REFLECTIONS

What are some of the feelings that you sense in your body right now? How does your body feel in this moment? What was it like to imagine extending compassion to others in this way? What thoughts and emotions come up? Take a few minutes to journal about the image, feelings, and sensations that arose for you during this practice. Resolve to explore ways of bringing the wish for self-compassion and compassion for others more to the fore in your everyday life.

People have various reactions when I talk about compassion practices for the self and for others. Some readily understand the importance of bringing awareness to the way we hold these matters in our hearts, including the woundedness that each of us carries. Others find it difficult. They worry that the self-compassion aspect seems self-indulgent or too "touchy-feely," or they just can't make themselves vulnerable enough to admit that their hearts, too, need healing.

For some, it is hard to imagine extending good feelings to others, but for many, that part comes easier. It can also be a challenge if you are sitting with others. Fortunately, we can practice compassion alone, or while taking the commuter train to work. We may do it while resting in a favorite chair on any given morning, noon, or night. And we may do it while recovering from illness or when we feel like giving up.

I encourage you to simply be open enough to give these practices a try. Experiment. See what might happen if you just do the practice. It may, at first, feel inauthentic. As I tell my students, and as my teachers have said to me, "Practice anyway." Be open to what might arise if you just give the practice a chance.

As Juan and so many others can attest, showing compassion for ourselves and others tends to take care of a great deal of the rest. Exploring race and racism in our lives, when engaged with lovingkindness for ourselves, can itself be a pathway for healing that leads to liberation and deep peace.

Because while it is undeniably true that our lived, embodied differences in experience do matter, we are also capable of deeply meeting one another as human beings who suffer and desire to be free of it. And while our particular home communities and neighborhoods may not look at all the same, we remain one human family that has forgotten who we are, profoundly shaped by our interactions with one another.

So take a moment to pause. Take a deep, cleansing breath. Feel the support that exists for you here and now. Take note of the goodness of your heart, the compassionate concern that has gotten you to this page and helped you stay with this challenging effort to connect more deeply with your own experience and with that of others, in a world in great need of deeper human healing and mutual concern.

Spend a few moments honoring this part of you. Write a short reflection in your journal to mark your self-awareness, your increasing insight, your bravery, your deepening love. Describe what you most want to remember, and why. And when you are ready, turn the page for even more of what may open up along the path of ColorInsight, even through the moments of conflict and challenge that commonly arise.

CHAPTER FOURTEEN

ENTERING A ROOM FULL OF PEOPLE (AND ELEPHANTS), AND LEAVING A COMMUNITY

Racism is still with us. But it is up to us to prepare
our children for what they have to meet.

—ROSA PARKS[1]

Creating Robust and Resilient Spaces Through the Mindfulness Connection

The body-based awareness practices that we've explored here do more than help us live with greater ease and clarity. They also help us move into connections with others because whether we want to see them or not, race and racism are so often the proverbial elephants in the room. The more we try not to see these aspects of our lives, the more they can crowd out our ability to effectively see anything else.

While we may admire others who seem to be able to come together across lines of real and perceived difference to talk about race, we may find that the most we can do now is begin to talk a bit more about it with people who look like us or make us feel safe. We may feel inclined to explore spaces where groups of people who share our identities—affinity- or heritage-based groups—come together to share and acknowledge the particular challenges that "people like us" face and to collaborate on ways to free ourselves. Yes, this means holding spaces where whites come together with other whites to discuss race in their lives, and people of color gather separately in their groups for the same.

In such relatively homogeneous spaces, and with the added support of our self-compassion commitments, we can settle in and unpack what's going on without having to worry about the fragile feelings of others who might not understand. We turn to our familiars for help in putting our life stories, our Race Stories, into historical and cultural context. We rely on the compassion and safety that we may find in these spaces. We revel in being able to jump right into the heart of our intense feelings and experiences. And we rely on the group's understanding. Whether as a prelude for coming together in more diverse, multicultural groups, or as an end in itself, we may well find that in such groups, we can *really* breathe again. How we organize such safe spaces is often difficult. Do I need to find a group comprising only black women? Or women of color? Or people of color? Any one of these might offer support in a given moment.

Then again, we may be willing to join in discussions in more diverse groups whose members have had experiences that differ significantly from our own. It is essential that we look inside and ask whether we have done enough personal practice—exploring our own habits of evasion, confusion, anger, or shame around race—to be able to see our identity-based barriers to deeper awareness and connection. Are we ready, willing, and able to sit with compassion for ourselves *and* for others, and to engage in mindful, empathic listening as others share their experiences? If we are white or see ourselves as closely allied with whites, we may need to look especially closely at the ways that the most dominant patterns of identity-based privilege in our culture—whiteness, maleness, heteronormativity, and so on—may make it difficult for us to see how we contribute to the suffering of others. And if we are not white, and see ourselves as allied with nonwhites, we need to be willing to consider how our experiences of subordination and disrespect may make it difficult to see our own agency in the work of disrupting the patterns of racism and race-based suffering of all kinds.

Having done some of the work of seeing and healing—alone or in safe spaces with others—we may feel ourselves better able to move with courage into more challenging conversations. In my experience, it helps to prepare for being only partially understood, not as fully embraced as we would like to be. We may come in with our guard up. Becoming aware of what we bring into mixed groups is an important step in creating the preconditions for our own greater strength and resilience in such settings. We can look at how we might be triggered and mindfully attend to signs that we need more self-support, even if we need to leave the room to take care of ourselves and come back when ready to begin again.

Depending on the circumstances, we may choose one approach over another—working with a group that we consider to be "our own," or coming together with a more diverse community. There is a great need, then, for a range of spaces necessary to support us wherever we find ourselves on the journey. People of color—only sitting sessions? Yes, please! "White Awake" groups? Certainly. And equally important: groups that have been developed intentionally to bridge the gaps across different affinity groups, bringing us together in communities that are enriched by the time we have spent in more focused groups. Given that most of us need support for our own liberation and healing, but still have to leave our comfort zones at some point, we may find ourselves toggling back and forth among a variety of communities of ColorInsight practices.

What is crucial is that we commit to staying close to the marrowbone of our experience, and to working to alleviate our own and others' suffering around race, which takes courage and compassion. As we take one faithful step at a time with the support of our practices, we'll develop greater capacity and skillfulness for the lifelong journey.

Reflecting on Race with Our Familiars

Because the North Carolina community in which I grew up was all black and not given to protesting, we didn't see a particular need to discuss racism or the concept of race on which it depended. Whites came into our home daily on a little black-and-white television in my GranNan's living room, but we didn't discuss the differences that we saw in their lives compared to our own. When my family moved to Virginia, our neighborhood was a bit more integrated. Over time, I learned how race mattered and found value in talking it over with friends.

As you begin to notice more about race and racism in your everyday experience, you too may find it helpful to talk with others about it. The most logical place to begin may be with those closest to you—family and friends. Often, given the patterns of self-segregation that persist in our cultures and communities, these will be people whose backgrounds are similar enough to your own that you can feel at least some level of comfort in broaching the topic.

Reflecting on Race in Mixed Company

James walked slowly toward the open door of the meditation room at a retreat center. With an effort to appear casual, he peered inside. He had read that this session would be on the subject of diversity. He had not been happy about it.

He knew he had skin that marked him as white. When combined with his gender, he felt particularly vulnerable in spaces where the topic of race came up. So he'd debated whether or not to skip the session and spend his time napping in the room. Finally, he'd decided to go. But he had a strategy.

James entered the room and took the seat closest to the exit door, in the very back. He'd leave as soon as it got to the point where, in his experience, so many other conversations on race had gone—with white men under attack. He worried he would end up feeling, once again, like the fall guy for all of the ills of the world, with little he could say in response.

As James settled down, Shellette entered. She had not realized that she was holding her breath while reading over the retreat schedule, looking for something, until she saw it. She breathed a sigh of relief when she read the description for the session with "diversity" in the title.

"Finally, we'll get to talk about the whiteness of this place!"

Nevertheless, as the room began to fill, Shellette felt a rising sense of anxiety, even dread. Once again, she was one of the only African-American women in the room. She wondered if this would end up like so many others she'd joined before in majority white spaces—with the experiences of white people shaping the conversation over that of people of color, and with most whites "just not getting it." She worried she would either end up feeling, once again, like wallpaper in someone else's dining room, with no real seat at the table herself, or feeling called upon to bare her pain for the teaching of others.

What makes it difficult for you to talk about race in settings like this—with people from a range of backgrounds, most of whom you've never met before?

What makes it easier for you to do so?

What feelings, thoughts, and sensations come up for you when you reflect on this now? How might these reactions shape your willingness to enter rooms where it will be discussed?

If you are like most people, the demographics of the space—who is in the room—is a big factor. When we peer into such rooms, we notice race. And the greater the number of people who appear to be "like us," the higher the likelihood that we will feel some sense of safety.

Then there's the question of who's in charge. Most of us need to know who is leading and facilitating the discussion. We try to discern whether we will be safe enough with the person "in charge." We've seen such conversations go off the rails before, and in case that happens again, we want to know something about that person's level of skillfulness in getting us back on track and minimizing the damage that may be done.

We all know that discussions about race among people of different backgrounds are fraught with tension. If we bring mindfulness to our own experiences, we know something about why this is so. These tensions are rooted in the knowledge we all carry—that racism has done a great deal of harm to a great many people, in our communities and beyond, across generations. And we recognize that we cannot all relate to these facts in precisely the same way.

For example, if we are white (and especially, white and male), we have often been trained to avoid these topics. The training may be subtle and hard to see, and once we recognize it, it may be hard to grapple with the reality that this training holds the structures of racism in place. This is why we need compassion meditation as a base for our work. Research in the fields of cognitive psychology and neuroscience has shown that engaging in compassion practice provides support for us as we turn toward the suffering that racism causes, by minimizing the fear-based reactivity in our brains and lessening the sense of physical distress. Compassion practice also helps us minimize self-criticism and judgment.[2]

And so, let's return to James and Shellette as they each in their own way join the group. Aware of the challenges we face in feeling our way toward just enough safety and trust to keep us moving into deeper connection together, I offer an opening practice bringing mindfulness to our experiences of breathing in our bodies. We move from there to a practice of self-compassion, and finally, to compassion directed toward others. Taken together, this series of practices serves to ground us in a way that most of us can feel in our bodies. It is a Grounding Practice, one of many that I use to support the work of mindful social engagement.

As the last element of our opening practices, I invite everyone to look into one another's faces and take in the measure of our deep histories and our will to connect as we move into the next phase of our work together. I call this practice "I See You," or "Ubuntu Practice." It is inspired by the multicultural concept of *ubuntu* from South Africa, which has been shared with and translated to me by a member of a culture in which it is practiced as: "I am because you are; and because you are, I am." It is a concept that conveys awareness of what philosophers call "intersubjective humanity," the idea that our very existence and well-being depend on one another's existence and well-being. It resonates with the sense of interconnectedness that may be supported by skillful mindfulness teaching and practice. The basic idea is simply that each of us comes to have a sense of "who we are" in the world based on the interactions we have with one another.

And herein lies more potential for healing. While we tend to interact with others based on past experience, with awareness we can interact with others from someplace new. Simply looking into each other's faces, for example, provides a break from the typical masked and defended way that we hold ourselves with people we do not know well. Turning toward each other with kindness is a move we can feel in our bodies. And as we do so together, the sense of the larger group shifts toward what feels more like connectedness, safety, and concern.

I check in with the group, awaiting eye contact, noticing shoulders dropping, eyes softening. Here and there, I see a gentle smile.

"How is everyone feeling now? What was that like?"

In a variety of ways, they tell me that there has already been a shift, a growing sense of trust and ease in the room. James and Shellette feel into this shift, each in their own way, and become just a bit more comfortable within the group. Only after building this sense of safety in the space do I invite another reflection.

"So how do you usually deal with questions of race as they come up in your life? Think of a recent incident where racism seemed to be a part of what was happening. Does everyone have an example in mind?"

Heads nod.

"Okay, good. Now bring this moment back to mind and body, as vividly as possible. Where were you? Who was there with you? What did you see and hear? What sensations come up for you? Pay attention, especially, to any subtle feelings arising in the body right now. Also notice what thoughts, images, or explanatory stories are coming up."

I didn't know it yet, but inwardly, James decided he was willing to take a look.

"What comes up for you when you're invited to talk about race and racism?" I ask again, gently.

James settled into silence and allowed his thoughts, feelings, and sensations to emerge. He didn't feel the need to deny what he was feeling, nor to move away from the discomfort of it.

After a bit more silence, I ask for volunteers to share what had come up, and James raises his hand.

"I am feeling shaky saying this. My heart is actually beating a bit faster. But what I noticed is the thought that I don't have much experience with racism, that I don't know much about race. Then I noticed something else: that I actually work on *not* seeing race, on *not* knowing about racism because unpleasant feelings and discomfort come up. And I want to avoid it. I don't want to feel that. So it isn't that I haven't come across racism. It's that I *turn away* from conversations or news reports that deal with it."

We all paused, listening to James, hearing the shakiness in his voice, and sensing that something important had just come to light for him. He was expanding his own awareness. His face was more alive. He was sitting forward on his chair, literally leaning in.

Shellette found she could not help speaking her experience into space. "I almost feel like running out of this room, away from people like you," Shellette said to James. "I'm sorry, but I want people to understand something about my history, about the life I have lived. I am so tired of feeling the pain of everyday racism that is everywhere I turn, and that so many others—that white people—somehow don't see, or are not willing to see. That you can all just turn away from." Tears were flowing now.

James did not know what to say, but he could not deny what he had heard. He practiced just sitting with the desire to move away from the pain in the room. Drawing on his mindfulness practice, he allowed himself to listen and to be present to his own reactivity. He noticed the temptation to defend himself. He put it aside and took a deep breath. He realized that he could listen without taking what he had heard personally. He took a deep breath and noticed he was willing to hear the pain in Shellette's voice; that pain was not an attack. It was just pain. He was committed to staying in the conversation. And he found himself wanting in some way to help alleviate her pain. One moment at a time, he was working on developing his own capacity to be with what he knew to be true through the experience of another, to see the world through another's eyes. And feeling that we were with her, Shellette found she could stay in the conversation as well.

As a country, the U.S. has never fully acknowledged the racism of our history for what it is—the personal, interpersonal, and systemic ways it channels the whole spectrum of violence and suffering disproportionately to racialized Others, while providing a buffer of protection against skin-based vulnerabilities to the racially privileged. As a result, we have become fragile rather than strong in our ability to work toward healing. Like Shellette, we may be carrying resentment from past interactions. Like James, we may be bringing hurt feelings from some prior experience that did not go so well for us. And on top of such "lessons," we have been fed messages about the harms of simply naming white supremacy as a part of our histories, whether personal or collective. We have been subtly and not-so-subtly discouraged from coming together to discuss racism and to work to redress it. We have been led to believe that our humanity is measured by our ability to speak in terms of the universal and to avoid, at all costs, discussing the particular—including our own experiences around racism. As a result, we find ourselves coming up short again and again in our capacity to see, to accept, to explore, and to courageously move through racism in our history and in our present in ways that might lead to a less racist and more equitable, just, and loving future for us all.

Awareness and compassion practice guide us onto a radically different, shifted plane for relating with one another. As we enter this plane, we are grounded in kindness toward ourselves and others for the purpose of becoming stronger. No matter our age, we grow up just a bit more. No matter how robust, we heal just a bit more. And in these encounters we are doing the work of rebuilding the world.

Mindful awareness calls us to do more than soothe ourselves in the face of pain caused by this history of racism and its contemporary ramifications. It calls us to recognize the suffering that continues as a result of our history. It calls us to see the interconnection between our current lived experience and the experiences of generations that have come before. It calls on us to know ourselves as one family. We are called, then, not merely to see racism and bias around us, but also to see racism and bias *in* us. And our compassion practices aid us in sitting with what we see, accepting and acknowledging it in ways that change us and pave the way for collective transformation.

And so, with compassion for all that we have inherited, for all the ways we have suffered, and for all the suffering that has gone before, we turn directly but gently toward racism with the will to see it together. We have no choice but to wade into the muck and mess of it. There is no way out of it but through it.

But by now, perhaps we have begun to see more fully that going through it need not be a source of further suffering. We will feel the pain of it, yes, if we are open to feeling as we go. Yet we have begun to know and to trust, through that process, that we will move through that pain and feel more alive. We will also feel more capable of deeply connecting with ourselves and with others. We will feel our way to becoming more fully human again, together. And we will not only be willing to have messy conversations, but to stay in connection with one another for the next one, and the next, to remake the world as we go.

How do we do this? We do it through mindfulness that goes deeper than simply becoming aware of the breath. Through deepening practice, we are able to see and to feel our interconnectedness. As we continue, we are able to see our own views and identities as important, but still only part of the story. From these more porous and compassionate ways of experiencing ourselves and others, we create the space within ourselves to access the new possibilities that are always available to us, just a moment away. We become adept and nimble at creating spaces that make those present feel safe and heard, so we can grow together; we gently dismantle these spaces when they no longer serve us and lightly take them up again as needed. Over time, a new identity, shaped by our experiences of being together in new ways, emerges and grows.

MINDFUL REFLECTION

Think of a time when you've been invited to talk about race or racism in mixed company. How has it been for you? Would you have preferred discussing it first in a group made up only of others more like yourself? Why or why not?

UBUNTU PRACTICE

Inspired by the South African philosophy of *ubuntu*, this is a practice for two people. Sit or stand facing each other. Take a breath and ground yourself before resting your gaze gently on the face of the other. Silently call to mind the definition of *ubuntu*—"I am because you are, and because you are, I am," and repeat it inwardly, directing it at your partner. Take a deep breath and continue, reciting the following phrase inwardly: "Just like me, this person wants to be free. And their freedom is connected with mine." As you sit in silence together, reflect on the possibility that liberation for each of you exists through connections like this one. When you are ready, close by offering any appreciations that have arisen to your partner.

CHAPTER FIFTEEN

FROM IDENTITY-SAFETY TO BRAVERY

❧

People who frequently experience being in the minority often sense that the spaces we inhabit are implicitly imbued with race—whether they be classrooms, courtrooms, neighborhoods, banks, or legislatures. We know that these are not race-neutral spaces. We know that the world has been constructed, mostly but not always unconsciously, in ways that make the dominant group more comfortable, more at home in public spaces. In other words, many of us know that how we use spaces and relate to one another in them are important factors in the making of race and racism in the world.[1] We also know that even when the demographics, the raw numbers are skewed against us, some spaces feel safer, or more regulated around inclusive norms and expectations, than others.

A recent mindfulness and compassion conference session, simply titled "Let's Talk about Racism," illustrates these dynamics well. Let's explore the scene through the eyes of Adila as she enters the room. She looks around a bit nervously, then settles into her game face. She appears neither engaged nor disengaged. This look has traditionally kept her safe from being drawn into engagements until she is ready. She has decided that she will only join in this discussion if it feels right, but she is not sure whether or where she fits in.

Adila scans the faces and checks out the body language of the others in the room. Based on outward appearances—the primary means by which most of us determine race—she concludes that no one looks particularly like her. She notes that there are more white people here than she would have expected, although based on her reading of appearances, about a quarter of those in the room are people of color.

There is an open seat next to another woman of color and Adila moves toward it. As she sits down, the two women exchange smiles. Subtly but perceptibly, Adila feels a slight shift in her body, a movement toward settling in and feeling a sense of belonging in the space.

Still, she sits on the edge of her seat, rather than settling in completely. She has not yet decided whether this space feels safe enough, but she is willing to give it a try. To Adila, the space *feels* white. And in her experience, spaces that feel white are not spaces where she has felt safe talking about race.

What does it mean to say that a space *feels white*? It means that the space has been shaped by a culture that has privileged the experiences of white people—it can be characterized by hyperindividualism over collectivism, entitlement to material comfort (if not luxury) in a world of presumed scarcity, and a sense of disconnectedness from the broader contexts in which we live. Often, such spaces are devoid of bright colors or of depictions that include references to people of color. These and other subtle trainings that comprise whiteness help shape what is and isn't possible and who is or isn't welcome in such spaces. They communicate in an unspoken but powerful language some of what we are up against when we seek to connect anew.

Shaping the Path We Walk

Eventually, Adila takes a long, hard look at me. Later, she tells me that something about my way of being—my own outward bearing as a cisgendered woman with brown skin, as well as something about the quality of my presence—puts her at ease a little. She notices the words that I am intention-ally choosing in an effort to open a variety of doorways into the conversa-tion, to push these doors open as wide as possible, and to reopen them when they begin to close. She can feel herself settling into the space just a bit more.

After introductory remarks, and a chance for everyone to say their name and engage in meditation together, I put a question to the group.

"How would you answer the question, 'What race are you?' As you gather your thoughts, notice any emotions or sensations that come up for you when you think about this."

Everyone in the room takes time to pause, reflect, jot down a few notes to themselves. They may turn them in to me if they like, or not. They can raise their hand and share what they've written, or not. I may call on them and invite them into the conversation, and yet they always have the right to defer or pass. In these ways, we are creating a supportive space to explore what keeps us silent and what helps us open up.

Adila has to be invited to participate in this conversation. She's still not sure she wants to open up yet to this group of people she doesn't know and doesn't yet trust. She is afraid that discussions about race aren't typ-ically centered on people whose backgrounds are like hers. And she's also not sure whether what she'd say would be welcome. Later, she tells me, "These issues are difficult to talk about sometimes because you don't want to offend. I don't think my words would be offensive to anyone—but you never know."

Because this session has been advertised as a discussion of race that's rooted in mindfulness and compassion, people rightly expect that we'll be addressing this issue in a way that provides some support for the chal-lenges that will no doubt come up. As you've already seen, mindfulness helps us by grounding us in a sense of deeper support and capacity to withstand conflict, challenge, and change. Mindfulness and compassion practices, both explicitly and implicitly, help us to regulate the emotions that arise when we encounter situations that make us feel vulnerable; tap into the sense of common ground that exists between us and so-called Others; and from there, engage in discussions based on critical, constructive thinking through which we may reason more effectively together.[2] Because I am the facilitator of this conversation, my ability to self-regulate, to relate, and to reason compassionately with those in the room will be important in helping others do the same.

The details of just how we come together or remain apart matter. For example, I often have people sit in a circle instead of rows in which they look at the backs of one another's heads. I ask people to bring awareness to what it feels like to sit together in different ways. In this instance, as the size of the group increases, people are tempted to take a seat against the wall.

"Could we please bring a few additional chairs in, so that everyone can join our circle?" I ask. We practice adjusting. We make room for a bigger "inside."

And here lies another subtle difference from the norm of engagement in this busy life: as each person enters, I try to look into their eyes and say "Welcome" or otherwise express gratitude for their presence in the room, and I note the adjustments that others are making, inviting them to continue greeting new arrivals as well. Expressing appreciation and receptivity seems like a minor point. But in fact, it is essential to healing and embracing more fully our common humanity. My intention and hope is that each person feels that I see them and am open to what they have to say. In these and other subtle ways, we practice making space for the new, the "stranger"—both within ourselves and in our social world.

Although entering every conversation and workshop is different and uniquely scary, there are some things I've come to expect: That every person involved is completely different, having walked an unpredictable path into this conversation. That every single one of them is carrying some sort of anxiety, holding on to some sense that this conversation might not be for them. There will also be many different kinds of elephants in the room—a range of issues, some predictable and others not so much, that people would like to discuss, but are afraid to raise. Many of us are not used to giving people the benefit of the doubt when it comes to these matters—we are quick to judge and interpret their words through the limited lenses of our own experiences. Expressing empathy is important, then, to opening up the space to us all.

I do what I can to speak intentionally and from the heart, to gently make it clear that this gathering really is for all who enter. "We'll get started shortly. To help ground us in this space, I'd like you to take a few moments to settle in."

"Welcome, everyone," I say. I look around the room slowly and try to make eye contact with every person that I can. "Thank you for coming. I mean that sincerely. Whatever we are able to accomplish here, it will be because of who is in this room. Your presence matters. Your voice in this conversation matters. And how we are together as we listen and speak matters."

Here again, I offer a version of Ubuntu Practice. "We're going to be talking today about race and racism," I begin, "and we only have a short period of time. Because this is a learning community, a place where we have come together intentionally to learn and to grow, I want to invite everyone to take a look around and see who is in this room. Take a moment to look into one another's eyes and greet one another. Really take in who is here, and perhaps any categories you believe may not be here." Most people readily notice the majority in the room is often white. They notice something about the gendered makeup of the group—often mostly female.

"Before I offer some comments, I want to invite reflections on what has brought you each into the room. So take a few moments to turn your attention inward, to the sensations of sitting here and breathing. Bring a gentle sense of compassion to this moment—compassion for yourself, for each of us in this room, seeking to support one another in deepening our understanding."

We practice sitting in silence. People in the room have varying degrees of experience with mindfulness practice, so some may struggle, but eventually we join together in our efforts to come home to the body, in this place, in this time. We are becoming intimate with the particular chorus of our minds and bodies, separately and together.

Here now, we practice a version of grounding.

"Notice the ground beneath your feet. Allow your mind to rest on the sensations of breathing—this is an anchor to the present moment. Sense into the support that exists for you here and now."

From this place of grounded support, we are able to move into more focused contemplative inquiry. As we continue to sit together in silence, I offer the following gentle prompts.

"Why are you here?" I ask. "What is it that you hope to take away from this conversation? Allow this question to arise in you, and simply notice what responses come up. Let the words come without judgment. There may be a memory coming up, a scene, a snippet of a conversation. Just notice it and see if you can identify a few words that capture why you are here."

We sit in silence for a few more moments. Again, for some of the people in the room, this alone is an invitation into a new way of being with other people. In time, we will get used to these unfilled moments. For some, these pauses will offer an immediate respite, quenching some thirst they did not know they had. For most, it will require some getting used to. And yet, slowly, we become a little more comfortable being in solitude, remembering our innate dignity, together.

"What emotions, thoughts, sensations arise as you prepare to enter into this conversation? Just allow these to arise, and meet them, as much as possible, without judgment. Because everyone knows something about how our social identities shape our experiences in the world, and we will learn and grow from sharing what we know with one another."

As we go around the room, Adila finds her voice. "People don't usually ask me about what race I am. They just ask, 'What are you?'" She pauses, noticing that others around the table are nodding, and some are smiling knowingly. With this encouragement, Adila continues.

"Usually, this comes after someone hears or sees my name. I don't always know what they are asking. Where was I born? Where does my name come from? Or where do I live?" Adila pauses again, looking around the room. She can tell that some of the people who had appeared not to notice her are now examining her features, trying to guess what she will say next about her background.

"If someone does ask me my race, I say I'm white, because my skin color is white and I am perceived as white and get by in the public as a white woman. But I'm ethnically Middle Eastern and Jewish. It's just that . . . these identities are not written on my skin."

The challenges that Adila overcomes in entering this conversation—the mixture of desire to be heard and hesitance to allow this group of relative strangers to be in on her experiences—are not uncommon. As we know, most people find discussing race in mixed settings difficult. Researchers say that this difficulty has many roots, including deeply ingrained, pervasive yet subtle cultural trainings against being vulnerable; differences in perceptions about the nature of the racial problems we face today; tendencies to forecast the most negative outcomes (and a "negativity bias" that leads us to look for and amplify confirmations of these expectations); and unhealed wounds from prior efforts. In short, the work we do to find common ground is not easy, and it may never be. The outcomes of the efforts we make are not always and may never be predictable. Mindfulness helps us sit in the place of not knowing, without feeling lost or as if what we are doing is somehow not worthwhile.

As we continue going around the room, Kelly, a white woman in her twenties just entering her first post-college job, speaks to us slowly, checking out how each word lands as she goes. She says that she has lived a very sheltered life, and she's come to see what it has meant that, for most of it, she has lived only among white people "like me."

A few heads nod slowly in dawning support. Kelly pauses. She looks around and continues, describing how she, as a public school teacher, will soon enter her first classroom where she will encounter a larger percentage of students who are not white. She is afraid, she says, that she isn't ready to deal with the issues that will no doubt come up. "I don't know *anything* about these issues. But I know I need to learn."

Her voice is tentative. She doesn't say it, but I can sense that she's hoping she won't be shamed. Or ignored. At some point in her sharing, I can see that she is stepping more fully into her vulnerability and trusting me to help keep the space safe. I place one hand over my heart and I look into her eyes. She smiles at me and breathes a sigh of relief. I thank her for sharing. I will do this again and again after each person speaks, encouraging others to give one another as much nonjudgmental space as possible, so that their truth can be spoken here.

Next to her is a young, white, queer man named Chris, who has been to one of my sessions before. He says quietly that he knows that I hold a safe space "for looking at this stuff" in a way that makes him feel comfortable enough that he can learn. Because I, too, am a little nervous, I appreciate his affirmation, knowing that it may make it a little easier for some others in the room, who have never met me before, to move closer toward trusting the space.

Then there is a middle-aged white woman named Marta, who, I can tell, has been in discussions like these before. She talks about how she's spent years working with privilege, and so supported having this conversation at the conference. She does not say it then, but she will tell me later that she is frustrated with other white people who, as she puts it, "haven't done the work" of looking at the world through the eyes of people of color. They don't know anything about white privilege. She has been working on her "own shit" for years. She has no patience for their "cluelessness." I understand what she is saying and can certainly empathize with her frustration. By the time she reveals this, I've already sensed this frustration in her demeanor toward the whites in the room, as I suspect others have as well.

Part of our work will be to try to bring awareness to the ways that we are each tempted to look with contempt on others who have less information or awareness than ourselves. Mindfulness asks us to consider whether we are claiming the mantle of being "woke" as white, or "righteous" as black, to reinforce our sense of being different from "the others," or in some way superior. Are we offering our analysis and critique from a place of compassionate response, or from a place of bitter reactivity? Is it based in ego, or in service to something more?

I hope we remember that we are all human beings, caught up in deeply entrenched social patterns and practices. We are all trying to make sense of a world we did not create. We are all recipients of cultural trainings that we did not choose and generally are not well prepared to critique or to resist. And we all struggle to learn new ways of seeing the world. With mindfulness as a support, we remember how we, too, were once in the position of not knowing what we now know. We work on being humble as we engage others, aided by the awareness that we also still have our own learning and growing to do. We become aware that, even as we do what we can to make the world a better place, we, too, will make mistakes sometimes. We work on creating safer spaces for getting it wrong so that we may get it wrong less frequently elsewhere. And we work to build the will to repair, to reconcile, and to keep coming back to one another in hopes of building resilient relationships and robust community together. As difficult as it can be, we work on bringing empathy and compassion to missteps that arise. We work on caring for ourselves and one another as we reveal aspects of ourselves that we are embarrassed to see. As we do this, one conversation at a time, we are building the trust necessary to be vulnerable together, to share what we see with one another, and to listen long enough for the truth to be revealed—all in the service of deepening our own learning and transformation.

As we continue going around the room, I notice a young black man named Avery. From his demeanor and posture, I suspect that he is angry, hurt, and tired, and yet, is also open. He is ready to offload, to share the burden of some of his pain. Avery is exhausted by the effort of sitting through conversations like this where the group is mostly white and most people's experiences are very different from his—less violent, less painful than what he has lived and witnessed over the years. Although he suspects he will have to do some of it here, Avery is tired of having to teach white people about race. He is also worried that this conversation will be oriented around white experience in a way that will make it hard for him to share and receive understanding-based support around his own.

In prior discussions like this, he eventually shares, so much time has been spent trying to get white people to feel comfortable talking about race, or to see the experiences of people of color as worth listening to, that there is no time left for him to talk about the hurt feelings he's carrying, or the fresh wounds he's experienced. For example, he notices that as they entered the room, several white people looked at him and the empty seats beside him, yet chose to sit on the other side of the room. He doesn't know if race is a factor when something like this happens, he says, but it's part of what he has to think about every day of his life—whether people are looking at him and seeing a stereotype, avoiding him, not seeing him for who he really is, seeing their perceptions of him instead.

"When Charlottesville happened," he says, referring to an incident in which white nationalists rallied and left a young white counteractivist named Heather Heyer dead, "it didn't surprise me. I fear for my safety every day of the week. As a black man, my very presence is cause for suspicion in most places. You don't know what it is like to be hunted, to be targeted because of your race until you've experienced having the police called on you for jogging through town, or having a gun drawn on you multiple times after a traffic stop. Racism is real, it's every day, and people who claim to care really need to wake up to it."

A white woman, Anne, who has thus far been silent, says, "I fear for my safety every day, too . . ."

Avery responds, "If you can be convinced that your safety is tied to me simply being in a place that you don't expect, then your fear will lead you to collude in my oppression."

Anne nods slowly. The room falls silent. I intentionally do not invite anyone else to speak yet. I thank Avery for sharing his experience. After a pause, I thank Anne for commenting.

I don't rush to fill the space or to provide analysis here, as these moments speak for themselves. We are, in a sense, bearing silent witness to what we have heard from Avery and Anne. And we are noticing what came up for us in response. If we had more time, I would inquire about what else each speaker might have felt when listening to the others, where these feelings showed up in the body, and so on. But sometimes I defer to silence as the teacher we need in moments like this, trusting that people learn as they reflect on what took place, in their own time.

Looking on sympathetically is Robert, a middle-aged white man, a teacher who says that he has "done some work" on his racism, which he grew up with as a white person in this society. He believes that he is privileged, has unconscious bias, and still has work to do. He is feeling a combination of anxiety, frustration, anger, and shame.

When he speaks, his voice carries a sense of urgency that, from time to time, conveys a flintiness that ignites us all. "I just keep coming back to this: the *history*, the *legacy* of white supremacy is *real* in our society, and we don't talk about it. It's what we're up against and we don't know it. *We have to keep talking about it.*"

Another white man, Jim, is less sure of himself. His body temperature has risen, and he is tempted to go emotionally numb with disengagement. He is wondering why he came, when he realizes that he needs to find a way to talk about this, too. He has willed himself to stay.

When asked what might get in the way of his speaking up, he gets right to the point: "Feeling vulnerable, and feeling the unwillingness to be vulnerable here."

I nod, understanding. "How many of you also feel a bit of that?"

Hands go up around the room. I have placed my hand on my heart already in a gesture of compassion for those expressing anxiety and fear. "Yes, this is something we all feel in some measure. It's okay to feel fear and to acknowledge it here. You are not alone in feeling this," I say.

As we've seen, research in the field of compassion has shown that seeing and acknowledging our painful feelings and knowing that we are not alone in feeling them are crucial. Taking this practice into conversations with others can be of real benefit in helping minimize the potential for unhealed trauma to arise or for creating a sense of emotional dysregulation that makes it hard for people to move on. Interpersonal compassion makes the conversation safer. Pausing to name and offer support for these feelings allows us to open to a sense of self-compassion and feel the empathy and compassion of others rather than move toward the connection-ending experience of humiliation. Thus, encouraging Jim to name what he feels and bear witness to that feeling, allowing it to connect us with the similar feelings within ourselves, we have a way of transforming this fear into courage and may ultimately begin to feel the joy of being more real with others.

And then there is an older Native American woman, Jewel. She is a community activist. She is leaning back from the circle, in a way that appears to convey some degree of skepticism—toward me, toward the group, maybe toward the entire effort.

"I'm holding back a bit," she admits. "I'm grateful for what you're trying to do. And I'm glad that Avery spoke up. I hear your pain, brother," she said, looking directly at Avery with palpable empathy and compassion for his suffering.

She pauses. I stay present to her as she chooses her words carefully.

"I decided years ago that when people of color try to guide such discussions where whites predominate, everyone tries so hard not to hurt white peoples' feelings that nothing real gets said about racism and systems of oppression. And even when something does get said about such things, nothing ever gets done."

I feel myself suddenly under the heat of a spotlight. My own body temperature is rising. *People like me,* she is saying, who facilitate conversations about race in ways that center attention on the white people in the room, may be more a part of the problem than the solution. This is a real statement. It's edgy.

"Let's pause and take that in." I need a moment to collect my thoughts in response. And I also want what Jewel has shared to be heard and considered deeply by those in the room.

Her comment is a profound one. It touches on some of the structural difficulties that we face when we come together to discuss these issues. The demographics of the space matter, in part because it affects who feels comfortable and who doesn't. On the one hand, if we are committed to speaking from our own experience and encouraging everyone to speak in a predominantly white room, we will find ourselves diving deeply into the experience of whiteness. This can, and often does, I'm afraid, leave precious little time or capacity to delve into experiences of the more vulnerable people in the room. On the other hand, when people of color disproportionately share their experiences, it can feel as if they are, again, doing all of the work of trying to upend racism and raise the awareness of whites—work that is more appropriate for whites to do.

I thank Jewel and acknowledge the truth in what she is sharing. Others nod, and lean in. "You are right, there is a risk that we face here. If we look around the room, the majority of the people in this room are white. And when it comes to racism in America, despite much effort to convince you all otherwise, white people are simply not the ones who are most vulnerable to its worst consequences. Is that something we can agree on here?"

I pause, and people nod with differing degrees of vigor. They know we live in a world in which claims of "reverse racism" get a generous hearing in white-dominated institutions, like courtrooms, schools, and workplaces. And yet the white folk who are here in this particular workshop are here in large part because they know that when they see those most vulnerable to the pain and violence of racism, it is generally not people who are white.

"And yet," I continue, "the people in this room are here. They want to be here. And so we have an opportunity to learn something and to teach something. Because we have all suffered something as a result of the cultures of dehumanization that we live in. And we need compassionate spaces, places where whoever is in the room can explore their experience with the intention of gaining insight and turning toward their own deeper work, even as we who are people of color explore our own."

I pause, and then continue: "What we are doing here is only offering a beginning, a place where we can all begin to share some of the ways that race has impacted us. If we are serious about looking into this, we will have to do more. We'll have to commit to ongoing work. That will mean looking at whiteness as a facet of the dominant culture in America and examining how it has impacted all of us. We all know more about whiteness, the most 'invisible' of racial experiences, than we have been given space to acknowledge. And those who are experiencing whiteness and reflecting on it for perhaps the first time will have ongoing work to do that is different from the work that perhaps you or I have to do. And yet, here we are, offering one another support for the journey, whatever our path will bring."

The room is quiet with the intentionality of close listening. We are practicing listening mindfully to one another, and with as little judgment and reactivity as possible. Listening to one another in this way has already created more of a sense of safety in the room that we can feel.

Moment by moment, our conversations, learning, and practices help us to deepen our capacity to trust one another. We share our stories and build a sense of mutual respect and concern. We grow in the sense that we can, indeed, work together. And if we are willing, we begin to imagine efforts to address systemic and institutional drivers of racial and other forms of identity-based injustice.

By the end of the session, Adila, too, has warmed up to the group and is sharing more readily about her background. She notices that as a result of increasingly hostile political rhetoric around Muslims and Middle Easterners, she has felt the stigma of "Othering," and has been challenged to figure out how much to assimilate and how much to stand with increasingly vulnerable people who share some of her cultural affinities.

She has come to see that while some of what she and other Middle East-erners are dealing with is based on ideas of cultural and religious differ-ence, some of it is rooted in very American notions of physical difference tied to "race" and its proxy, "color." What she would prefer to see as eth-nicity and culture, it turns out, are being crafted as a new form of race and animating a new kind of racism.

Whiteness, we have come to see, is about embodied power, privilege, entitlement to belong and even live. It is the experience of being given the benefit of the doubt by police, though it will not protect one completely from the risk of harm in an increasingly militarized world. As a light-skinned person who is sometimes considered white, and sometimes considered "of color," Adila occasionally experiences skin-tone-based privileges. But she also feels an affinity with those who experience a heightened level of threat, whether because of their religion, the way they dress, their accent, or their skin tone.

Slowly, through sessions like these, each of us gets to know ourselves better. One conversation, one reflection at a time, we're building trust in ourselves and in one another in ways that lead to true community. And we are learning how to be with the dynamics of race-making and of racism in ways that not only begin to dissolve these, but does something more: it builds within and between us the feeling of rich interconnectedness that can soften our hearts and encourage us to be braver in this moment, and in the next.

CHAPTER SIXTEEN

PARTICULARITY AS THE DOORWAY TO EMPATHY AND COMMON HUMANITY

It has taken me many years of intensive study and practice to be able to recognize and articulate how I am shaped by being white, and this in itself is an example of whiteness (while there are exceptions, most people of color do not find it anywhere near as difficult to articulate how race shapes their lives).

—ROBIN DIANGELO[1]

Being in Context

In understanding race and social injustice, context—time, place, history, and culture—matters greatly. As one part of that context, it is important to see the structural-economic problems causing material distress across all racial groups. A recent study showed that 43 percent of working U.S. households have trouble paying for both food and rent in any given month.[2] It is important, then, to see that people of all races and backgrounds are suffering from food and housing insecurity in the United States and around the globe.

And yet, it is *critically* important to see that the pain of this insecurity routinely and disproportionately falls on some more than others. In Michigan and other states, for example, blacks and Hispanics suffer the highest rates of poverty and income insecurity.[3] This is precisely why a focus on socioeconomic issues or "class rather than race" will not solve this problem. Our class system depends for its stability on racism, and vice versa. As experts on the intersection between poverty and race help us to see, "There cannot be racial justice without economic justice."[4] And in our age of surveillance capitalism, with implicit and likely explicit bias being built into the artificial intelligence by which predictions about human behavior are monetized and exploited, we are especially challenged to unpack the complex interaction of racism and capitalism in our lifetimes.[5]

Racism makes poverty more biting, and income, housing, and health care insecurity more precarious. It also means that even blacks whose incomes place them in the middle or upper class suffer higher levels of stress and worse health outcomes than others of similar means. Because of their vulnerability to racism in housing and other markets (combined with their proximity to a wider network of economically distressed family and friends), middle- to upper-income black people generally have lower levels of accumulated wealth than similar others. Thus, increases in wealth may soften the edges of our vulnerability, but do not protect any one of us or our children from the threat of racism. If we care about justice in America, then, we must confront the fact that racism at every level makes poverty and distress more likely. Otherwise, patterns like these will persist.

And yet, we are routinely led to think about these problems against a historical-cultural backdrop that favors whiteness, and increasingly, white nationalism. We are reminded on a near daily basis that "illegal aliens" are coming and "taking our jobs" and "bringing crime." We hear such fear-based rhetoric, again and again, in tones often loud and shrill. Rather than addressing the real and devastatingly important underlying causes of societal problems, we seem to have little choice but to settle for the politics of scapegoating, of fear and anger, of division and polarization.

But as we deepen our mindfulness practices, as we bring insights from our practice more fully into the problems of our everyday lives, we begin to see the interconnectedness between our own well-being and the well-being (or lack thereof) of others. We develop the stamina not only to look at the social identities of those who are suffering most, but also to see how that suffering is linked to power politics, and how the dominant culture's inclusion/exclusion practices and fearmongering around identity obscure structural problems that threaten us all.

Further Widening of the Lenses

The reported rise in diagnosed anxiety, as well as drug and alcohol abuse and in some cases criminal behavior, reveal some of the consequences of these existential threats on the well-being of people across all of our communities. What looks like acting out, on closer inspection, may be but one or another way many have sought to cope.

As a result of increasingly devastating circumstances caused by war, climate change, and economic and political collapse, people around the world are compelled to move, to get out, to undertake cross-cultural journeys in search of safer, more peaceful, and just plain better lives for themselves and their children. However, this also leads to destabilization, uncertainty, and distress. And in moments of distress, we are susceptible to the siren song of racism, xenophobia, and resistance to the tides of change.

Alas, we have seen most, if not all, of this before. We have seen fear and fear-mongering lead to nativism, racism, hate crimes, and generations of suffering. Unfortunately, these things may reassert themselves because we have not yet found a way to disrupt their capacity to hijack our brains and make us prone to more of the same.

The False Hope of Color Blindness and the Promise of Mindful Perceptual Awareness

Part of the problem is that we've spent the past generation trying to tell people that race and racism are things of the past, to convince everyone that we and our institutions—our schools, our workplaces, our system of justice—are (or should be) racially neutral or "color-blind." As we turn a blind eye to racism in our societies, we implicitly and unconsciously contribute to racist systems and the harm that they do.

Research findings in the field of cognitive psychology help us see that, in reality, the notion of color blindness, the idea that we can somehow just not see race, is a fiction. Our brains just don't work that way. Our brains actually perceive race, and these perceptions affect how we interact with one another, whether we intend this to be so or not.

We may be better able to understand why this is so through mindful inquiry. We've managed to get where we are as a species because we figured out a long time ago how to quickly size up all manner of threats to our existence and take action to minimize risks. Since race has mattered for so long, we all have become very good at not merely "seeing" race, but mapping our perceptions of the value of various groups of people and organizing our relationships accordingly.

Research on implicit bias, from ongoing studies at Harvard University[6] and elsewhere, confirm the widespread existence of unconscious views about categories of people—the elderly, women, blacks, Asians, and so on—that belie our conscious, stated views about them. (If you want to see how you fare, check out the online tests at ProjectImplicit.org.) Bias causes all sorts of unnecessary suffering and material harm in the world, and as we have seen, suffering flows disproportionately to a society's traditionally vulnerable or disfavored groups over others.[7]

So, it is impossible, actually, to be "color-blind" in a world in which color and its analogues have been made so relevant to outcomes in our lives. To believe otherwise is to be more confident in our capacity to control our thoughts and behavior than the research suggests we should be, and to be less aware of the workings of our brains than we might wish or need to be, given the present challenges and past moral tragedies.

Yet we can see that in various ways, we are rewarded for our ignorance in dealing with race. From retaliatory employment actions to social shaming, we have been punished for naming the ways that race contin- ues to matter and that bias continues to show up. Knowing all of this, I try to meet everyone who enters into conversations about this issue with me with an awareness of both their particular situation *and* our common hu- manity in a world of great and increasing distress. Here's the thing: the fact that we *all* see race and tend to associate differently racialized people with different value doesn't make it okay. Similarly, the fact that much of what we experience in the way of disparity happens as a result of struc- tural or systemic dynamics beyond our personal control does not mean we lack the moral agency necessary to have an impact. The things we are up against do not absolve us of moral responsibility to try to make a dif- ference. They do not render the differences in our experiences somehow equivalent, and they do not let you or me or anyone off the hook for ad- dressing identity-based bias and working for racial justice. As inheritors of a world that has made race so consequential, we all have some measure of responsibility for minimizing the role of race going forward.

Our perceptions precede the formation of the racist concepts. For ex- ample, when someone fails to give us eye contact, what do we make of it? Do we perceive this as being unfriendly or rude, and then make assumptions about all people "like this"—e.g., "Indian students are rude"? Or, might we notice our temptation to do so, pause, and disrupt the perception-to- thought-to-concept process? If so, we might learn that among recent South Asian immigrants, a lack of eye contact may indicate a show of respect—the very opposite of being rude. In this way, research and practice reveal some of the ways that we can become more aware of our perceptions, overcome our biases, and work together to promote greater harmony and peace in our communities.

Racialized Spaces as Sites for Multiracial Collective Action

The specific racial demographics of a given space contribute to its "racial character," especially for those in the minority. In workplaces, communities, campuses, and even countries in which the demographics are skewed so that one or more social identity groups' members feel more "at home" than others, the views of the more populous group(s) will shape the sense of what is true or acceptable there. When minority views are expressed, they are less likely to be recognized as valid. White-normed spaces can feel less welcoming of the whole person, more cognitively than emotionally vibrant. As a result, racially skewed spaces do not feel equally safe to everyone inhabiting them. Mindful awareness of this— what we might call "racial spatial awareness"—is critical to the everyday work of undoing racism. It is important, then, to develop the will to see the particular in our midst, the situatedness of our experience—not to the exclusion of a sense of oneness, but as a means of more authentically entering into it. Particularity and common humanity are two sides of the same coin. By being lovingly present to the real and perceived differences between us, we create pathways toward meeting in our rich and full humanity together.

We might bring mindfulness and compassion to bear on our encounters with one another by taking time in advance to consider the social dynamics of the engagement, including the demographics and power differentials we are most likely to encounter, or if we have the power to do so, to create. We might develop the capacity to talk about racial demographics and address the concerns of those who are in the minority, with a view toward holding ourselves and our organizations more accountable to those suffering the most. And we might develop the will to see the complex connections between these aspects of our environment and other variables that, when read together, help us more effectively understand what is going on. Indeed, if we understand the ethical implications of our being interconnected, of *ubuntu*, we may feel compelled to explore these things and more.

Our formal practices of mindfulness and compassion can increase our ability to have not merely difficult but increasingly complex conversations. We can, without anyone noticing, pause for a second or two, take a conscious breath, bring awareness to the thoughts, emotions, and sensations that are arising, and choose how we want to respond to comments that trigger us. We can strengthen ourselves enough to ensure that we are able to stay in the conversation necessary to collectively organize structural change for the better, and to keep coming back when things get difficult.

Becoming more aware of how race matters is essential to building our capacity to make not only personal and interpersonal changes to minimize bias, but structural and institutional changes that make bias less likely to hold fast among the generations to come.

Awake, Alive, and Well

As you deepen your mindfulness practice, see how you can bring it into every aspect of your life. Start with increasing your awareness throughout the day of what is good, what is peaceful within you. Doing so helps bring us into balance and grounds us. We need to be able to see that even as we focus on our identity-based suffering, we are alive and well. If we have practiced the art of bringing mindful awareness to what is well and at ease, we have the strength, flexibility, and stamina to take in the *un*-well, the *dis*-eased.

From the ground of expanded awareness, we have the energy to notice and then to investigate what is beneath any particular difficulty we're experiencing in a given moment, including racial suffering. We might consider how our feelings relate to the social demands of our lives, the trainings of our own cultures and of the dominant culture, the ways we have been chided, shunned, punished, or rewarded for noticing these things in our organizations and communal spaces. If our community members have disproportionately experienced race-related trauma, or if we see signs of anyone feeling exceedingly overwhelmed by our efforts to work together, it may be best to pause and to proceed only after ensuring appropriate sensitivity and care.

As we continue to learn and to practice mindfulness and compassion every day and everywhere, we deepen our capacity to live in the presence of all things, including race-based suffering and its intersection with other aspects of our lives. As our ColorInsight deepens, we may begin to imagine a way of being in the world that supports us in the ongoing work of making the world a bit more fair and just for all of us.

EMBODIED RACIAL AWARENESS PRACTICE

As with the practices we've already covered, please be aware of the need for self-care. Only follow these instructions as far as you can go without being overwhelmed. If it would help, seek the support of a friend, counselor, pastor, or other advisor before delving deeply into your most painful memories or experiences.

Consciously sit in a way that supports you in experiencing a sense of your own dignity. Again, if possible, place your feet flat on the floor. Feel the support that exists for you from the ground beneath you.

Take a few very deep breaths. As you do so, allow yourself to focus your attention on the sensations of breathing in and out, in and out. Notice the way simply breathing provides life. Appreciate the support that exists for you in this moment as you simply sit and breathe. Gently and with kindness and appreciation for your being in this moment, bring your attention back to the breath again and again.

Allow yourself to turn toward what you have personally experienced around race and racism. If necessary, take it very slowly. What memory or memories do you still carry? What have you not spoken about in years—if ever—that conveys something about what you have learned about race over the course of your lifetime?

Now expand your awareness to take in the sensations in your body at this moment. What thoughts are arising? What emotions? As best you can, allow yourself to feel the full measure of your emotions. Whether sorrow, confusion, anger, or even rage, experience as much of your feelings as you can in this moment, without becoming overwhelmed.

Reflect on what you know, deep in your bones, about race and its inter-sections with other aspects of your experience (gender, class, sexual ori-entation, and so on). For any one of us, this may be difficult to do. But the difficulty varies depending on our experiences. For black or brown peo-ple, the sheer number of painful memories may be difficult to bear. Then again, you may find that you feel relatively numb. If you are not black, you may also have been shielded from the ways in which your experience bears the marks of America's ongoing race wars. If you are white, this may be difficult to do for other reasons—experiences that travel with your race are often extremely subtle. It may feel as if you have nothing to reflect on here, but you do. If you are Asian, or what in our history has been known as yellow, you may find it easy to recall experiences of dis-crimination, and this reflection may be painful. If you are a member of the vast and varied communities racialized as red, you may have memo-ries of identity-based injury in your own experience or that of your fam-ily or tribe. And if you consider yourself multiracial, or have not identified with any of the above groups, reflect on your experiences as well, includ-ing those that have led to your understanding of the various races of which your background is composed. How have the ways in which these groups are perceived influenced your own thoughts about yourself?

In fact, each of the racialized groups that we have created in the United States comprise people from various cultural heritage groups with unique stories and histories. There is much pain, complexity, and denial woven into our experiences of race.

Breathing in, consider both silent and explicit teachings about race and its meaning in your life. Consider what you have come to think about these various ways of labeling people in terms of race and your level of comfort or discomfort with such terms. Stay present to what comes up in the body as you do so.

Now think of how the spaces in which you spend time these days may be thought of as having a racial character or feeling about them. What about these spaces might be difficult for people who are "raced" differently than you? Are there ways you can readily imagine alleviat-ing that difficulty?

As we turn toward closing this practice, check in with yourself. If necessary, allow yourself a moment of self-compassion. Place one hand over your heart, and one just below your belly button.

Sense into the suffering that you are experiencing in this moment, the causes for this feeling of suffering, and the way this experience connects you with all of humanity and so many sentient beings, as suffering is a part of being alive. Allow yourself a few moments of kind attention, breathing in and out.

Take a few moments to journal about your experiences with this practice.

BRINGING AWARENESS TO STRUCTURAL RACISM IN YOUR LIFE

Set aside at least twenty minutes for the following reflections and meditations.

We need to come into contact with the ground from which we engage others on matters of social justice as we examine how race plays a role in our own lives. We call to mind where we've been on this journey to date.

To be able to tell the truth about intentional and unintentional racism in its various forms—personal, interpersonal and institutional or structural and systemic racism—we deepen the practice of just this sort of grounding in our own experiences. We slow down, put aside our judgments, and simply look back on our histories and turn toward the patterns of our lives today.

Begin by taking your seat and resting in the sensations of being in this moment. Drop into this moment with openness and with kindness.

Reflecting on your heritage and lived experiences in particular places, social identities as pathways to connecting with a deeper ground of being, interconnection, and common humanity, we ask the following:

Looking back on the places I most identify as home, what was the racial makeup of the neighborhoods in which I grew up?

How exactly did this community come to be that way?

At some point, you may take the time to learn a bit more, looking into specific questions like:

What laws, public policies, or private policies with racially disparate intentions or outcomes were in place? What were their effects on my predecessors? My parents? On me?

How then are the legacies of these structural conditions shaping my life experiences—my opportunities, my challenges—now?

And what more do I know or might I learn about my family's journey? How did they come to live where they did? How were they received? Did they experience legal restrictions on becoming full citizens? On receiving a decent education? On experiencing a sense of belonging? What immigration/migration and social policies smoothed or inhibited their journey?

In what ways has my own life been affected by this history? What about the lives of people in my circle of friends and family? How has this history framed my own starting point in the journey to where I am now?

And finally: What might I do now to better address the legacies of these practices in my own life? In my community?

PART FOUR

Doing

Mindfulness is the courage to practice
doing what needs to be done,
investigating, inquiring, that more and
more of our actions might embody
wisdom in the here and now.

We recognize that when black lives matter, whenever that
happens in our history, that will mean that all lives
matter. . . . This is what Dr. King called "the indivisibility
of justice."

—DR. ANGELA DAVIS[1]

CHAPTER SEVENTEEN

"FUCK!" AND OTHER MINDFUL COMMUNICATIONS

Ultimately we are beyond race. Relatively, we must deal with the
harm that racial dominance and subordination produce.
Each of us must ask, "What kind of society do I want to live in?
How can my life be a reflection of racial harmony and an
example of well-being for future generations?"

—RUTH KING[1]

Holding the Space for Complexity and ColorInsight

Constantin has been coming regularly to class discussions about racism
and other forms of bias. He has taken my course on race, mindfulness,
and law. And when he describes these efforts, it is not uncommon for
people to ask him, "Why?"

Constantin looks white. The vast majority of our race-making is
based solely on sight, but Constantin's background is complicated—he is
of Jewish descent on his father's side, and of Greek descent on his mother's. He identifies as nonwhite and has, in that sense, experienced a sense
of marginality and embraced a kind of ambivalence about his own racial
identity.

In his mid-twenties, he became fascinated by the arbitrariness of
race and began to sympathize more and more with those who are racialized as nonwhite. After reading about a massacre of American Indians

that he had never heard of before, Constantin came to a class session with a new level of outrage.

"*Fuck!*" he shouted loudly. "I just can't believe this happened. And at the same time, I can't believe I didn't know about this!"

The class was silent.

Constantin continued, quieter now.

"How much must I *not* know about racism in our history?!"

This moment captures a point in the process of bringing mindfulness to racism in our lives. To experienced meditators or mindfulness teachers, it may sound like reactivity to what we see, or unmindful "strong emotion." However, creating space for strong emotion is necessary for developing deeper understanding of how race operates in our lives. Being able to feel *all* of our feelings, and being able to name them without shame or disapproval, are crucial steps along the path—from seeing what is there, to accepting the reality of it in a way that enables us to acknowledge it more fully. Only from there might we realistically be able to take actions that more effectively transform the dynamics by which racism is perpetuated in our lives.

In this chapter, we will explore more deeply how to listen and speak about race and other forms of social identity bias. We will learn more about how to bring simple awareness to bear in our interactions with others with the help of nonviolent, mindful, and awareness-based communication practices, specially designed to support mindful engagement with our own voice and in meaningful conversations with others.

Think about how your own experience may compare with that of someone of a different race. This may seem difficult to do, but our imaginative capacities are much greater than we typically acknowledge. If necessary, call to mind someone you know well, a friend of a different race. If you do not have any good friends of a different racial background, consider what you know about how other races are viewed in your community. You may know more than you feel comfortable acknowledging at first, but if you stay with this prompt, you will find that you are more capable of thinking through this difficult topic than you might at first realize.

Some people will struggle with this inquiry. John Powell, a law professor and scholar of race, once shared that his students often claimed not to know how to put themselves in the shoes of other-raced people. He developed a practice of inviting students to imagine themselves as dolphins, rushing through water, encountering sea vessels, and so on. He would suggest then that if they had the capacity to so vividly imagine themselves as sea creatures, they likely had much greater capacity than they would admit to imagine life in a differently racialized body and related social location.

To assist us further, we might rely more explicitly on our mindfulness practice, noticing our thoughts that tell us that we cannot relate to people of different races and that we can't imagine what life might be like for them. We slow down the reactivity long enough to sense into what we know about the experience of people of color in our communities, and to hold the space for complexity, for both/and, for nuance and ambiguity. From here, ask things like:

How will I deepen my ability to understand how differently racialized people experience the world in various contexts? How will I keep up this effort?

How does race intersect with other identity variables to complicate my understanding of injustice and of what responses might be better suited to make things right?

What comes up for me when I learn about a painful aspect of history?

And: What can I do today to disrupt my habits and conditionings around what I've learned?

Over time, the basic sitting practice described in chapter two permits a way of seeing, being, and working with others that allows us to see more fully how race operates not only in our lives, but in the lives of others. It allows us to slow down our reactivity long enough to learn more about what is happening when we find it hard to take in certain information. The subsequent practices have offered doorways toward deepening these insights, but it all rests on the basic ability to focus attention and calm a busy mind—gifts of the Awareness of Breathing practice.

When we paused together with Constantin, we invited ourselves to ground in the body, to sense the support that we feel when we bring our attention to the ground beneath us. From there, we settled in and opened up to insight: What are the emotions that arise when we read such histories? Anger? Shame? Numbness? Pain? Naming our emotions assists us in the important work of becoming less governed by them. Seeing and naming our emotions helps support us in choosing how to respond to what we feel.

As we've seen, mindfulness supports us in staying with or reconnecting with the body, which is essential in developing emotional self-regulation. On some level, we are almost always judging the body's raw experience of the present moment. If we turn our attention to the processes by which we arrive at these perceptions and calm things down, we might learn something about how our minds and bodies often automatically *react* to stimuli in our lives. By slowing down when we notice ourselves reacting, and by bringing mindfulness to these moments, we start to perceive an ever-present, great range of options for responding.

Returning to Constantin's reflections and the class's reactions, I invited the group to reflect on what emotions, thoughts, and sensations came up for them as they read about this particular massacre in American history. For me, as facilitator, it required the willingness to relinquish control.

We sat together in silence.

"I feel numb," someone said. "I find it hard to really take in story after story, so that some part of me just can't feel anything at all."

"Well, I'm with Constantin," said another. "I really *feel* angry. And also, shame. But I also feel resistant to saying that. What good is it to feel anger? I guess I just want to better understand how this relates to where we are now, and what we can do to prevent such injustices in the future."

Pausing long enough to allow ourselves *to not know*, or to feel all of the often conflicting emotions and sensations in our bodies, is really important if we are ever to truly change the patterns and habits we have created around race and racism. Our basic mindfulness practices—from sitting to Body Scan, to Mindful Moment, to Lovingkindness—all deepen our capacity for this, when engaged in on a regular basis.

Mindful Communications about Race and Racism

Here's what's more, my friends: any communication may be seen as a chance to practice deep mindfulness. Even the simplest or most routine contact with another person presents the chance to wake up to the precious value of our own human existence, to become present to the same in another person, and to perceive what exists between us with greater insight. Mindful listening and speaking might appear easy. In fact, they are more challenging than we might expect, but are often exquisite opportunities to practice and to grow.

Mindful listening is an essential practice for us when talking with others about race. As we ground ourselves and breathe into the moment, we set the intention of listening to another's story. For me, I open my attention to how *I* react to the comments I am hearing, noticing the sensations in my body, emotions, and related thoughts that come up. I drop my story, and I once again breathe and *just listen*. I let go of the typical practice of silently trying to construct my response before I've even heard what there is to hear. I focus on not merely hearing and reporting, stenographer's style, what has been said. Instead I listen for ways the speaker is conveying deep meaning—through words, gestures, and tone—and do what I can to help them find their true voice.

When things get difficult, when I feel myself moving into reactivity, I notice a temptation either to go into my own pain, or to move away from it. It can take the form of an impulse to interrupt the other, or wanting to end the conversation. It might look like suddenly wanting to make a joke that might shift the intensity of feeling in the room or even to shift my own feelings.

Mindful listening, however, brings attention, loving and kind attention, to this series of physical sensations, thoughts, and feelings, and gives me the space to decide how to respond rather than react. My mindfulness practice helps me to meet awareness of these feelings, too, with compassion—the desire to alleviate the suffering that the other may have experienced: "Okay, I'm now judging him. . . . And I don't know his full story. Let me let go of that and just be present to his voice, to what he wants me to hear now."

I may notice then a quiver of self-criticism: "Okay, I'm now judging myself for judging him. . . . I have seen this before." I realize, in that moment, that this is just how my brain works. So even as I listen, I silently continue bringing in a measure of self-compassion. I might place my right hand over my heart or belly as I listen to something that arouses the feeling of pain in my heart; I might simply visualize myself doing so in that moment without changing my posture at all. These subtle gestures of support are helpful to me. They help me let go and return to a sense of my deeper well-being. They help me to begin to attend to the movements of my own heart long enough that my presence might be a space for the healing of another.

Some of the workshops and classes that I offer target people who serve under-resourced communities in San Francisco, nationally, and beyond. My attendees in such workshops may be predominantly people of color. The classes I teach at my law school are often similarly diverse. When I offer general public workshops on race, diversity, and the like, however, my attendees are often predominantly white. These offerings are often situated in the broader Western mindfulness field, which is still predominantly white, even as demographic change is under way. This, in many ways, is good news. As we've seen, people who are racialized as white are often among the least experienced in discussing and working with issues of race on a regular basis. White people need as much support in discussing race and its implications as any of us do. And in some ways, because of the silences in which whiteness is often held, they need more.

But the fact that these conversations take place in predominantly white settings points to some of the structural underpinnings of the ongoing struggle against racial inequality. We live in communities that have become resegregated to such a degree that organically engaging in conversations about race with diverse groups of people is less likely simply because we don't often enough engage in adequately mixed groups at school and work.

And because whites predominate in places of power and influence, if we are to change these dynamics, we must engage with how the still-most-powerful racial group typically avoids and lacks the skills they need to engage effectively with race and racism. This is a serious problem. It reveals our greatest racial literacy need. Turning the distress we all feel these days into fear about demographic changes is just one reason for the rise of racist rhetoric and policies facing immigrants in the United States and beyond. This is just one of many examples of how the failure of our communities and institutions to provide spaces within which whites and lighter-skinned or white-identified people can learn about and come to terms with race-making and racism is a serious problem. But it isn't, as much as I'd sometimes like to view it that way, a "white" problem. At the same time, it isn't merely a problem for those most affected, for those people of color most vulnerable to the indignities of racist treatment. When you see how all of us are affected by such policies and delusions, you see that these practices and policies not only harm us all but create exploitable fissures that can put our security as a nation at risk.

Racial Constructions "In the Air"

Although, as we have seen, most social scientists believe that race is socially constructed, the notion of race remains tied to notions of differential value triggered by perceived physical differences. The notion of biological race has not somehow gone away.

References to biological racism arise and fall in our interactions with one another, whether in person or online. For example, just the other day, while searching online for information about a Ray Charles song, I found this reminder that old-fashioned, biological racism is quite simply everywhere (and surprisingly popular):

> The black, especially female voice and the soul they put into music is unparalleled. Margie Hendrick's [*sic*] solo at the 1:29 mark is *the* great black voice. You don't teach it. It's a gift and part of their DNA. Think of some of the outstanding black R&B/Soul female vocalists of the recent past: Aretha, Etta James . . .[2]

On the face of it, the comment about the inimitable Margie Hendricks's singing talent sounds like a compliment. Indeed, in a world in which blackness is so often tied to some disability, one might be tempted to applaud this attribution of value to the DNA of black people, this "gift." In the comment stream following this one, there were, in fact, a number of comments by apparently black people in which they applauded this biologically racist claim. In a racially ordered society, we are all tempted to perpetuate the notion of biological race.

The fact is, however, that anyone who believes that all black people have a "gift" for singing like Margie Hendricks as part of our DNA has not heard most of us at a karaoke mic. And anyone who believes whites or others cannot develop similar abilities, should they choose to devote themselves to doing so, has not really listened to any of a number of singers who have learned much from Margie Hendricks and other greats— people like Amy Winehouse, Adele, and Sam Smith.

The problem, however, is that biological explanations are not merely wrong, they are also double-edged. Putting aside the way such claims reduce serious effort, cultivated skill, and well-developed talent to a feature of the inheritance of perhaps a fifth of the world's population, if one can believe that "black people" are biologically, naturally suited for singing, it is equally believable that black people are biologically, naturally *unsuited* for education—one of the many stereotypes that have been cultivated about black people for centuries. And if that is so, wouldn't denying education to blacks, or simply providing only the most minimal one, be the rational, efficient, even humane thing to do? The truth is that biological notions of race have long been advanced in support of ridiculous beliefs like this one. For that reason, the problematic nature of even the most benign-seeming of those beliefs must be brought to light through mindful reflection.

The Social Deconstruction of Stereotypes and Racism

In white-oriented, white-normed societies, whiteness is more than a personal identity. It is more than a notion of culture or heritage. It is an ideology that has been formed in relationship to a mostly pernicious notion of blackness, of colored-ness, or "not-whiteness." If the explicit stereotype is that Asians are "foreigners," the corresponding, often implicit stereotype is that whites are "American." If the explicit stereotype is that blacks are not successful at critical thinking, then the corresponding, often implicit stereotype is that whites are naturally better suited for it. If black people are born able to dance, whites are not. And so on. These concepts of race—whether black, white, Asian, American Indian, or Latino—are social constructions that arise in relation to one another. When we invest in one such concept, we are correspondingly investing in all of the others.

As we've seen, stereotypes like these are picked up in countless ways over our lifetimes. But because the teachings are often as subtle and invisible as the air that we breathe, whiteness-norming can be very, very hard for people to see. With mindful awareness, we may become more cognizant of the manifold obvious and not-so-obvious ways that race and racism are perpetuated, how any one of us may contribute to the maintenance of stereotypes. If we really slow things down, we can catch ourselves in the very process of "making race," of constructing a story about another person or group that bears the imprint of racism in our culture. In addition, if we bring to mind the harm that all of this does, we are on the road to personal transformation at a level that cannot but change the world.

Nevertheless, we often struggle to *be with* those realities long enough to develop deeper insight into what we're facing. But with mindfulness, we can develop the capacity to sit with these hard truths of "the way things are" long enough and profoundly enough that we might not only see more, but also begin to disrupt the patterns within ourselves that help perpetuate racism. In so doing, we begin a crucial process capable of creating real change in the only place we can be sure that real change can happen: our own minds. We can actually experience the social *de*construction of race—the reversal of the cognitive process by which race is constructed—one moment at a time.

Reframing the Conversation

Awareness practices have been shown to assist in setting the stage for conversations about race. Thus, if we have the chance to establish some guidelines for talking about race, racism, or other potentially divisive issues, we should reflect on how we might include mindful, perception-expanding elements. Whether we call them mindful or not, naming our intentions and motivations, and incorporating openness, curiosity, and mindful awareness into these discussions at the beginning, will help make the space more open to new possibilities for being with and learning from one another.

So, even where mindfulness practice is not well established among dialogue participants, consider how you would use techniques like sitting in a circle; opening with a moment of reflection on our own backgrounds, histories, and Race Stories that might impact our point of view;

encouraging mindful listening and speaking; and bringing awareness to habits of perception that place ourselves and others in preconception or prejudicial boxes. Consider in advance some of the ways in which you will demonstrate as much mindful presence and perception as possible, to embody the sense of respectful inclusion that you hope the group will extend to one another, and to set the stage for experiences of interpersonal liberation.

PAUSE AND REFLECT

Take a few minutes to jot down your reflections on how you might bring mindfulness to bear in preparation for a personal conversation about race.

And now consider this: each one of us may be called upon to share our views about these matters in our organizations or communities. How might your mindfulness practices support you in structuring a *more formal presentation* about how race operates in our everyday lives?

Finally, consider ways that you might *incorporate teachings and practices* on mindful perceptual awareness to open up space for seeing how our race-based preconceptions about ourselves and others may limit our capacity for being together in new ways.

MINDFUL SPEAKING AND LISTENING PRACTICE

Invite a friend to support you by practicing mindful interpersonal communication. Read through the following instructions in advance and then together.

The purpose of this exercise is to practice mindful communication. You will alternate between the role of listener and speaker, so begin by deciding who will speak first. Each person will have uninterrupted time to speak. Set a stopwatch or timer at three or four minutes so you don't need to keep an eye on the clock.

Now begin by sitting across from each other, ideally without anything resting between you, with your knees nearly touching.

Take a few moments to just sit together, allowing yourself to explore what it feels like to be in close proximity to this friend.

The person who will serve as the first Listener plays the important role of cultivating a space within which the truth may be spoken, honored, and held in confidence. The Listener sits and listens, paying attention without judgment, and in a way that supports the Speaker in speaking truth from the heart in response to the reflection questions. Be mindful of your facial expressions and other gestures in reaction to the speaker, keeping them moderate and modest so as not to have too great an impact on the Speaker's process.

The Speaker listens to the reflection prompt; pauses and reflects on the thoughts, sensations, emotions, and stories that arise; and shares them when ready. As much as possible, move into the heart of what wants to be spoken, or the pearl of truth that seems most vibrant and forthcoming. As always, use your discernment and only speak about what you are ready to share.

The reflection question is this: "Think about the experiences you have had in speaking and listening to others about race. What is the story of yourself you bring to these conversations?"

When you are ready, the Listener will press the start button to allow the time to count down and will settle into the role of supportive silent partner.

When the timer sounds, pause where you are, even if midsentence. Allow the words to come to an end. Notice whether there is a feeling of having not said enough, or of having said too much. Practice allowing yourself to feel as if what was said was what needed saying, and that is indeed enough for now.

Now the Listener is to set the timer for two minutes. It is the Listener's turn to reflect back what was spoken. The goal here is to help the original Speaker hear their own truth. Note what you recall, including the gestures and tone of voice that you perceived as emphasizing a particular point.

Finally, the original Speaker is given one minute to reflect back on what they have heard, including clarification on anything that was not correctly conveyed.

Following that opportunity to close the loop, you are to switch roles and to repeat the entire sequence.

After both of you have had a chance to share, give yourself three minutes of "cross talk," asking questions or deepening the reflection by adding new thoughts that have arisen.

Close by offering one another any appreciations that seem appropriate.

MINDFUL REFLECTION

What was it like for you to practice mindful speaking and listening in this way? How might such ways of communicating support you in working for a more just world? Take a few minutes to write a reflection in your journal.

CHAPTER EIGHTEEN

DECONSTRUCTING WHITENESS AND RACE

On the plane of ultimate reality, race does not exist, and racism causes no suffering. And even on the plane of relative reality, race is a biological fiction. But it's a socially constructed reality that has been incredibly popular and effective in structuring the distribution of benefits and burdens in societies. Still, if race can be constructed, it can just as certainly be deconstructed. And yet, since it took centuries to construct racism and race, we must be prepared for it to take at least as long to deconstruct it. For now, the struggle is ceaseless.

—RHONDA V. MAGEE

As an essential part of the work of ColorInsight, we have to spend some time in the shoes of people of different races and racial groups whose experience is most often left out of discussions about race. We have to explore how Asian Americans experience race and racism differently than do blacks. We have to explore how Latinos experience race and racism in ways that differ from the experiences of each of these groups. We have to explore the often underappreciated experience of the indigenous within our borders, and of those who think of themselves as multiracial. And in order to deepen our understanding of all of this, we all have to engage with the echoes of whiteness within and apart from all of it.

Reckoning with Whiteness

On the one hand, as a result of white supremacy, whiteness has become a means of signaling embodied power. On the other hand, being "of color" has signaled embodied vulnerability. Whiteness is more than an identity. It is an orientation toward the privileges associated with white-racialized people, through the systems of white supremacy and the philosophies that underpin them.

Educator Peggy McIntosh famously described the privileges that accompany whiteness. I see them as similar in power to the privileges I have been afforded as a result of being what some call "cishet"—cisgender and heterosexual—in a world that continues to privilege those identities over those who identify as transgender and homosexual. Such privileges make it harder for us to see the suffering that others experience. Privilege and the resulting acquiescence toward the legacies of white supremacy make addressing the racism among whites—and others—difficult.

To an outsider, whiteness may look like the presumption of innocence, while color (especially blackness or brownness) looks like the presumption of criminality. Or, the presumption of creditworthiness compared to the presumption of credit unworthiness. Or, the presumption of full humanity compared to the presumption of being semi- or almost human.

The work of ColorInsight requires building the capacity to see the experience of whiteness-based privilege as an aspect of pervasive whiteness. I have had thousands of conversations with people who are racialized as white, and years of experience supporting groups in deepening their understanding of whiteness in everyone's lives. Over the years, I have come to see that it is important for all of us to engage in practices for contemplating whiteness as the "normal" way of life in the United States, or as the standard by which others are measured as worthy of acceptance. Separately and distinctly, we might explore practices for contemplating whiteness as an aspect of one's chosen identity in the world.

Whiteness as the "Normal" Experience: The Evolution of Race and Races

Though we have all been exposed to whiteness as the normal way of life in America, many of us have not really thought or talked much about whiteness in this sense. To understand this use of the term *whiteness*, we need to step back and think about whiteness as an idea, as a dream—about inclusion, success, exceptionalism on the world stage—in Western history and culture.

From the time of the colonial era in the early 1600s, Europeans justified the practices of enslavement and conquest of indigenous people across the Americas with notions of European religious and cultural superiority. In the United States, from the first immigration law enacted in 1790 (just two years after the ratification of the Constitution), whites have been systematically privileged as full members of the political community. The law granted the right to be naturalized as a citizen solely to "any alien, being a free white person" who had been a resident in the United States for two years.[1] This was not the first law to grant privileges to whites that were not available to others—states had been doing so throughout the colonial period. And it certainly would not be the last such law.

Throughout this period, the emerging field of anthropology gave the veneer of scientific legitimacy and rigor to racist notions. Thus, an interlocking set of narratives—religious, political, legal, and anthropological—combined to create whiteness: a unifying racial identity applicable to a diverse group of people sharing similar physical characteristics who were deemed (by its own members) to be superior when compared to all other racial groups. Correspondingly, notions of the other major racial groups came into sharper cultural relief. In this way, modern concepts of race and races developed to support the law, policies, and practices of white supremacy that were already in progress. In the early twentieth century, we would begin using the term *racism* to describe the ideology and practices that justified the exercise of power over racially marginalized others.

Whiteness as an Aspect of Chosen Identity

As we have explored through the stories of Jake, Seth, and Constantin, white people know about whiteness as an aspect of their personal identity through their experiences. But they often have not been given support in exploring or reflecting on how it was created. It is important, then, to create spaces in which white identity may be explored more fully, as a means of understanding the attachments, aversions, and confusion that travel with conversations about race in white-majority spaces.

The tricky thing is that looking at what it means to be white (or white-identified) entails the risk of being seen as *feeling entitled* to race-based privilege—as *embracing* white privilege—in a racist society. One can and should look at one's own racial experience without embracing the pernicious teachings and seductions of it. Indeed, doing so might be necessary to fully understand the particular blind spots and interpersonal habits and conditionings that often travel with whiteness. This sense of risk, however, must be brought skillfully into awareness and confronted with intentionality in order to deepen conversations about race among white people.

As we may have begun to see, the social histories that shape our reality are in the rooms we enter, whether we acknowledge them or not. In the early twentieth century as a post–Civil War period of Redemption took hold in the South and gave way to a period of Restoration, white people enthusiastically and proudly embraced their racial privilege, in a way that we would call racist today. Characters in classic films from that period used terms like *prestige* to describe what their whiteness granted them in the world. They used phrases like, "I'm free, white, and twenty-one!" to claim their sense of superiority and status above others.[2]

A version of this survives in what we call "white privilege," a legacy of racism. Just because we no longer hear the phrase "free, white, and twenty-one" this doesn't mean that the ideology that created that phrase has died off. What's more, because the degree of white privilege that people experience may vary by proximity to whiteness, light-skinned people and people with ancestors from a range of ethnic groups may experience some level of privilege—what sociologists call "colorism." Those of us who have experienced privileges associated with lighter-toned skin know some version of this. We know we may be considered more acceptable by some because we are presumed to be nearer to whiteness (and among "our own" may be subject to distrust). Sitting with awareness of these facts is not easy to do alone, but is especially difficult in groups comprising people from mixed backgrounds. Still, bringing awareness to these aspects of our experience, and the social or cultural habits that sustain them, can bring important nuance to our conversations about race and its implications.

When I am an "of color" body in a white-majority space, I know that I have my work cut out for me—when I turn attention not only to my racialized experience (which naturally differs from that of the majority racial group and so gives rise to cognitive dissonance) but to racial disparities in the distribution of power, which lead to injustice. To redress this injustice would feel like an injustice to those who previously benefited. The most *invisible* and least understood racial experience, whiteness, is also the most powerful in Western cultures, where whiteness has been constructed as a valued and privileged racial category. It is considered normal—the racial experience against which all other experiences are measured. Yet it is the most difficult for all of us to see, examine, and experience with integrity. Anti-racist educator Robin DiAngelo argues that all whites in white-majority society have internalized the message that whites are superior, and must work hard to upend this message, especially given the social pressure for "good" whites to *not* name their internalized racism.[3] Even as we deepen our understanding, being with others as we try to do this work is a challenge. For that reason, it is important for us to act with compassion, integrity, and the will to act for justice, moment to moment.

Coming Together in the Practice of ColorInsight

If we create a compassionate and supportive space for group discussions about race, people will be more likely to take the risks necessary to engage. And as more people discuss how they came to know and develop some level of consciousness about race in their own lives, the sense of comfort in the room often slowly increases.

When I do this work, I am often in spaces skewed in favor of white experience. This may be because the majority of the people in the group are white, or simply because the space has been shaped by those who are. Still, each experience is different, shaped by the many differences that emerge among any group of people. And yet it is through reckoning with our diversity in all its particulars, including diverse "white" experience, in interactions with others and alone, that we may grow.

In time, the lived experience of our common humanity helps. If we feel safe, we can feel ourselves soften as people share some of the funnier ways in which others have inquired about their backgrounds. We express our sympathy, or allow our tears to fall, as we allow ourselves to hear the more painful stories in the room. We spill into the shoes of those around us, walls dissolving as time well-spent together turns a meeting into a gathering of chosen family. What we are doing is developing trust in one another—by being vulnerable and caring together—in ways we have been trained against all of our lives. We have been trained to fear one another. And we all know that when we are afraid, we are simply not our best. Here, we start to see and to feel that we have more in common than not. And to see that we have a lot less to fear from one another than we once believed.

As we engage with one another, we take time to notice what is arising in each of us, including ways we are defending against revealing too much and ways we are feeling unsafe or afraid. We see for ourselves how mindfulness and compassion practices help us to stay with what we are noticing and keep moving toward connection. To use the language of so-cial psychologists, these practices help us to *self-regulate*—to bear with the challenge of strong, even negative emotions and remain grounded enough to pause our more automatic reactions. They help us relate to our own experiences and to the experiences of others in the room with greater empathy, compassion, and resilience.

With the self-compassion that you've begun to develop, and with a bit of guidance, you'll be able to identify your emotions more effectively. You'll more easily name the anger and the sadness you feel. But what about the vague sense of resistance, or of "spacing out" that feels like boredom? How precisely does shame feel to you? What about hopelessness? How does that feel in your body? How does it show up in your interactions with others?

As we deepen our emotional intelligence, we may also deepen our so-cial intelligence—the capacity to sense the emotional state of others and to see the world through their eyes. This relational skill often flows from sustained mindfulness practice. We are mindful not only of our own ex-periences, but of those of the people around us as well. Developing these skills generally takes some practice. Along with self-compassion, pa-tience as we and others work on these areas of our lives is essential to building the capacity for racial justice work.

Building trust takes both the will to trust and the commitment of time. Over the course of our practice, we are working on the commitment to stay in difficult conversations. We build trust not just in one another, but perhaps more important, we build trust in ourselves and our sense of groundedness for facing disappointments and unexpected revelations. It is this ground that enables us to keep trying. We are deepening our ca-pacity to stand in the fire of conflict and ambiguity. As we develop a sense of community, we are more regularly met with a sense of common hu-manity rather than blaming or shaming. This is why mindfulness and compassion practices are so essential to the work we are doing together.

Becoming more aware of the range of dynamics surrounding race and bias is empowering. We start to see how we can build trust in one another when we listen without judgment to each other's stories, and remain in the room and in the conversation when things get difficult. And we feel more confident talking about our own and others' experiences when we develop the language to describe different aspects of the problem.

In groups where I am one of the few people of color, I know that I may stand out. This experience is one to which many of us can relate. If you are not familiar with this experience, pause and take a moment to reflect on why that is so. What structures—economic, racial, cultural, religious, or otherwise—help explain why you have lived most of your life among "your own kind"? Now take a moment to reflect on what it means to have lived a life in which you have been in the majority most of the time.

Whiteness and Structural Bias

Over the course of the work of ColorInsight, we examine some of the structural and systemic drivers of racial disparities in the world. For many people, focusing on systemic rather than personal drivers will cause another round of cognitive dissonance. Most of us have, after all, been taught to think of racism as personalized, individualized, and intentional, rather than depersonalized, systemic, and often unconscious.

But we are starting to see—and are becoming willing to admit—just how racism and racial bias are part of the structures underlying our upbringing. Segregation in our neighborhoods is one of the most prevalent systemic structures of racism in our lives today. Because of segregation, we may have only seen people of different racial backgrounds in restaurants or at a country club, and then only in particular, subservient roles. We may have had a father who taught us that "the only good n—— is a dead n——," as a black hairdresser of mine once surreptitiously overheard her coworker, a man of Mexican heritage, teaching his two-year-old son. We may have grown up in communities in which we did not see people of other races, encountering people of certain backgrounds for the first time as adults. These structural aspects of our lives that we do not control have lasting implications for us.

When we live in a world in which whiteness is privileged in ways generally not spoken about, and where people of other backgrounds remain at the margins, *everyone* learns and internalizes the tacit rules that privilege, empower, value, and protect some over others—according to their proximity to the ideal of whiteness.

Whiteness, then, becomes a way of not merely naming and claiming embodied power, but orienting self, community, or culture toward embodied structural power, and in that sense, claiming embodied-structural power—whiteness—indirectly. When we face subtle and not so subtle demands to assimilate—to speak English, to straighten our hair, to stay out of the sun—the demand, generally, is to assimilate to whiteness. We are all tempted, by the siren song of greater inclusion, to perform in ways that accord us some of the privileges associated with whiteness. In other words, whiteness is not only the province of so-called white people. We must understand that anyone raised in segregated societies inevitably imbibes some version of white supremacy. We all have learned that a "good neighborhood" is defined by the majority in part by the absence of people of color. The spell of racism, the addiction of it, the appeal of it, makes anyone in racist societies vulnerable to its reach.

Working with Our Own Biases

The good news is that researchers have shown us over the years that there are things we can do to minimize our reliance on stereotypes. We actually can change the way we process the world. And given the great harm that flows from unchecked stereotyping and other forms of bias, we should be motivated to do so—it is essential to working well with others as we move more deeply into an increasingly diverse world. Doing so is not easy, but it is possible.

We start by telling ourselves the truth about our own lives—about where we have been privileged and sheltered, where we have seen racism in ourselves and in others, how we have put up walls to avoid dealing with this issue, both within ourselves and with others. With mindfulness as a support, we slow down and listen for the deepest truths that we know. As we listen to ourselves and honor our own experience, we are building up the muscles that will allow us to listen to other people in ways that inspire truth-telling in them. It is about not merely creating spaces for truth-telling, but actually becoming, in our own being and presence, a space in which the truth can be spoken.

Turning toward the difficult with steadfast care is a basic foundation for the work of developing insight into the nature of the problems of social identity bias, this work of examining how things like race, gender, religion, and so on affect all of us. As we develop the capacity for self-love, for a way of being with our own struggles around identity that creates the capacity for healing and growth, we find that we have more capacity for looking at the aspects of our lives that we have, in the past, chosen not to see. We find that we have the strength to revisit some of the painful memories that we have buried or decided we'd "gotten over." Indeed, for many of us, as we orient ourselves to a way of being that allows us to hold the painful realities of what we know about race and racism more gently and with greater self-care, we find that, indeed, we actually know more.

As you've been reading this book, you've probably had to put it down from time to time, to engage in The Pause. Perhaps memories have appeared in your mind—some long-buried incident finding its way back into your consciousness, now that you are ready. Or you may be thinking about a group of people who are suffering today, and wondering how to hold the pain of your awareness as it increases.

We all need to take time, to slow things down during this particular stage in our awareness practices. Whether you have been thinking about your racial identity for the better part of a long life, or are new to reflecting on this aspect of your experience, you will find that pausing and taking time to reflect here and now will be of benefit as we go forward.

We cannot rely on what we have been told by others in some documentary, book, or workshop about how racism shows up in our lives—even though we all very likely need to learn a lot more about the histories that have shaped our worlds. We need to look more deeply within, to take in what we have seen of how deeply embedded racism and other forms of bias are in our lives and communities. Because we all know something about practices of exclusion and belonging, the most important practice may simply be coming to terms with what we know.

We know more about the prevalence of racism today than we did ten years ago, in part because of the rise of the Black Lives Matter movement and the immediate availability of recorded images of everyday black experience, thanks to the tech revolution. More than likely you've seen one or more videos that depict police force against a person of color. It's not easy for any of us to take in this information. And yet, if we are to deepen our awareness of reality and work for justice, we have to be able to stay present with depictions of what we are truly facing together.

One way of expanding our ability to sit with these difficulties is through a practice known as "Bearing Witness." This is a practice that calls for being present to suffering in a way that acknowledges it completely, in as close proximity as possible, with the willingness to be touched deeply by it. I shared a version of this practice with a large group of mindfulness teachers and researchers at the 2015 conference of the University of Massachusetts Center for Mindfulness. On the main stage, I asked participants to reflect on how they respond to evidence of bias in their lives, and how their practices of mindfulness might assist them. After previewing the exercise and giving participants a chance to leave if they so desired, I shared a video recording of a person injured in an altercation with police. Participants were asked to remain present and then to reflect on the thoughts, emotions, and sensations that arose as they watched the short but painfully explicit video. I asked them to examine how mindfulness and compassion practices might be available to assist in the difficult work of addressing social injustice, and we had a group discussion about the practice afterward, exploring what we'd learned together and might learn from similar practices in the future.

I was told by more than a few people that the practice had a powerful impact on those present. It spurred mindfulness teachers around the world to think about how the practices and training we provide may help us engage the most difficult social challenges of our time.

BEARING WITNESS TO WHITENESS AND RACISM

For this practice, select an image or short video, one of no more than one minute, that depicts both whiteness *and* an individual suffering from racism in a contemporary setting.

Settle into your seated meditation posture. Sense into the ground beneath you and center yourself by focusing your awareness on the sensations of breathing.

Focus your attention on the image or video.

Notice the thoughts, emotions, and sensations that arise for you as you take in what you can.

When you have completed the practice of Bearing Witness to Whiteness and Racism, ask yourself: "What did I notice? What did I find hard to see? What are the links I see between this representation of whiteness, race-based suffering, and the suffering of other vulnerable people in my community, and in the wider world? How can I take this experience into the world and be a more effective witness to the hidden or under-acknowledged suffering of others?"

MINDFUL REFLECTION

To deepen your reflection, take a few minutes to write freely about what came up for you during this practice. What are the stories you tell yourself to justify societal segregation or other forms of contemporary structural racism in your life? Capture your reflections in a "free write" of notes in your Mindful Reflections journal. Try not to edit these reflections. Simply write. Do so for no more than twenty minutes.

When you are finished, allow yourself to engage in embodied movement practice—walking, dancing, or singing—that supports your processing of experience. If you continue to be drawn to thoughts about the image, bring mindfulness carefully to bear. Return to the body and breathing. You might also set aside another twenty minutes to free-write about what you are thinking and feeling. Repeat your journal practice for up to five days in a row. Then see if you can more completely allow the experience to recede in your mind as you return to practicing one of the core mindfulness practices on a daily basis instead.

CHAPTER NINETEEN

COLOR-BLIND RACISM AND ITS CONSEQUENCES

Refusing to recognize difference makes it impossible to see the different problems and pitfalls facing us. . . . And true, unless one lives and loves in the trenches it is difficult to remember that the war against dehumanization is ceaseless.

—AUDRE LORDE[1]

Science is confirming what contemplatives have been telling us for thousands of years: we are all radically interconnected, and our brains are literally shaped by the communities in which we live, grow, and learn. Cognition, the functioning of the brain, does not take place in the space between our two ears. Rather, it develops in the contexts and environments in which we live and breathe. And emotion has much more to do with thought than we realize.

For these reasons, we need to be mindful about all aspects of our experiences and those of the human beings with whom we spend our days. This includes becoming more aware of patterns of racial isolation that make it difficult to see race-making and racism's many variations. We need to be able to talk about race and acknowledge the differences in our experiences that we often are afraid to admit or name, especially in mixed company. We also need to become more aware of the ways that deeply ingrained notions of race—the set subtle rules and orientations based on skin color, hair texture, facial features, and the like—shape our sense of our own importance and that of others. We need to be able to see more clearly how these notions have shaped our experiences, and how they shape our lives still. Indeed, if we are willing to look for it, we might see evidence of these ongoing effects and of investment in race-making every day. Whether old or young, people are "doing race" around us all of the time. And we do it, too.

Just yesterday, for example, I happened to overhear the conversation of two young women, each no more than twenty years old. With their backs toward me, they discussed whether a mutual acquaintance of theirs was "white." I could not help noticing that for some reason they did not make explicit, it was important to these two young white women to come to an understanding about whether the label "white" should be applied to someone who had evidently claimed or implied that it might. Why did this matter to them? Why was it important to these two women to discuss how someone else they knew socially signaled *her own* racial status? What did it really say about *their* wish to be seen as somehow different from her, and as somehow entitled to something that she was not?

If they are like the majority of whites who report that they are color-blind when asked, they would deny that they have any investment in the question of whether or not some other person in their circle was indeed white. And they would certainly not consider their conversation to be racist. But they were committed to coming to a consensus that this friend was "not white," and certainly "didn't seem to be completely Caucasian," even though this person was "always saying that she looks too white."

"No," they concluded outside of her presence, "she definitely *isn't* white." Self-designation of whiteness by the absent Other seemed to be of little consequence to these two women who considered *themselves* unambiguously white, and therefore in a position to determine where the color line fell in relation to another. It also didn't seem to matter to them just what other race the other woman might be—it was simply important that she be seen as "not white."

Sociologists would have much to say about the social implications of this behavior.[2] About how the conversation itself reveals how race is constructed in the very lives, interactions, and conversations of people today. In this instance, whiteness appeared to be a matter of some consequence—for these young women, race was *not* irrelevant. Whatever they might say if asked, this conversation reveals that they are not "color-blind."

At some point, the two young women changed the topic of their conversation. It seemed to me that the transition was rather abrupt. Whether or not the pacing and timing of the shift had anything to do with their having noticed my nonwhite presence within earshot, I cannot say, but it would not be a surprise if so. Much of contemporary race-making is done either in our own minds or in interactions with others we deem racially similar enough that it is safe to reveal what we really think about these matters.

Pause for a moment and reflect on your own experience of such conversations. Consider what you know about the rules that govern conversations about race in your own social circle, whether currently or in the past. Is the topic forbidden entirely? If not, what are the basic rules? Are there certain topics you can address, or time limits that seem to be implicitly observed?

Give yourself time as you think about this aspect of your life experience. If possible, call to mind specific conversations you have had about race as it applies to particular people you've known or come in contact with. Now focus in on just one. What details do you recall? Note the particular social context, what groups were represented, what perspectives were absent. Have you witnessed or participated in conversations in monocultural or monoracial groups that would not comfortably be repeated in mixed groups?

Silence about conversations like these is an essential part of the culture of contemporary racism in the United States and around the globe. Another problem is that when we do talk about race, we often use coded language—"inner city," "urban," "low-income," and the like—to signal a racial Other or to reflect notions of inclusion and exclusion. We also use a variety of culturally reinforced moves to advance, in color-blind ways, our commitment to confusion about the relevance of race in our own lives and the prevalence of racism in our communities and organizations. What may be seen as the preservation of racism through its transformation—the maintenance of racial hierarchy despite a raft of antidiscrimination laws and a generation of Americans taught to consider themselves color-blind—is thus aided by what sociologist Eduardo Bonilla-Silva refers to as the four frames of contemporary "color-blind racism":

(1) abstract, general statements professing equality commitment ("I believe in equal opportunity" but those people "lack merit")

(2) naturalizing socially created patterns ("This city isn't segregated, people just naturally prefer to live with their own kind")

(3) cultural racism ("Latinos don't believe in education," "Blacks aren't interested in the construction industry," "Whites are more normal")

(4) minimization ("You're overly sensitive. What you described just isn't that big a deal.")[3]

These reinforcing frames have kept us comfortable with maintaining racial inequities as the status quo—in a sense, hidden in plain sight. For example, recent analyses reveal how mostly invisible policies and practices, including some that might be considered illegal under current law, have maintained neighborhood segregation in cities across the United States in the decades since the civil rights movement.[4]

In many places, economic and racial segregation goes beyond market forces or personal choices. That segregation is buttressed by local laws and ordinances that effectively exclude or discourage poor and working-class people from moving into certain communities, keeping those areas primarily the domain of the white and wealthy. . . . The laws do not specifically mention race, but because African Americans and Latinos have on average far less wealth and income than white people, the laws do tend to drive people of color out and keep neighborhoods more uniformly white. That's in keeping with the racist history of "snob zoning."[5]

This book is filled with stories of people who have seen how race is constructed, negotiated, discussed, and remade daily, through housing law and policy and through so much more. It requires bravery and openness to reflect on these moments, with the support of mindfulness and compassion practices. We can learn and teach one another about the largely invisible, generally under-acknowledged dynamics that hold the structures of racism in place. We can identify and dissolve the underlying emotional impulses that shape our thoughts and actions when race comes into the picture. And we can support one another in bringing these issues to the fore through discussions about any social justice issue, highlighting how racism interacts with other forms of oppression, and by disrupting these structures. Individually and collectively, we can live each day in ways that create both change within ourselves and the commitment to continue taking action for change over all our days.

Life Lessons in Color

Mackenzie is from a Midwestern town. Growing up, she wore secondhand clothes and was often anxious about whether she would have enough lunch money to last her through each week at school. Nevertheless, she felt that her life chances were helped by her attractive features and white skin. "Even now as a student," she said, "I can sense that people expect me to be successful one day, to be able to afford a home, to have a position in life. I can tell that other people around me, black people in my apartment building and neighborhood, aren't given the same benefit of the doubt. And I know that when I walk around the city, my white skin gives me a kind of protection and welcome that my friends of color do not enjoy."

Like Mackenzie, we all know something about race and racism through personal experience. Yet we often don't talk about what we know. We rarely invite reflections on or discuss the questions we have about how race impacts our everyday lives. And when the topic comes up, we may feel that it's best to take the safest way out—to remain silent rather than reveal what we know. Or we may feel that, given the prevalence of racism in the world and its persistence over time, it is complicated beyond any understanding, and so, better to ignore.

But one thing is for sure: if we are ever going to change these patterns, we must change our own habits and conditioned patterns of thinking, feeling, and behaving. And we will need a great deal of support, through friendly acceptance, lovingkindness, and compassion practices. Kindness toward ourselves is essential to building the capacity to take the risks required to learn in mixed company and to move toward taking action together for change. Kindness toward people who look and think differently is essential to creating safer spaces for telling and hearing the stories that reveal what we're up against and prepare us for the struggle ahead.

Over the following few pages, we will look at what cognitive scientists, sociologists, multicultural educators, and others say about racial dynamics in the contemporary United States. Using examples from my classes and workshops, I provide a window into just how our own perceptions, thoughts, and emotional reactions get in the way of experiencing true freedom and real community. Finally, we'll examine research suggesting that mindfulness and compassion practices can help.

Much of what we know about race and racism may lie fairly dormant in many of our lives most of the time. And again, this is especially so if we are white or light-skinned in a culture shaped by white supremacy. But we have all been trained not to see or recognize racism.

Yet we know that if we sit with our experiences long enough, we learn some things. We learn that we each carry the subtle, often invisible teachings of a society that has devalued groups of people by the workings of racism. We learn that these teachings have shaped our own habits. And we often learn that we have developed sophisticated yet subtle ways of remaining unaware and comfortable. Even when we are willing to see and to address racism in our lives, we are often ill-equipped for the very real challenges of doing so.

Mindfully Confronting Bias

As a black woman, Gesmine knew what it felt like to be the victim of microaggressions on a daily basis and to see the effects on the people she loved. "It's difficult to separate out one instance," she said when asked to give an example of harm she has seen. "Every day feels like violence, and I experience or witness some form of it all of the time."

Because of the everydayness of her experiences with racism, Gesmine felt ready to have hard conversations about it. But when she confronted her white friend about a microaggression directed at Asian Americans, she found her friend backing away, feeling hurt and attacked. Knowing what to say did not prepare Gesmine for the challenging emotional work of remaining connected with her friend with compassion while also challenging her to see why her behavior might be harmful.

Paul, a young white man, wanted to learn how to talk about race and bring people together across racial lines. He soon found, however, that whenever he opened up to other whites about it, conversations quickly stumbled, and then one way or another, whether quietly or with anger and defensiveness, ended. Again and again, Paul noticed that other white people changed the subject or literally found a reason to walk away. He had to admit that despite his good intentions, he was feeling mostly alone in this effort. He was beginning to think that it might be best if he left the work to someone else.

The fact is that sitting with and talking about our experiences of racism is incredibly difficult. This is one of the reasons why having effective conversations about race, and expanding our capacity to stay in such conversations with diverse groups of people, takes so much work. And yet, all of this is possible with a commitment to self-awareness and compassion when we see something in ourselves or others that reveals bias that we hadn't previously recognized.

Buddhist scholar John Freese described bringing awareness to his encounter with a racially different "Other": "When I looked closely, I came to see that there was this fear of annihilation that arose in me when I went into a predominantly Mexican-American neighborhood in Texas, not far from where I lived. [I realized] this is coming up out of my gut consciousness, this fear . . . It wasn't until I was back in the place where I grew up that this deeper stuff came up that's more hardwired in my system . . ."[6] Returning to his hometown helped him to see the deep-seated nature of racism within himself. His mindfulness helped him stay with what he saw long enough to deepen his understanding and be a source of teaching and learning about whiteness for others. In John's words, he "learned from Thich Nhat Hanh that racism is compost that we should transform into the wisdom of interbeing, and that purity and compassion arose from that same gut consciousness when connected to the heart-mind, when we awaken to the Ground of Being."

Better understanding of these issues and doing the work of supporting other people on their journeys have been the focus of my life's work for many years. Part of my commitment to this work grew out of my upbringing in what I believed at the time was a desegregated America in which full democracy and true equality were really just around the corner. My heart broke again and again as I came to see that America was in the throes of cycles of repair and reversal, reform and retrenchment, some progress followed by return to the old hierarchies that have often been accompanied by rhetoric justifying their existence. Professors like Reva Siegel, Kimberlé W. Crenshaw, and John Calmore suggest that given this historical pattern, we all need to be more skeptical of the rationales and justifi-cations that seek to blind us to racial disparities and racist actions. We need to be comfortable with skepticism about claims of progress in ongo-ing repair, redemption, and justice. We need to seek to change the broader consciousness in ways that make systemic, structural changes possible. We need to commit to doing these things for the rest of our lives, and we should cultivate these ways of relating with injustice and pushing for jus-tice as the heart of daily, engaged mindfulness practice.

Working Toward Universal Human Dignity

Over the course of U.S. history, we have experienced brief periods of col-lectively reaching toward justice for all—that sense of basic fairness and human dignity, and understanding that harming and handicapping oth-ers because of race or other characteristics beyond their control is simply wrong.

These moments have often been followed by longer periods during which we collectively reach backward to the past, bringing back the "good ol' days" when unfairness was the norm, when America was once "great." The "progressive" New Deal policies intentionally created racially segre-gated subsidized public housing. The federally subsidized suburbs, the Levittowns and the like, eventually drew lower-income whites (and some Asians) out of public housing in the urban centers and into neighbor-hoods from which blacks were explicitly, and often illegally, prohibited.[7] The schools and neighborhoods in Virginia that had been intentionally desegregated, making my relationship with Jake possible, have now be-come resegregated through market-sanitized means. The North Caro-lina town in which I was born has instituted a more severe form of racial segregation through increasingly isolated, racially concentrated public housing and denial of access to resources. These patterns of separation maintained by state housing, policing, and education policies are lega-cies of the explicit racism in the U.S. that goes back centuries.[8]

Our reactions to these "color-blind" indicia of racism vary significantly, often depending on which side we fall on what DuBois called "the color line"—that line separating whites from Others, designating who would be included in the promise of liberty and who would be treated as subordinate throughout American history. Black people and other people of color have often been especially aware of the consequences of these practices, and of the underlying antiblack racism that drives them, because our families lived through them. Although the dominant culture has often sought to have us proceed as if the color line has either dissolved as a result of the civil rights movement, or continues where it does only because of inferior culture (if not genes), a closer, more mindful engagement with our lives, communities, and histories can help us see that this is not so.

To engage in such a sustained, hard look at who we are and who we are not takes a kind of commitment to letting go of the stories we have been told about "American exceptionalism" (the idea that we in the United States are or were uniquely distinguished in our commitments to democracy and freedom). This opens us up to more than a little discomfort. And so we cultivate the energy and ability to work through the pain.

DEEPENING INTENTIONS FOR JUSTICE, BUILDING STAMINA FOR CHANGE

Begin with The Pause. Sense into your body as you sit and breathe.

Whatever your own racial background, allow yourself to consider how whiteness has been the primary racial category of embodied social power in our country and elsewhere around the world. Being nonwhite has opened countless people around the world to vulnerability to harm. Nonwhiteness has been constructed as embodied social vulnerability.

Consider how our state-sponsored laws and institutions were, for generations, explicitly aligned around the commitment to maintaining white supremacy, and, in a capitalist society, explicitly white wealth-building. Reflect on the vast implications of this. Even now, whiteness is associated with privileges, blackness with subjugation, while other groups are compelled to stand in support of this hierarchy (as, for example, "model minorities"), or to try to avoid getting involved. When consciousness supports it, people of all backgrounds— white allies and an array of people of color—come together to fight for dignity for all.

Breathing in and out as you take this in, notice any emotions and thoughts that arise. Notice these and then let them go.

What choices do you make on a daily basis to ally with others in the fight for equity and transformative justice?

What thoughts, stories, habits, or patterns get in the way of taking additional steps to ally with those fighting for universal human dignity and transformative justice?

What are some of the specific steps you personally would need to take to break through the barriers to working with others for justice?

Whiteness and Other Race-Making in Support of Racism

The core idea of racism is that differently racialized groups have essential characteristics that make them more or less suited for respect, full political inclusion, leadership, wealth, and ultimately humanity. And as we have seen, what has mattered legally and socially in America, and in many parts of the Western world—as a legacy of the ideology and practices of white supremacy—is the color line separating whiteness from other forms of racialization. Other parts of the world deploy hierarchies based on shades of color, height, religion, and other social identifications.

Gently notice what comes up for you as you turn toward the legacies of white supremacy in your own life, historically and now.

Again and again, stay with the commitment to practice mindfulness of your own experience here. Using the RAIN process presented in chapter nine, see if you can keep coming back to reflections that raise your awareness—that support you in recognizing, accepting, and investigating with non-identification. What memories arise? What discomfort? Where do you feel these in your body? What are the sensations that you attach to them? Where do you feel pained or stuck?

The truth is that racism is so thoroughly embedded in our culture that it is with us always. It is a consequence of the work of our ancestors, who built, sustained, and were often crushed by centuries of systems of race-making and place-making that organized our social, economic, and political lives to privilege the few on the backs of the many. Thus, it should come as no surprise that race, the product of racism, continues to impact our thoughts, feelings, and reactions to one another.

Race, as my "Anita Hill" story reveals, is in all of our meetings and encounters with one another. Exactly how it shows up in our lives will no doubt be different for each of us and will vary from day to day, place to place. For some, it will show up more in the guise of acceptance and access than injury and rejection. Both our inherent interconnectedness *and* the ways we co-create one another's suffering are ever-present. If we examine these dynamics closely, we cannot help but begin to see that *we are all part of the problem and may all play a part in the solution.* Seeing this in a culture that continuously seeks to have us do otherwise demands our ongoing wakefulness.

When we see that race is not simply a matter of "diversity"—the putatively benign notion that we are all "different"—but instead that race remains part of a big lie that justifies racial hierarchy (i.e., that people of different races are of unequal moral value and social worth) so as to justify economic exploitation—the ethics of our awareness practices invite us to do more than pause.

Developing Racial Emotional Intelligence

Mindful social justice work demands acceptance of the full range of emotional reactions that come up when we see what there is to see. We feel angry because anger is appropriate in the face of injustice. It is important to allow ourselves to feel what we feel, to understand that all emotions carry with them messages that help us to heal and to grow if we are willing to attend to them. Explore what is beneath the anger—is it pain? Is it vulnerability? Is it fear? In this moment, look into your feelings and the feelings beneath them. See whether you have a preference for certain feelings—do you actually prefer to feel anger over fear? Or pain? Or fatigue? Can you simply be open to feeling what is there, without, for the moment, needing to change it?

When we are ready, we can work with our anger and other raw emotions in service of our own and others' empowerment. Transforming anger in ways that help us heal is possible. Through our strong emotions, we might see how racism leads almost inevitably to real, often daily suffering. Rather than allow difficult or strong feelings to rage on in ways that may harm ourselves or others, we might channel that energy toward the work we wish to do in the world, awakening our senses to racism, developing the courage to act toward preventing it.

Deciding to Work Against Racism and for Thriving Humanity

The social processes by which race is made and white supremacy is perpetuated are in our communities, our workplaces, our political organizations, everywhere human beings gather. They are present regardless of our own personal efforts to live with kindness, to be color blind, or to minimize our biases. Seeing this can provide a measure of compassionate understanding between us as we seek to work across lines of real and perceived difference. And even more important, seeing this might assist us in developing a deeper set of commitments to working for change.

Although I am aware of the complexities behind the labels of race and of the intentions of many to work for the end of racism, I still see the difficulty of disrupting these patterns. Despite years of practice, I sometimes struggle to find ways to trust in the possibility of change. When I move through the social world, especially in areas that I do not know well, where I am not known, I often notice a lingering feeling that I might be in danger—that I could, at any time, be discounted, rejected, disrespected, injured, or even killed for no reason other than my perceived "blackness." Because race was created to support white supremacy, and white supremacy has so often required violent demonstrations of its power to maintain it, a sense of real, race-based vulnerability may arise in me when I am among white people I do not know.

Racial dynamics are at play in everyone's lives, even the most talented and privileged among us. Pop singer Bruno Mars changed his last name from his given name, Hernandez, in response to the reactions he received from music industry executives who saw him through the lens of his race. They reportedly wanted to label him a "Latin" singer and even tried to convince him to sing in Spanish, even though Mars was born and raised in Hawaii, was of mixed heritage, and presented his music and persona through a generic pop lens. Although he was part Puerto Rican, Latino was not Mars's identity of choice. His name carried racializing implications that he could only avoid by dropping it. So he dropped it and picked up a name that could not be associated with any racial cues, one that allowed him the freedom to be, as he put it, "out of this world."

The appeal of racial identification as a support for racial order and hierarchy, however oversimplifying, is everywhere. It is how we have come to know so much of the world. However clumsy and partial, notions of racial identity—as we apply them to ourselves and to others—sometimes open doors to being accepted, to feeling at least somewhat safe and understood, to feeling as if we know where we stand. If we let ourselves open up to the feelings of rootlessness and meaninglessness that often arise when we reject those cues, we may, at least momentarily, be terrified. There are many ways that we seek to avoid these feelings, one of which is making meaning around race and becoming blind to the ways in which the notions of race that we are willing to embrace—black people using the N-word among ourselves, for example—harm ourselves and others.

If you really listen to people talk about their experiences of racism, you will hear just what I am saying here. You will hear stories of black and brown people who had guns pulled on them by police officers time and time again in their youth. You will hear how some people are followed, threatened, asked to leave when they enter a neighborhood or a Starbucks or a park where someone believes that they do not belong. These experiences take place in neighborhoods, schools, churches, courtrooms, and so on that have been made and shaped in a world of bias and social and political hierarchies. In the United States, the ideology of white supremacy—which enabled every system of racial oppression from the Native American conquest and genocide, to slavery, to the anti-Asian exclusion acts—continues to provide a sense of comfort to too many.

Race reduces each of us into categories, keeping us at safe distances from one another's suffering and from our own hearts, systemically channeling the surplus pain of our society to racially disadvantaged groups. These patterns have existed for a very long time and persist for many reasons, including everyday conditions that, as we have seen, sometimes appear to confirm that what we see is simply the "natural" order of things. And for white and light-skinned people, there is the work of rejecting, again and again, the psychological comfort associated with stories of white nobility and innocence and of deciding to be a part of the ongoing struggle against racism.

White supremacy wants us to believe that segregation happens simply because of free choice, because people want to live in communities of their racial tribes. That over-incarceration of brown and black people happens simply because there are higher levels of criminality in some populations than others. That the U.S. Department of Homeland Security's policy of separating children from parents at the southern U.S. border happened simply because our immigration system was "broken." That the failure to adequately respond to Hurricane Maria in Puerto Rico happened simply because, well, it was Puerto Rico.

The decision to work against racism means that we will regularly look beneath the stories that support the racial status quo. When we do, we are willing to really see the evidence of unjust distribution of resources—including cultural esteem and moral worth—that contributes to these supposedly "natural" outcomes in the world.[9] We see ways that individual biases lead to—and are shaped by—systemic and institutional biases. We see the ways that race intersects with other aspects of our lives to create challenges that must be viewed with greater nuance than is typically encouraged (or allowed). And we are willing to feel the pain of the cognitive and moral dissonance that will come up again and again.

The difficulty we face as mindfulness practitioners is to see that race is an illusion that is nevertheless real in our lives in ways that cause deep and avoidable injury every single day, and that we can and must work to end that suffering, too. Our practices of mindfulness and compassion prepare us to meet the patterns of oppression in our midst without becoming mired in them, without making that which we seek to redress more real than it really is. We do not have to remain stuck in notions of difference as we engage in the work to repair the harms that difference makes. Mindfulness gives us the capacity *both* to confront injuries caused by conventional ways of thinking *and* to let them go and experience moments of true freedom when we see that racism and its injuries no longer either haunt or serve us.

With mindfulness, we begin to see that all of our notions about race, our inclinations to hold on to privilege or to ideas about who belongs where, are just emotions and thought patterns that we've adopted to make us comfortable. We are seeking to make solid that which is inherently shaky and morally problematic. Importantly, mindfulness ultimately helps us see that our thoughts, emotions, and sensations are impermanent and not the whole story.

Mindfulness helps us to see that our identities are not merely foisted upon us. They are constructions that we also participate in creating. And so they are constructions that we can dissolve and reshape in service of the decisions we make to live out our highest and best vision of ourselves. Mindfulness can support us in deploying our identities to engage in work for justice and equity with clarity and without making others our enemies. Along the way, we open ourselves up to the gift of our own empowered life energy and inner freedom! We become more open to the warmth of living in connection with all others. In other words, as we let go of our fixed notions about race and other identities, we develop the capacity to let go of the ways we have succumbed to the teachings of the dominant culture that keep us feeling alone and needful. We learn that our tendencies to grasp what feels good, to push away what does not, and to otherwise choose ignorance are at the heart of our participation in race-based injury in the world. We learn that these habits and conditioned ways of being in the world are also at the heart of what keeps us disconnected from the rich life that we were meant to live and the joy in being human together on this beautiful planet that we were meant to feel. When we practice deconstructing race and racism, we practice deconstructing separation. We are practicing the healing power of interconnection and the transformative power of true freedom.

Mindfulness for the Sake of Personal Justice, Interpersonal Justice, and Collective Liberation

By now, you have seen that the ultimate purpose of ColorInsight is healing and liberation. We begin with ourselves, working to raise our capacities for attention, focus, kindness, and deeper awareness that may lead to insight into our inherent interconnectedness and belonging. This includes awareness of what is happening, of who is suffering, and why and how, which is essential to creating just practices and policies for all.

We are choosing not to be at war with reality. Instead, we are willing to stay with what is present in the here and now, to investigate it and see what we can learn. We resist the temptation to identify with what arises, to see what comes up as a more or less permanent part of who we are. We realize that we can experience anger, for example, without identifying as an "angry person." We see how we can feel sadness and fear without drowning in them. We can name a feeling and feel the shift as it falls away. And in these moments, we experience a kind of freedom grounded in embodied, presence-focused, and heartful reality.

Mindfulness practices have been a lifeline for me, keeping me steady as I step up each day to do my part in the ongoing struggle for racial justice and liberation for all. With the support of mindfulness, I can come back into a sense of clarity and mental flexibility when I experience or witness racism. I can stop the experience of trauma before it further traumatizes. I can face the next challenge without the added baggage of the last.

Over time, mindfulness has helped me to see, hear, and feel more clearly and readily the effects of racism on me—on my psyche, my body, my sense of well-being. It helped me to develop an understanding of how to deal with this illusion of race that has had such real and visceral impacts on me and on the world around me. It helps me to maintain resilience in the face of the ongoing challenges of dealing with racism. And it helps me better relate to others who are struggling in similar ways.

The practice of expanding awareness to take in the sensations in the body and the thoughts and emotions that are arising helps us to see that these things are not permanent. If we turn toward them with clarity, we can see that what we think is never the whole story. In that sense, mindfulness practice helps us to participate in the actual deconstruction of race, racism, and its wounds in real time, giving us space to reconstruct ourselves and our relations with others from a place of radical possibility.

And when we allow ourselves to feel the full measure of what we feel, we are not merely deepening emotional intelligence, but we are also increasing our capacity for deciding how to engage with the world in a way that keeps us in touch with our humanity and ability to work for good. Whether we are meeting sorrow, confusion, anger, or rage, we can sit in the fire of our feelings, knowing that we make it through the heat. We can choose to go through these emotions and remain in connection with those who have triggered them. Research has shown that with the support of compassion practices, we can deepen the well within us from which we can allow in more and more of our own and others' suffering without going into overwhelm.

Even more important, however, is that these practices open the door fully to our liberation from the conditionings of our cultures, the pervasive trainings and teachings that seek to tell us who we are in relation to one another. They assist us in stepping out of all of that, and in moving toward greater comfort in simply being with one another.

And yet, however skillful, practiced, and earnest we are, we must approach this work with the openness to be undone, to fall apart, to leave our comfort zones long enough to develop trust in our deep being. Our expectations should be modest. After all, it is not easy to deconstruct race and experience the dissolution of some of our most cherished beliefs! We need the real social-psychological support of awareness as we move through these changes. And of course, we must continuously work to increase our love for ourselves and others as we go. Opening ourselves up to vulnerability and reaching out to those whom we have been taught to distrust, we seek new levels of aid and comfort in our practices and in the community of practitioners with whom we may experience collective healing.

Take your seat and take a few conscious breaths. Consciously ground yourself in the present moment. When you are ready, call to mind one of the many groups who suffered because of the efforts made to colonize and later build the institutions of your country, whether on your country's soil or in colonies or territories abroad that helped build the wealth of the nation.

You may think about indigenous people (in the United States, Native Americans/American Indians), whose lives were lost to clear the land on which you may now be sitting. You may reflect on those whose labor was exploited and who were otherwise dehumanized (in the United States, that would include African Americans who were enslaved, Asian Americans and Latinos who were worked and then discriminated against in their efforts to become citizens, and so on).

As vividly as you can, bring to mind faces that reflect individual members of the racial groups who have suffered. And now allow yourself to reflect on what you know about how the members of that group actually suffered. Visualize this suffering as much as is safe and possible for you to do right now. Allow yourself to explore what it might have felt like to endure that suffering. More important, consider how their descendants continue to suffer the legacy of these policies.

What thoughts, emotions, and sensations arise in you as you sit with these images? And now, as we prepare to bring this meditation to a close, open yourself up to the possibility that the people whose suffering you have brought into focus have something valuable and important to teach you today. In what positive way might their experience be more of a part of the world even today?

Finally, let the images and thoughts that you've been holding dissolve, and allow yourself to sense into the present moment from this place of expanded awareness of connection across space and so-called difference. Feel the quality of the heart that knows its connections with others.

A year before announcing his candidacy for the U.S. presidency and nearly five years after the assassination of his older brother, Bobby Kennedy did what no other presidential candidate before or since has done. He traveled through the regions of the country where the poorest people were struggling to eke out a living and take care of their families. His visit reportedly included a crucial few hours in the Mississippi Delta, one of the poorest and most racially oppressed regions in the country. After stopping to ask men, women, and children what they had eaten that day, whether they had the money to buy food, Kennedy returned to Washington with a clear sense of the need for a federal program to end poverty in America.

Kennedy showed us how pausing, being willing to turn toward the suffering in our midst, to see and accept it fully, without rushing to change it, just might possibly change a life. For the remaining fourteen months of his life, Kennedy kept returning to what he had learned on his one afternoon in the Delta. His stories and his efforts to report what he had seen helped wake up a good many people to these realities.

Broadly speaking, our dominant culture does not place a great deal of value on pausing to enable feeling empathy, or on the work of personal transformation. But those of us who have engaged in contemplative practices aimed at healing ourselves and others have a name for what Kennedy was doing on that trip. He was *bearing witness* to others' suffering as a path to his own and others' awakening, in service of healing that would touch us all.

CHAPTER TWENTY

THE WOLF IN THE WATER: WORKING WITH STRONG EMOTION IN REAL TIME

Mindfulness can increase the chances of our successfully integrating trauma by enhancing self-regulation. As an adjunct to trauma treatments, mindfulness can assist in our turning toward trauma with greater mental stability, an improved faculty for self-regulation, and the ability to cultivate courage and compassion in the face of dysregulating symptoms.

—DAVID TRELEAVEN[1]

I don't like to talk in terms of race, but we have to.

—DAN RATHER[2]

Triggers Happen

What's your reaction to Dan Rather's quote, above? What reactivity is he describing in that statement? Does it sound familiar? If you've read this far, you've probably experienced some discomfort along the way.

And I know that if you've been talking with anyone about what you are reading, you've experienced—perhaps for the one-millionth time, perhaps for the first—what it's like to wade into the deep streams of conflict and unhealed trauma that so many carry when it comes to these issues. It is for these reasons that some people—the privileged among us who have a choice—often do not want to talk about race. At all.

As I write this, Brian Crooks's essay about growing up black in a predominantly white suburb of Chicago has gone viral on Facebook. He describes having had his first girlfriend break up with him because her racist father demanded it. (Sound familiar? Almost scripted?) Crooks also describes that day when a "good friend," in the midst of an argument, called him a "n——r."

Each of these incidents resonates with me. They call to mind some painful memory or another of my own. And given the number of people who are responding to Crooks's post, I can see that I am not alone.

Yet his prescription for what to do next is surprising. In a televised interview, he said, "Everyone says we need a conversation about race. . . . But what we need is a series of monologues."

For twenty-one years, I have taught lawyers and law students how to increase understanding across diverse communities and to develop the skills necessary to have conversations about these topics. For most of those years, people would tell me that race was no longer an issue.

Not anymore. Although most of us remain unsure about what to actually do to address racism, we are clear of at least one thing: the notion that race is "no longer an issue" is just wrong. Racism is not only a serious issue, but it may be as devastating to our society today as it ever was in the past. Hate crimes are on the rise. With gun ownership and access rates at historically high levels and the threat of terrorist violence like what we saw in Charlottesville in August 2017, we have to do more to build a culture of caring in which everybody matters and white supremacy and racism are no longer seen as American values.

Yet when we try to address these issues, we often find it so frustrating that we are tempted to give up. Mr. Crooks's message seems to say that given how painfully difficult it is for us to actually talk about race, to listen and hear others' stories, we should instead simply tell our stories one at a time. Post them on Facebook. And have an actual conversation with . . . no one in particular. I see the value in Mr. Crooks's suggestion. It would at least allow each of us an accessible, supportive structure for having our say. And even more, I understand the frustration behind it. Having experienced so often the difficulty of not being heard on these issues, and of having my own reactivity triggered as a result, I truly get it. I think most of us get it.

Yet I hope that the mindful awareness and communication exercises that you've been practicing here have helped you see that there is another way. It isn't an easy one, and we cannot get there overnight. But through personal justice work, combined with mindful communication practices, we can develop the capacity to skillfully engage with ourselves and one another around these very difficult issues.

Handling Difficult Emotions

The key to handling emotionally fraught issues is to notice and work with our reactivity—the thoughts, judgments, underlying sensations, and root emotions. This requires deepening our practices of mindfulness and compassion with a view of our own worth, or a commitment to personal justice. We have to deal in particular with the core, the root of the issues— the feelings we have that overwhelm us, the ones that make us crazy. We have to wade into the feelings we are often ashamed to admit.

Years of working with people from every background and walk of life to process racism have taught me a little about how difficult it is to face the realities of the pervasiveness of bias, its impacts, and the truth that none of us is entirely innocent when it comes to its operation in our social world.

As I thought about my own reactivity and how much it resembled what I'd seen in so many others, I pictured a deep ocean, in which an animal, a wolf, struggled mightily in rough waters, the waves nearly overtaking the beast as it fought against the tide. That's what racial reactivity often looks and feels like—a mighty spirit battling a roiling sea. On the surface, it can look like fragility, an inability to accept and to cope well with what we see. On the inside, it can feel like the temptation either to snap our triggers in two, or to sink rather than swim.

We've all seen it, haven't we? In ourselves and in others? We've seen the need for emotional savvy as we work through these issues of racism. The good news is this: the ability to swim with the currents of racism and racecraft in our lives is right there inside of us. With emotional awareness, we can learn how to tap into it and feel it as a support for us.

Handling strong and difficult emotions as they arise is one of the central challenges of working with others around issues of race-based and other identity-based injuries. Anger will arise. Shame will show up. Vulnerability and defensiveness, resentment and distrust will pretty much always be in the room. There will be tears. If we cannot handle these emotions and reactions in ourselves or in others, our efforts—however well intended—are headed for failure. And if we cannot do so with compassion, we may end up promoting more injury than healing.

And so, as we've seen, one of the pillars of ColorInsight is to develop racial emotional intelligence. With racial emotional intelligence, we are able to name the specific emotions that come up for us in our racial experience, to see how we tend to react to them, and to develop alternative means of responding that support us in living with intentionality and purpose. One of the keys to developing racial emotional intelligence is realizing that emotions like fear and anger are normal reactions in the body—our "fight-or-flight" mode—when we discuss issues related to racism. First described by physiologist Walter Cannon in the 1920s, the fight-or-flight reaction is the first part of the body's stress response system. When we perceive an interaction as threatening (largely based on the brain's tendency to overextrapolate from past experience), our body's stress response system activates a cascade of signals from the brain. A wide range of physical sensations arise as a result—heart racing, flushed skin and sweating, the onset of quick and shallow breathing, and so on.

When this happens—and it almost certainly will when we engage in real talk around racism—we can practice easing ourselves back into a kind of equilibrium, the sense of harmony within our bodies and minds that stress researchers call "homeostasis." It is important for our well-being and healing that we also create conditions that minimize our stress. If we experience chronic stress—and due to the prevalence of racism, many people of color already do—our capacity to recover is impacted, showing up in higher rates of illness, depression, and signs of early aging.[3]

The good news is this: mindfulness meditation has been shown to help us handle distress and heal our old wounded places while actually reversing the processes of overload and aging that can accelerate with the stress of dealing with racism over time. The regular practice of meditation increases the capacities of our brain and body to deal with stress in our interactions with others. While it is not a panacea for the pain of dealing with racism, mindfulness meditation *can* help us stay with the difficulty and discomfort of seeing racism and promote deep, cellular-level healing.[4] It won't *automatically* help us deal directly and compassionately with our own bias, but it can certainly help reduce it.[5] Even with mindfulness, we must deepen our own intentions and cultivate the will to minimize whatever bias we carry inside. Research has helped us see all of this, and over the years, I've had the chance to check this out for myself.

One of my own most difficult moments teaching about race happened when I encountered strong emotion and intentionally provocative behavior from one of my students, Dan. As I think back on this moment, I realize that dealing with it and continuing my own mindfulness practice over the course of that entire semester many years ago is what solidified my decision to bring mindfulness and compassion practices directly to bear on teaching and facilitating conversations about race and law. I realize that what had been my own, personal strategy for dealing with difficulty around these issues—compassion-based mindfulness practices—needed to come out of the closet and into the center of my work.

Dan was an Asian-American, cisgendered man who was, I might add, physically quite a bit larger than myself. Having been assigned to my Torts course in his first year, he'd voluntarily taken a seminar with me the next year. Now, in his last semester of law school, he'd signed up for his third course with me—this time on contemporary issues of race and law.

A major component of students' learning in the course was through a research paper and presentation on a topic of interest. As they each took turns discussing their thoughts on their projects, we came, toward the end of the class, to Dan. He said, "I want to do a paper on the Rodney King beating." His likely "thesis," he announced, was that the beating King received at the hands of police "was deserved."

Even as I write this now, years after what turned out to be a semester-long struggle with Dan's effort to address a deep-seated trauma from a prior classroom experience, I can feel a blip of reactivity. I can see the policemen in that grainy video that we've all seen, appearing to let loose with as much force as they could muster on Mr. King, raining strikes with their batons on the head and torso of a man already on the ground beneath them. And I can feel the empathetic pain, sadness, and anger coming up for me as a result.

So when Dan made this announcement to our small seminar-style class sitting around an oblong table, I could sense the tense silence that fell across the whole room. And I could feel my mouth go dry with fear and a bit of intimidation.

I felt my temperature involuntarily rise, the blood seemingly rushing to my head. "This is what anger feels like," I knew enough to admit to myself silently. And I certainly felt viscerally and immediately the sense of energy of judgmental thoughts arising in my own mind ("You are wrong!") and indignation ("How dare you?"). This was what confusion, anger, and dismay all mixed up together felt like. And it was what deep concern and compassion for my other students felt like—several of them were black and brown, and had felt the direct impact of nationwide patterns of over-policing of black men. Finally, on top of all of this, my own ego was on the line—I'd been tasked with facilitating this conversation and guiding it productively, and this moment certainly wasn't feeling like success.

There are times when the best way to handle strong emotion is to give yourself a time-out, to give yourself space to figure out the best way to address a difficult situation. This felt like one of those times. To be clear, this was not an avoidance strategy—I knew I would come back to the issue at hand. But in the throes of reactivity, my first strategy was to notice my distress and to take steps to find my centered self.

So in that moment, feeling just a bit of the ground beneath me, I realized that Dan and I would need to talk one-on-one. I would need to find out a bit more of what he was thinking and why. And I knew I would need to follow up with the whole class after that.

Standing before the class in that moment, though, sensing the ground beneath me, coming back to the breath, I wasn't ready to talk with Dan. As best I could, I stayed as centered as possible in the full-on experience of reactivity and judgment.

"Dan, I want to remind you that this is a legal research paper and not an opinion paper," I said, feeling supported by the structure, in this case, of a law school course and its stated objectives. "So as you think through your topic and thesis, be sure to keep that in mind.

"And," I continued, "we should discuss your thinking about this project, and about this particular topic, one-on-one."

And so we did. During the first of several one-on-one conversations with Dan, I invited him to sit down with me and talk this through. We had both enjoyed our interactions over the course of the other two classes he'd taken with me, so in preparation, I did what I could to refocus us both on the positive history between us. After a bit of small talk, I told him I appreciated his interest in this topic. "I am always curious about what draws students into one topic or another," I said. "What is it that draws you to this particular topic? Has it been an interest of yours for some time?"

It didn't take long for me to uncover the prior, related trauma Dan had experienced. And herein, another lesson: beneath every aggression or effort to attack is a wounded human being.

"Well . . . yes," he said. His voice slowed as his gaze turned inward. "Actually, I tried to write a paper about this a long time ago, and . . . it did not go well. In fact, it was the worst experience I've had in school. Ever."

Dan told me that years ago, in a class on multiculturalism—the only other class he'd ever had with a black female professor, in fact—he'd sought to make that argument. According to Dan, that professor had reacted with what felt to him like fury. Flooded with anger, she had shouted him down for what to him had seemed like an eternity. She'd dismissed his proposal and whatever thought or experience went with it in a way that left him shaking and undone.

Not surprisingly, as a result, he had not written the paper he'd proposed. Instead, he had withdrawn into his own feelings of anger and shame. From that day on, he held something against this teacher, this particular black woman. And, he came eventually, slowly, to see, maybe all black women. And he had decided, it seemed, to figure out whether he would be able to hold it against me, too.

My own meditation practice sustained me as I sat with Dan and he recounted this story. Years of sitting and breathing and noticing what arose allowed me to stay present to my own racing heart and fluttering stomach without investing it with a story of what had to be done next. Somehow, despite my original impulse to run away, I remained right there with him, my eyes on him with openness. I maintained awareness of my own breathing, in and out, and feeling the ground beneath my feet and the chair supporting me at my core. I remained grounded, even as I felt my own emotions arise and subside as the words tumbled forth from this student sitting across from me. And I kept coming back, again and again, to the intention of listening to Dan—my student. And listening to him, I began to actually put myself in his shoes. Empathy and compassion naturally opened my heart.

Here again, my meditation practice helped. As I listened to Dan, I intentionally sought not only to hear his voice and story, but to listen as deeply as I could to what he wanted me to hear. It wasn't easy. When my own reactions arose, I noticed them. Relying on my practice, I sensed the ground beneath my feet. I came back to the sense of my role as professor and guide. Sitting with him, I returned my focus to his words and the sense of the feelings beneath them.

I listened to him in a way intended to help him feel safe enough to share deeply about his experience. Knowing that he had truly suffered over this, I wanted to alleviate his suffering by truly listening to him—in a way that would enable him to feel a sense of my caring for him, while at the same time staying in touch with my own feelings and guarding against any emotional reactivity that could get in the way. I realized that I wanted him to sense that my concern for him would not be disrupted by what he had to say. Doing so required more than intent or will; it required the support of a nervous system whose capacity for just this had been built up through the regular practice of mindfulness.

So with awareness of what was happening, but as little judgment about it as I could muster, I could guard against my own reactivity enough to actually hear Dan's words. I could see and feel the complex set of emotions running through him as a result of what he had experienced in that classroom so long ago: anger, fear, confusion, and the most toxic feeling of all—humiliation. I could see the suffering he still carried with him.

Sitting with compassion, with the desire for Dan to experience relief from his suffering, was not easy for me. The Rodney King beating was something I'd experienced some years ago from afar, in the same way that Dan had—by watching a video. Seeing that video again and again had shaken me to my core because it revealed the needless beating of a man by police officers, which we only knew about because of a surreptitious videotape. Watching it had left me feeling that the beating was not only *not* deserved, but that it was an instance of police brutality that would leave me more fearful of police for years and years to come.

Despite my reactivity, however, I understood that my role as teacher in that setting was not so much about me. It was about creating a space in which Dan's truth could be uncovered, unpacked, and given a chance to be met with other truths that would allow learning, healing, and potential transformation to take place.

As Dan and I took the time to have a series of difficult talks together, outside the spotlight and group dynamics of the classroom setting, I learned that in that very first moment when I decided to pause, to respond rather than to react, and then to take a time-out before meeting with him again, I'd not only reconnected with my own center but had also taken the first steps in helping Dan find healing. And by the end of the semester, he'd come to realize it too.

In the final week of the class, after giving a presentation in which he sought to make an argument that hewed closely to his original premise, Dan told the class, "I realize I have been holding on to some of my own pain around this incident. And it's something I have to let go." He wasn't necessarily a completely changed man. But he could see a glimpse of a way forward that no longer involved painful, unnecessarily provocative confrontations with others whose looks just happened to remind him of his earlier trauma.

So much of what we know as reactivity begins as an emotional charge in response to what we see, hear, read, think about, and otherwise experience in life. That charge leads us to act in ways that may appear to be fully rational, but on reflection, often are not rational at all.

Mindfulness has long been shown to play an important role in helping us deal more effectively with strong emotions and transforming them into something else. With practice, we begin to see that our emotions are not necessarily negative or positive, but that what we do in reaction to them can be. And so we must develop mastery over our responses. Mindfulness gives us space between stimulus and response. In time, we learn how to respond rather than react to even the strongest emotional triggers.

Mindful awareness and regulation of our emotions, especially as they arise in our conversations with others, is essential for working together more effectively in a world historically run by racism. When we combine mindful awareness with tools of effective and nonviolent communication, we are on the road to becoming agents of change and healing. Dr. Marshall Rosenberg—a psychologist focused on communication, human rights, and intergroup healing—taught that beneath our strong emotions, particularly anger, is so often found the more raw and shame-inducing feeling of fear.[6]

Indeed, much of the emotion that motivates racial reactivity across a wide range of scenarios is some form of fear. In many cases, this fear stems from experiences in which people who look different from us made us feel physically unsafe. In rare instances, such experiences can lead to an internalized fear that approaches terror.

One young white woman I taught, Jill, was raised in a big city where whites had largely abandoned the public school system for private schools in the city and its suburbs. Jill brought deep wounds to the class, memories of being bullied and even jumped because, she believed, of her race. Looking around at the black students in the class, she saw not only people who reminded her of this torment, but in at least some cases, she also saw economic privilege unlike anything she'd ever known.

It was extremely hard for Jill to get past her feelings of hypervulnerability and woundedness in my class. She had virtually no capacity to listen to the concerns of these black "rich girls." Not surprisingly, the "rich girls" reported having sometimes felt slighted because of their gender and race. It was difficult for Jill to open her heart and feel safe or empathetic in that group the whole semester, and this made the women of color feel unsafe, too. To my dismay, the only person in our group that she seemed able to trust—*a little*—was me. The degree of her trauma appeared to have been just too great to release in the course of a fourteen-week semester. In all honesty, I wasn't sure she'd made any progress by the end of it. But I knew I had done my very best to be at least one black person who could hear her, with whom she could begin to acknowledge the depth of her injury. There was at least one black woman with whom she could be a little vulnerable and share some of her suffering and be met with compassion. I knew from experience with my own woundedness and reparative work with a white female thera-pist that sometimes, if we're lucky, that's enough.

Anger, fear, and shame are not the only emotions that regularly ap-pear in our conversations about racism. Another emotion that shows up is what seems like disgust. Although most of us do all we can to hide it, it still exists; and sometimes we meet individuals who don't try to hide it—they believe that whole groups of people are just . . . categorically worthy of disrespect and contempt. If we are to do all that we can to heal the rac-ism that plagues us, we must explore the prevalence of these feelings and challenge their supposed justifications.

In at least some cases, we have been trained into these feelings. Some years back, my (white) boyfriend at the time reported that a mutual friend of ours, who was white and had a physical disability, said that his father "just doesn't respect black people," and so, neither did he. I experienced more than a little reactivity when I heard this! After all, though he was certainly white and southern born, I knew that he must have known at least a little about being dismissed due to physical characteristics be-yond his control, and from that, I thought, he might have developed at least some empathy. Oh, boy. Not so. And even now, in thinking about it, I feel my temperature rising a bit.

And so, in these most difficult of circumstances, when we encounter old-fashioned, unreconstructed racism, I have learned to quickly bring in mindfulness and compassion practice—if for no other reason than for my own sanity and well-being. As just one example, I sometimes use a portable mindfulness practice known as the STOP practice.

STOP FOR MINDFULNESS IN STICKY SITUATIONS IN YOUR EVERYDAY LIFE

Now that you've experienced mindfulness meditation practice, you may be starting to see how certain "portable" versions of it might sup-port you as difficult moments arise at any point in your day.

The four steps of the STOP practice can take as little as a few seconds to a few minutes to complete. Try it out and see how long you prefer doing each step.

So let's practice *STOP*.

To begin, the "S" stands simply for *stop*. Literally. Just stop what you're doing, whether it is typing or rushing out the door. Here the practice resembles The Pause, with which we began our practice journey together in chapter one. Give yourself a moment to come to rest, pause, and collect yourself.

The "T" stands for *take* a conscious breath. Now that you've paused, take a deeper breath, or two, allowing yourself to feel the expansion of the belly as you breathe deeply. Notice the sensations of being here, now. As you do so, it may help to bring your attention to the sensations of your feet meeting the floor. Feel the support of the ground and of your own relaxing breath as you do so.

Now move to the "O," which stands for *observe* what's arising in you, including any thoughts, emotions, or bodily sensations (such as tension, butterflies, tightness in the jawline). Broaden your awareness to take in the circumstances. Notice how you can be in this situation without being ruled by it. For added support, offer self-compassion as you release tension and stressful thoughts. As you calm down, open to the choices you have in terms of how best to move forward from here.

Finally, the "P" reminds you that when you are ready to close these moments of *practice*, you simply proceed with intentionality, taking the next step in your day from this place of strength, wisdom, and presence.

The STOP practice will likely come in handy as you bring awareness to racism and as you work with others. It can help whenever you're feeling distress, creating space to observe and tame your feelings, and to access the deeper resources within you.

Combined with simple mindfulness meditation practice—which helps you recognize more readily when you need to take a Pause—the STOP practice helps you develop the emotional intelligence and psychological flexibility required for greater mastery over the challenging moments when you engage with racism.

If you have become a regular practitioner of mindfulness, you are on your way to developing a deep well of resourcefulness to aid you when you find yourself pushed into the deep end. By incorporating everyday mindfulness exercises such as the STOP practice, you draw on their support as soon as you become aware that you need them.

ENGAGING THE STOP

There will be days when the STOP practice saves you. It is especially helpful if you need support to move through intense feelings so that you can note them and set them aside for the moment, with the intention of reflecting on them more deeply later. During a recent interview, I guided the questioner through the practice after I found myself sharing with her a recent incident of racial violence that she had not yet heard about. Afterward, we both got back on track with greater groundedness.

As we practice the STOP with others, we look deeply within while allowing space to be present with the other. We listen without becoming triggered by holding on to words tightly. We learn to be present to emotions, in ourselves and in others, without reactive judgment. With this practice, we remain close to our experience as we stay engaged. We get granular and we move from one moment to the next with awareness. We breathe in and out of that awareness, and after completing the practice, invite reflection on the incident as a whole, which can promote even further growth.

Maybe you've had trouble with a definition or a claim (or several!) I've made in this book. Maybe you've struggled with some of your own less-than-pleasant memories of trying unsuccessfully to work with someone around racial issues. Or maybe you've gotten into a thicket while talking about this book with a friend, colleague, or loved one.

As you know by now, all of this is reactivity. And it's part of what it means to be a human being. The question is this: How do we meet our reactivity without judgment, and with the intention of transforming it into effective responsiveness in our everyday lives?

We do it by practicing mindfulness as if our very lives depended on it, as Jon Kabat-Zinn says. Because in a very real sense, they do. More and more, our lives depend on our capacity for deep engagement with socially distant others. Engaging in conversations like these is difficult. The capacity to be lovingly engaged but not attached to particular outcomes, to keep coming back for more, to see the wholeness that can handle this moment of illusory disconnect, that one, and the next, is a complete and deep mindfulness practice in and of itself.

CHAPTER TWENTY-ONE

IN LIVING COLOR: WALKING THE WALK
OF MINDFUL RACIAL JUSTICE

Being willing to visit and hold our own pain and suffering, as
individuals, as a nation, and as a species, with awareness, compassion,
and some degree of non-reactivity, letting them speak to us and reveal
new dimensions of interconnectedness that increase our
understanding of those root causes of suffering and compel us to extend
our empathy out beyond only those people we are closest to. It means
that people everywhere have to have their basic human rights protected.

—JON KABAT-ZINN[1]

Raising Awareness of Our Internalized Woundedness

When I talk about race with other people of color, we usually focus on the
ways in which we have been harmed as a result of racism. Often, the primary response is one of appreciation for the space to share more safely in
this way, which supports our self-care and healing together. This compassionate holding of our experiences may be foundational to being able
to loosen our attachment to our own stories and wounds, and to being
able to help others.

As we have seen, the work of bringing mindfulness together with racial justice is about twin, intertwining paths of inner and outer work,
opening us up to the concerns we have about all suffering, and about race
as it intersects with all other forms of oppression. The notion of inner

and outer work is in some sense illusory: the two really are one, or, if you will, two sides of the same coin. The particular steps and practices that support our own personal healing, self-care, and liberation also subtly change the environments that cause so much wounding in the first place.

After many years of reflecting on race and racism and practicing love in action, I have noticed that much of what I have been taught about how to overcome racism has been about being the exemplary black person. It has been about, to paraphrase a beloved former First Lady, going high when other people go low. The trouble with this approach is, while it may win friends, it does not provide a pathway to ending racism. While I believe in being the best version of myself that I can be, I am also now clear on the fact that being respectable, resilient, and intelligent and dressing like a professional does not protect people who look like me from racism and the unnecessary suffering that it causes.

What protects us from racism, what keeps us in touch with our innate dignity and worth, is actually *not* minimizing who we are to be more acceptable to others. It is *not* trying somehow to blend in with others in hopes that difference somehow can't be detected. We live in a society in which racism is deeply ingrained, and differences will be discerned. As long as racism is a thing, race certainly will be, too.

Fundamentally, what protects us from racism, then, is working to end racism. We deserve the dignity that comes from living in awareness that we are already good enough. We deserve to know freedom and to know the support of people who are willing to work toward that with us across our lifetimes. Mindful communication helps us to listen to one another, to develop into loving, aware, committed communities. When practiced in groups of similarly experienced people, it gives us the renewing experience of being safer, more free, and often, more loved, together.

The Opposite of Fragile

Moving between racial awareness and awareness of our common humanity does not come easily. We have been trained to think in binary, "either this or that" terms. The notion that some aspect of our experience may be "both this *and* that" is something that we often find difficult to live with.

And yet, mindfulness practice, at its root, is about relating with reality in ways that support being in paradox, with the cognitive understanding and the lived experience of "both this and that." I call this the "flow of awareness," and interpersonal neurobiologist, mindfulness advocate, and psychotherapist Dan Siegel refers to this flow of energy and information as mind itself.[2] When it comes to moving between racial awareness and other lenses on our experience, this is the flow of ColorInsight.

In this chapter, we'll look even more deeply into our reactivity around race, including reactivity to moving between racial awareness and other aspects of awareness. We'll look at what cognitive science, neurobiology, and social psychology tell us about this. And I'll unpack more of the ways that you can work with reactivity to make you stronger.

Here's a practice to get us more deeply settled in the fluid strength of the true nature of awareness, and to explore the paradox of being grounded in our experience of the ever-changing nature of reality.

GROUNDING IN THE FLOW OF THE ELEMENTS

The following practice is meant to provide deep support to anyone, at any time, and anywhere, but it has special utility to help us deal with complexity as we stay in the fire of racial discourse. For some, it might serve as a daily practice. For others, it may be reserved for moments when they need an extra dose of strengthening as they sense the pull of reactivity.

The practice uses reflections on the five elements—earth, fire, wind, water, and space—as a basis for sensing into our interconnectedness with all things and the ways in which we are strengthened by the elements in every moment of each day.

This practice combines mindful awareness with self-compassion as you work through the challenges of attachment, aversion, and ignorance, allowing them to be seen, appreciated, and then to dissolve. Like the self-compassion practice that you explored earlier, it invites you to engage in visualization.

As you follow the instructions below, take time to allow each step to settle deep within you. If you have trouble with any, continue through to the next instruction, practicing openness and staying with it to the end. Or just revert to your foundational awareness practice, whether Awareness of Breathing, Body Scan, or a movement practice.

Begin by taking your seat. Take a deep breath or two and simply drop into the sensations of breathing and sitting.

Earth: Sense into the ground beneath you, the earth. Consider how it's been there for you all of your life, and in some sense, you have been there for the earth as well. The soil, trees, grass, and so forth. Notice the connection between your body and this earth in the present moment.

Consider how the earth feels solid until it doesn't, when there are earthquakes and floods. Recall the molten core that always rages beneath us, and the constant changes of weather. Notice that even as the earth provides support, it is ever-changing.

Now notice how our bodies are composed of the elements that make up the earth, in all of its colors and textures. Skin, bone, and muscle. Sense into the changes that constantly occur in the body as hair, fingernail clippings, and flakes of skin return to the earth. Whatever our outward appearance, whatever our colorful differences, we have in common the fact of being alive. And we have in common the experience of being different each day, of imperceptibly relaxing into the earth at every moment, without effort. We are sustained by the oxygen released in the environment. Breathe in and out the sense of your interconnection with this earth.

Now call to mind your own lineage—the particular people whose cultures intertwine with yours. Think of how those particular people and their practices were shaped in relationship with the earth. Sense into how you carry that lineage with you as you walk this earth. Reflect on the fact that the stories of our heritage are necessarily incomplete— only an infinitesimally small part of a vast, epic, largely unknowable story full of mystery and triumph.

See if you can sense how the various peoples of the earth—in all our diversity—are part of the ground on which we all walk. Reflect on how our ancestors, over hundreds of millennia, have survived trauma and tragedies much greater, perhaps, than those we face. Through their various ways of surviving over time, we are here. And yet, we do not know the great, vast majority of their names. Still, practice opening up to the thread of life that remains, this breath. Know the accumulated wisdom of all humanity and the desire for well-being that lives on in you. As you breathe and sense the body on this earth, know that it is this strength, this capacity to survive and thrive in a changing world, that is within you now and always.

Water: Breathing in and out, notice the element of water in each of us.

We take in water from the environment around us, borrowing it for a short while. Water is transformed by the body, and by water the body is transformed. Our bodies eliminate forms of water back to the earth.

Sense into the movements within you that invite you to engage with the streams of the ocean of life. Sense into the flow of all five elements and allow them to keep you fluid and open to motion. Feel the water element in you as it moistens the heart, soothes muscles, and quenches thirst, ever changing according to the needs of this life.

Fire: The energy of life is represented by the element of fire. The sun around which the earth revolves. The heat that provides warmth, the energy that supports the processing of the food to waste that is necessary to life. Even as we sit in stillness, the fire element within us goes on softly, giving us health and longevity.

We give off and receive the warmth of the fire element in our interactions with others. Call to mind one person who inspires you. Sense into the energy of that inspiration, the warmth of it, the intensity. This is one measure of the fire element that interconnects all of us.

Now call to mind a community or perhaps a particular person whose suffering you have witnessed. Sense into the feeling that comes with it—the pain, the anger, the desire for well-being. Feel the full measure of your wish to alleviate that pain. As you breathe in and out and sense the strength of your own motivation, your fiery will to help alleviate the pain of others, notice how the breath supports you. Allow the energy of awareness of suffering to support your resolve to take compassionate action. And witness the transformation by which even this desire may flow into nonattachment to action.

Bringing awareness to the depth of the in-breath, drawn up through the muscle group that forms the core of your body, allow a sense of strength to intermingle with the breath. See how, together, earthen body, ever-changing water, and the fire of will, meet the breath. See how, together, they strengthen, calm, and sustain in each ever-changing moment.

Wind/Air: Breathing in and out, sense the nature of the wind element within you. Sense into the breath as it cycles in and out. The wind or air element represents spirit, or chi, the very energy of life. Sense into what connects you with all of life, its suffering and its joy.

If you're willing, allow yourself to become aware of the spaciousness that exists in all things. The stories we tell ourselves about our own or others' suffering are not the whole reality. Allow yourself to open to what is not known, and the possibility that the whole story will never be known. Trust that there is some good nevertheless.

Space: Now sense into the element of space. Everything arises out of space and will return to it. And space, too, exists both within and without us.

As you breathe in, sense the spaciousness that exists within you. And as you breathe out, sense the spaciousness, the environment into which we breathe as we become present and connected with our surroundings.

As you reflect on the thoughts, emotions, and sensations that arise from your engagement with bias and racism in the world, recall this meditation. When you are feeling grounded, or even stuck in difficulty, consider that this is the earth element of your experience. Recall that the earth, too, changes—it's nowhere near as hard as the rocky parts make it seem, and beneath the surface is liquid, molten fire. However hard your experience in any given moment, it, too, shall pass.

Take a deep breath and feel the air/wind element rushing through and opening up more space to allow the truth to be present, to allow transformation to happen, to allow what wants to be released to be let go. When you feel anger or the desire to take some very immediate action, consider this to be the fire element arising in you. Meet it with a respectful appreciation of its energy and the will to transform it in the direction of your highest and best vision, through your choice to respond rather than react.

If you are feeling sad, weepy, swept away, or unstable, explore whether this might be the water element in your body. Recall its quiet, deep strength, like an aquifer holding an underground lake deep within the rocks, ready to be tapped when you need it. Recall the vast capacity of the ocean to hold all that arises.

If you find this meditation difficult, pull back from it and return to the earlier practices of sitting or mindful movement. Continue practicing the cultivation of compassion for self and others. And when you are ready, return to this Grounding in the Flow of the Elements Meditation, sitting with the instructions as best you can for as long as you can, with kindness toward yourself and your experience. This meditation offers support as you move into the more difficult trials of this journey, but it does so much more—providing deep insight into the impermanence of all things, including ourselves. It provides a felt sense, a lived sense of our interconnectedness with a vast, ever-changing universe to which the desire to love one another and to minimize harm is the only sane response.

Return to this meditation, then, as you feel called to deepen your insight into the nature of what causes suffering for yourself and for others, and what alleviates suffering and provides a pathway to peace. You will find it helpful as you move into the deeper levels of engagement—meeting other people in their reactivity and meeting yourself in your own, with enough kindness and compassion to enable dropping down into the deep beneath all of it, a dwelling in which, as Wallace Stevens wrote, "being there together is enough."[3]

Diving (or Being Pushed) into the Deep End

Mindfulness practice supports you so that as you develop greater insight into the nature of what you're up against when it comes to racism, you are also more willing and able to talk more about race with others. It requires daily practice with the intention of making good on the opportunities your life presents for you to wake up right then and there and to be of service to those seeking deeper understanding of what awakened justice looks like across lines of difference.

Now let's consider the following question that might come up in conversation: Since looking at race causes so much harm and suffering, wouldn't it be better to focus on what we have in common, not on what divides us?

When questions like this arise, I am reminded just why it is that I chose to commit myself to compassionate mindfulness as a support for racial justice work in the first place. This kind of question might trigger someone who's experienced a history of persecution, discrimination, and trauma based on race, often at the hands of people who bear identity characteristics similar to the questioner's. For me, it is obvious that this work is essential to helping illuminate and alleviate an often-buried dimension of pain running through so much of the world's suffering. Why isn't it equally obvious to others?

Rather than react, we need to bring mindfulness and compassion into the conversation. The following exercises have helped me in this process. Clarifying values has been shown to improve learning and performance over the long haul, to enhance decision making, and to support ethical action in the world. Our values differ, but when we come to clearer understandings about them, they can help us come to terms with what matters and why. The following is one among a number of practices that bring clarity to the values that underlie our work in the world.

BEING WHAT MATTERS: A VALUES-IDENTIFICATION PRACTICE

Set aside a few minutes for this practice.

Begin by settling into a position for meditation practice.

Take a few deep breaths, and then allow the body and breathing to settle into a natural, easeful rhythm.

Now, ask yourself the following questions and allow yourself to note what arises in response:

What do I value?

What do I *really* value?

How do the choices I make about how I spend my time reflect my values?

What else do I value?

Continue this practice until you have identified up to five values you hold dear.

Spend a few minutes journaling about what comes up for you.

When I engage in this practice, the values that come up immediately for me include loving, inspiring education, meaningful relationships, and change-making work in the world. When I ask myself what I really value, however, I see something more: awareness, spirituality, living in consciousness of interconnection, and acting with love. Because our values change as we all do, being aware of our values at this moment is just the beginning. Being aware of the relative priority we give to those values provides even more insight for wise action in the world.

I use the following practice to further clarify how to prioritize the values I hold most dear at any given moment. Knowing my priorities helps when apparent conflicts arise.

ENGAGING WHAT MATTERS: A VALUES-PRIORITIZATION PRACTICE

Set aside a few minutes for this Mindful Reflections journaling practice, which will allow you to reflect on and sort your highest values.

As always, begin by settling into a position that supports you in being present. Feel the connections between the body and breathing, and between the body and the surrounding environment—the earth, air, wind, and sky.

Call to mind your top three to five most important values.

Now see if you can sort your values in order of their priority to you at this moment, from highest to lowest.

If doing so is difficult, imagine having to choose only one value to focus on if you knew you had only one more year to live, or perhaps if you had only one month. Continue reflecting on this until you are able to organize your short list.

Now take a few minutes to come back to the present moment.

When I take the time to prioritize my values, I begin to see more clearly how they fit together. They form touchstones along my chosen path. Once again, I see living in consciousness of interconnectedness and acting with love, followed by spirituality more generally. These can help clarify actions that need to be taken. The practice also helps me to see the relationship between my highest values. And so when apparent conflict arises among values, I can rest in awareness that work in service of one value supports work in service of another.

Cultivating Kindness and Fierce Love

The next practice cultivates positive and calming feelings, especially in the face of anxiety. It's called the Lovingkindness Meditation for Collective Liberation. Research has shown that variations of this practice have helped increase positive feelings, including compassion, before challenging classroom conversations. It has also been shown to reduce implicit bias.[4] By practicing lovingkindness, we cultivate kindness of heart and the wish for well-being, first for ourselves and then for others.

LOVINGKINDNESS MEDITATION FOR COLLECTIVE LIBERATION

Although the name may sound light and fluffy, in my experience this practice can open us up to feelings that are far more challenging than the name suggests. When we engage openly and with a commitment to stay present, lovingkindness trains us in the kind of fierce love from which change agents the world over have drawn strength in times of distress.

While this practice can leave us feeling a dose of positive emotion, it can also be quite difficult. Traditional lovingkindness practice calls on us to visualize and call forth a series of images that, over time, may open our hearts to others and minimize attachments to conditions that will change over time.

So let's begin. We start by choosing a person from whom we have received care, nurturing, or support. Or someone from whom we have felt unconditional love. We sometimes call this person a "benefactor."

Call to mind the person, making the image as vivid as possible. Sense into how this person has cared for you. Feel into the heart region as you re-experience this person's love for you, and your affection for them.

Now repeat the following classic phrases, inspired by my friend and insight meditation teacher Jack Kornfield, directing them toward the person you've chosen to hold in awareness.

May you be filled with lovingkindness.
May you be well, in body and in mind.
May you be safe, from inner and outer dangers.
May you be truly happy, and free.

Continue repeating these phrases a few times. Then allow the image to dissolve. Return to the breath, sensing into the present.

Now call to mind an image of yourself. It may be an image of you now, sitting here, or it may be an image of you at some earlier point in your life—as an infant or as a child at an age at which you suffered some particular pain or trauma.

Repeat the following phrases, directed at that image of yourself.

May I be filled with lovingkindness.

May I be well, in body and in mind.

May I be safe, from inner and outer dangers.

May I be truly happy, and free.

When you are ready, gently allow this image of yourself to dissolve. Come back to the breath.

And now, call to mind someone you know, but not well. It could be the clerk or doorman at a building you visit regularly. To this person, direct these same phrases.

May you be filled with lovingkindness.

May you be well, in body and in mind.

May you be safe, from inner and outer dangers.

May you be truly happy, and free.

Again, continue sending these meditations out in the direction of this acquaintance.

Traditionally, we continue through a process of moving from person to person, to those more and more socially distant from ourselves. When you are eventually led to call to mind someone with whom you are experiencing some difficulty, direct the same traditional practices to that person. It might be difficult or feel insincere in the moment, but we continue with as much openness and intention as possible. From there, we imagine expanding the circle to include all people everywhere, especially the vulnerable, in every culture, everywhere.

Gradually, through this practice, we are expanding our hearts and widening our circle of concern. We are building the muscles for the flow of acceptance and peace that ripple beyond those about whom we care the most. And we are walking a path to the lived experience of equanimity that will be like a lifelong support as we look more deeply inside ourselves and as we engage with others, moving more completely into the work of transformative social change.

Now that we have intentionally brought other-regarding lovingkindness into our frame of mind, let's return to the question that someone might pose to you, the one I earlier described as potentially triggering for someone like me: Since looking at race and racism in our history causes so much harm and suffering, wouldn't it be better to focus on what we have in common, not on what divides us?

How do you answer? A mindful response might look like this: You pause and take a conscious breath. You sense into the compassion you feel for this person, and for yourself. The pause gives you a bit of space not only for grounding, but also for finding your own words and the wherewithal to say them while staying present.

You might begin with appreciation for the question (always a good start!), and then ask the person to share more of their thoughts: "I'm curious to hear more about what you see here. Have you felt pain or suffering when looking at race and racism in our history?" Or, "Are you willing to share some of the sensations in your body that are present right now, as you raise this question? Some of the feelings beneath it?"

If the person speaking is willing to be even a bit vulnerable, genuine questions like these can lead to an open discussion of some of the underlying anxieties that can cause us to shut down conversations before they even get started.

You might go further by following up with: "Does looking at race and racism really cause harm? Or might the opposite be true? Reflecting on race might not only be about looking at 'history,' but at a hidden part of the present as well—how, then, might we reframe this conversation about how race is relevant in this class [or office, or retreat center, or neighborhood]?"

As we move into inquiry in this way, we must be willing to let go of our own fears—the fear of being vulnerable, of not knowing, of causing greater upset. When we engage with others in racial justice work, we will inevitably do it imperfectly according to someone. We will be drawn to topics that touch on race but may be easier for some of us—especially whites—to handle. And yet, if we ground our work in our meditation practice and the awareness that flows from that, we will have a new set of skills to draw on, and a capacity to stay in the struggle of disrupting racism despite our sense of fragility, of futility, of "messing up," and other challenges.

Suppose that someone says this: "Since we're all about compassion, shouldn't we be compassionate toward those who commit hate crimes? Isn't it possible to love someone *because* they are racist?"

Such a comment will be especially hard for anyone who has suffered a hate crime directly. And yet, here again, if we are deeply practiced and have experienced some of our own healing, we can have compassion even as we seek to minimize someone's ability to do further injury. Compassion does not absolve a person of responsibility. And similarly, if we have done our own healing, we can love someone, regardless of their views, without making ourselves vulnerable to the harm they cause. The point is this: we can identify a transgression without making the transgressor an enemy. When we read or hear something particularly pointed or charged, we have the means of taking in what was said without clinging to it, and responding to it in ways that increase the sense of psychological and emotional safety for us all.

Meeting Suffering with Courage

Despite many years of bringing mindfulness and compassion to bear on issues of racism, I cannot say that the work is ever easy. Often, it requires the courage not only to be vulnerable, but to stay with an engagement through long periods of not knowing, of wanting things to be different, of seeing new levels of reactivity in ourselves and others. In short, ColorInsight is about deep mindfulness brought to bear on the healing of some of the most challenging interpersonal dynamics in our lives.

COLORINSIGHT PRACTICE: RACIAL SUFFERING
AND REPAIR PRACTICE

Take your seat. Take a few very deep breaths, and then allow your mind to rest on the sensations of breathing in and out.

Think of a time when you were in a conflict with someone on an issue of race. When you felt misunderstood. When you felt angry and wounded.

What sensations in your body do you feel now, as you recall this incident? Be precise: Where are you feeling this now?

What thoughts arise as you call this incident to mind?

What emotions are showing up as you sit with the memory and recall how it impacted you? Keep exploring feelings until you feel either a sense of having taken in enough or a sense of release.

If you are feeling overwhelmed with negativity, immediately shift back to a Grounding Practice. If you have been sitting, stand. Take a few very deep breaths. Feel the sensations of your feet on the floor. As you stand, notice that you are safe and that you have the support of the breath, the ground, and your surroundings. To help bring supportive nurturing, place one hand over your heart, and one over your lower belly. Call to mind a person around whom you have felt loved and safe. Bring forth the image of this person in your mind's eye, making your visualization as vivid as possible. Breathe in and out as you recall that you have known safety and love and that your body holds the capacity to assist you in calming and reconnecting to a sense of safety, serenity, and even joy, in this moment.

Feel into what is well, good, and at peace within you in this moment. Now sense into the strength that exists in you now.

Take the time you need to explore these and other ways of staying in touch with the ground of support around and within you.

When you are ready, call to mind the person with whom you had a conflict.

If you are willing to move toward connection, ask yourself this question: What safe-enough step can I take to move *toward* this person, to repair the harm of our interaction?

Note what thoughts, emotions, and sensations come up for you.

Now release them.

Take a few minutes to journal what came up for you in this practice.

In this practice, we are building the capacity to take steps toward our own healing, and toward healing our misconnections with others. As we realize that we have the ability within ourselves to take action toward healing, we see that our ability to heal from the wounds of racism does not depend on the actions of others.

Practices like these have helped me to see when I've been carrying a sense of woundedness around an interaction with someone, and how it is getting in the way of my own sanity and well-being. I've been able to discern what I need to do to begin repair, starting with myself. From there, I've been able to take steps toward reconnecting with others. Sometimes reaching out again and again is required. And navigating some conflicts will require the gentle intervention or mediation of a teacher or facilitator.

I once had a conflict with Pam, a woman of Jewish heritage who identifies as white. As we discussed our roles for an upcoming event, she told me that I had only been asked to step into a particular position—one that she coveted—because of my race. I felt unfairly diminished by this statement, as if the actual range of qualifications I brought to the work had been reduced to zero. It felt like a racial microaggression, and I told her as much.

She didn't take the information kindly. She did not think she owed me an apology. In fact, she thought that in calling her to attention to how her words had felt racially insensitive toward me, *I* had been unfairly attacking her. "I can't believe you're taking it this way," she said. "I can't believe you don't see that what I'm saying is a simple *fact!*"

As I reflected on the experience, I felt really hurt. I had made myself vulnerable to a white woman and once again been made to feel disrespected as a result. I continued to reflect on the incident, and how she might be jealous or threatened by me. I also knew that, from the perspective of the person who had offered me this position, my race and gender probably had played at least some part. In this way, reflecting mindfully helped me to see that despite my pain, there were two sides to this issue. When I thought about it against the values I held in relationship to the project at hand—minimizing harm, staying in connection with my fellow teachers amid conflict, growing in my own ability to work with others and again, demonstrating love in action—I concluded that the relationship mattered enough to me that I would make an effort toward repairing it. I needed to reach out to Pam and to be open to her efforts to reach out to me. We met in an effort to explore what had taken place as mindfully as possible. Each of us had long been students of mindfulness and compassion. And yet, we still felt the raw, painful disconnection that such an argument and harsh scene can leave in its wake.

Together we decided to take another step toward repair by reaching out to a trusted mutual friend and deeply practiced mindfulness teacher, seeking his suggestions on how we might work through our conflict.

After more than an hour of sitting together, sharing our separate experiences and expressing our intention to learn from them and deepen our relationship if possible, our teacher suggested the practice of lovingkindness.

"Practice lovingkindness with one another in mind. And keep doing it every day. For a year. Can you make a commitment to doing that?"

"For a whole year?!" I thought. Still, because I'd come with the true intention of doing what I could to repair this breach, I did not object.

My friend and I both said yes.

The next morning, somewhat begrudgingly, I sat in lovingkindness, directing the verses toward the woman whose words had caused me such pain. I sat daily, practicing lovingkindness. The days turned to weeks. The weeks, to months.

Over time, something happened. I started to lessen my grip on my story of what had happened.

Yes, her statement seemed unfair. This was clear. But at the same time, I understood how she might feel the way that she did. As I wondered, "What part of her statement might be true?" I could see that she might have arrived at this view without ill will. Though I felt she could have been more sensitive, I realized that her comment helped call attention to the lenses of bias through which I might have been regarded by others in our group. Might the person who had selected me for the role have been biased against her or in favor of me? Quite possibly, I had to admit. Either way, Pam's particular statement started to sting just a bit less. I took it less personally and started to see that it was not, after all, entirely about me. Or her. Or anyone.

As I allowed myself to look into my wounded feelings, I noticed my own attachment to being viewed as worthy "regardless of my race," to being valued, period. And yet, had I not also been focused on sharing my race-related expertise? If I substituted my "race" for my "race-related expertise" in Pam's comment, might it then be considered at least partially true in a way that even I, on some level, had to admit?

Over time and with practice, I felt myself growing in empathy toward my estranged friend. At the same time I felt understanding toward my own struggle. I felt a softening of the sense that I had been wounded in a way that held her to blame. Gradually, I felt a diminishing of the sense that anything needed to be forgiven. And at about this time, Pam reached out to me. We shared our feelings about where we stood, apologizing and acknowledging that we would need to continue reflecting on what had happened, but we also felt a mutual sense of connection that would ensure our ongoing efforts to make amends. To this day, we continue to work together and to grow together in our ability to make a difference in the world.

Through experiences like this over the years, I have learned that we can always do our part in the work of reconciliation. I have learned the value of patience, of seeing the long-term nature of the work that we do to repair the harms we experience in life. And I have come to see the futility of blaming others for the woundedness I feel around issues of identity. Given that we have the power to control our perceptions and our responses, we all bear some responsibility for the harm that we feel around racism and related identity-based wounds.

In the course of this journey so far, we have practiced opening and examining some of our racial wounds with kindness, giving them the full measure of compassionate response that assists in coming to terms with them. We have, in that sense, been acknowledging harm in ways that may set the stage for apology and forgiveness, as in the case with Pam. Indeed, the interpersonal repair that we experienced may be seen as a micro version of broader personal, interpersonal, and collective redemptive justice work. We acknowledge the injury that we and others have experienced, apologize to ourselves and to others, work to make amends to ourselves and to others, and engage in ongoing reflection on how to minimize the risk of such harm going forward.

Our responsibilities for repairing the wounds of racism will certainly usually not be equal, but we can each take up a part of the work. Indeed, I believe that we each must. Whatever the story of the original injury, if I am to stand in my own agency and integrity, the story of healing and repair must begin—and end—with me.

PART FIVE

Liberating

Mindfulness is the chance, in each and every moment, to begin again from an ocean of awareness, a place of infinite possibility. It is the very practice of freedom.

You can't stop the waves, but you can learn to surf.

—JON KABAT-ZINN[1]

CHAPTER TWENTY-TWO

WALKING EACH OTHER HOME

ॐ

There is a lot that needs to be done in society—work against war, social injustice, and so on. But first we have to come back to our own territory and make sure that peace and harmony are reigning there. Until we do that, we cannot do anything for society. Let us begin immediately.

—THICH NHAT HANH[1]

Expanding the Circle of Compassion

It has taken most of my lifetime to learn that my personal relationships, as much as they give me life, cannot be the sole source of my joy. If we are fortunate, our lives are enriched by many close and loving friendships and partnerships. And yet, they alone do not define a life worth living. My journey has also been about learning to remain open to compassion for others outside my close family and friends—to caring for a widening circle of others in the world around me.

Bringing mindfulness to bear has helped me to see the full spectrum of relationships in my life with a new level of awareness of how each can be a source of compassionate, friendly connection. Practices such as lovingkindness help build my capacity to meet everyone with greater kindness, even amid difficult moments.

A recent video of a conversation between two people on the topic of race that went viral on Facebook gives us a window into just how. In it, a black woman and public policy expert named Heather McGhee received a call from a white man who asked, with a palpable sense of vulnerability, how he might overcome his own biased beliefs. It was striking to see how McGhee was able to listen to him without bitterness or judgment, but rather with genuine care and concern. Instead of shame or derision, she offered him a genuinely curious, listening ear.

There are many ways to arrive at this ability to listen to another person with compassion. The kinds of practices in this book have helped me to do so. They can help you, too, to attend carefully to yourself in a way that leads to deep healing, humility, and the wish to do no harm, all of which support expanded compassion for others.

In this chapter, we look further at what is required to heal from the traumas of our own racialized experiences. From there, we will look into who we *really* are as we come together with others, seeing our relative positions and the challenges of living well with others in the given social and political world, as well as the deeper ground on which we stand. Finally, we will examine research and personal experiences highlighting the importance of other-regarding compassion—the desire to act to alleviate the suffering of others—in the work of racial justice.

Deepening Healing for Ourselves

Most of us come to interactions and conversations around race with varying amounts of anxiety that come from prior wounds. And we have experienced how mindfulness and related practices can help us during these moments of anxiety and even panic. We have seen how the practices can help us develop the intentionality and commitment necessary to address the conflicts that will no doubt arise. Mindfully accepting that racism and the notions of race on which racism depends exist in everyone's experience, and that they intersect with other forms of suffering, is the ground on which the work of racial justice is built. We cannot change what we do not see and are not willing to accept as worthy of our efforts to understand, redress, and redeem.

The practices in which we have engaged so far assist you in being ever more present to diversity and beauty in the social world around you. The practices in this section will support you in creating a deeper awareness of the diversity *within* you. In varying ways, we have each been hurt by racism, by the ways in which we have been miseducated and misunderstood. Often as a result of racism or colorism, we experience confusion and unawareness about our own identities. We have consciously or unconsciously found ways of defending ourselves against being harmed again. For some, this means having a tendency to get bored or to go numb when asked to look at these issues. You or someone you know may sometimes tune out these conversations or believe that those who talk about racism want to be seen as victims. On the other hand, people of color and white allies who have worked to see how whiteness has been constructed in their lives may find it difficult to muster the will to connect with those who are well-intentioned but have not yet learned much about white supremacy and the subtleties of racism.

Whatever the defenses we see in ourselves or in others, it is important to slow down—to Pause—and to take a good, hard look at them through the softening lens of our mindfulness practices. Here, in part five, we deepen our means of looking at our defenses, moving from accepting them to investigating them as fully as possible, without making them into a new excuse for throwing up our hands and giving up. Instead, we seek new ways of breaking through to freedom.

The defenses we have built up need to be explored with kindness, in order to support deeper understanding of what we are dealing with as we move toward healing. Here again, be prepared to give yourself extra care along the way. As we have seen, the particular wounds that we carry around race-based experience are varied. Looking at them and developing language to describe them is helpful for many people. For example, some of us have experienced many microaggressions over the course of our lifetime. While any one of these incidents might seem relatively minor on its own, the cumulative effect of microaggressions that occur on a daily basis can threaten our well-being. Moreover, they often inhibit our willingness to be vulnerable in situations where they may recur. When we attach to these injuries, when we guard against them in ways that make us hypervigilant, we may feel we are protecting ourselves from further harm. But the truth is that from such a place, we will likely continue to suffer. As we replay the incidents that have caused us harm, we become the sources of our own suffering.

When you look beneath racial injuries, you may notice that they are no more permanent than the moments, spaces, or bodies in which they occur. The pain we feel is increased by our defensiveness and our difficulty letting be. As you work with these wounds over time, you may find that you can hold these experiences in a way that promotes healing and feeling better about life despite the ever-present possibility that a microaggression may occur.

How do we explore the further healing that leads to liberation? I am not a therapist, and this book is not a substitute for therapy, but I can share with you some ways in which the practices described here assist us. We'll look at some of the variations in what might be beneficial, depending on the precise nature of our own and others' wounds. And we will do so knowing that the time may come when we need more expert support in finding and maintaining the courage to work toward greater well-being, remembering who we were before we were hurt or felt so afraid of being vulnerable that we closed our eyes to the suffering of others.

Who Are You Really?

I believe that some greater measure of healing and recovery is possible for each of us, whatever the degree of our trauma. Yet this can often take a long time and require much care and support. As we begin to heal, we can sense things changing, including how we think of and experience race in our own lives. Slowly we may begin to investigate our own racial and other social identities with more openness. We may begin to notice how we cling to a view of ourselves that places undue attention on our personal experiences with discrimination, a view that holds in place a pattern of woundedness that does not serve us. We become aware of the emotions that have accompanied this, including, in many cases, a very deep fear of being seen as an outsider. We begin to see how much of our identities have been shaped by the world around us, by the imperative to "fit in" and succeed, and by our families, friends, and their experiences.

The racial designations given to us and the assumptions that travel with them find their way onto the documents certifying that we exist and have a right to be here. From there, as we learn more about how our families have experienced race and racism, we generally develop a sense of allegiance to the racialized identities that we have been born into, in ways that range from subtle to intense. In an effort to find and to maintain a sense of belonging, we often look into our racial group's history and develop a sense of pride in these racialized identities. All of this is understandable, but mindfulness ultimately shifts our perspective to see more clearly that while such things help us find a sense of place in the social world, our true identity is much larger and deeper than the histories and heritages that we have been given. So while we hold our histories and cultures with respect, we loosen our attachment to them as more special than others'. We see them as part of the stream of human history in which we are all simply playing an infinitesimal part. And at the same time, we realize that just how we play our part during our limited time on earth means everything.

As we look deeply at our experiences of race using mindfulness practices, and as we continue reflecting on how we hold these experiences in our bodies, we begin to become more comfortable in witnessing that part of us, of our consciousness, that can observe our thoughts, emotions, and sensations and not identify with or hold too tightly to them. Experiencing race from the standpoint of witnessing is an important aspect of the liberation that mindfulness makes possible. As we spend more time as the Witness, we observe more of the processes and social practices by which we participate in the construction of race in our lives. And in those moments, we may participate in the deconstruction of race in our own experience. Then and there, we begin to glimpse psychological freedom, greater openness and wakefulness.

What is happening is that we are becoming more willing and capable of softening the stances we have held to get through the world. We are not rejecting our identities or past experiences. We know that our embodied characteristics—so-called white skin or black hair—signal racial meanings and cultural hierarchies that have impacted us profoundly, despite the temptation to believe we have evolved to be "beyond race." We acknowledge these realities while also holding any attachment to race as a matter of personal or political identity more lightly. We experience fully our responsibility to minimize identity-related harm, and we sense our capacity to breathe through it when it arises. We may even develop the capacity to loosen our focus on pain-points, to ease up on the vigilance we may have felt necessary to avoid being hurt again. We are developing the capacity to see who we are through the lenses of our particular identities and of the ground that lies beneath them.

Along the way, you might begin to notice a desire to act from this new level of awareness. We are all part of a larger whole—as my grandmother and community taught me when I was a little girl. We are all just one family who have forgotten who we are; with that awareness comes responsibility. When we see our inherent interconnectedness more clearly, we are called to do the work of real and lasting change within ourselves and in the world around us.

Deepening the Will and the Skills to Connect Despite Racism

At the heart of compassionate engagement with other people is the openness and desire to connect. We must make the decision each day to remain engaged with one another, especially when racism has made it difficult. We develop the will to cease struggling to be right in the interest of deepening connection and understanding.

We aim to alleviate suffering caused by racism, which requires staying in emotionally and socially intelligent connection with as diverse a group as possible. We investigate barriers to staying in connection with those who have been wounded by racism *and* with those who seem unaware of the effects of racism. As we have seen, this requires skillfulness in speaking and listening to others. We put down the explanations of just how the other person got it wrong—few people are moved to change by being on the receiving end of a withering verbal battery that leaves them swimming in humiliation or shame. But if we can speak from the heart and from our own experience, we give others what they need to hear and to learn without judgment. Practicing mindful and nonviolent communication is essential to the work of ColorInsight.

Living Ethically with All That We See

When we view humanity as one family whose members have forgotten who we are, we see ourselves in different ways relative to one another. And just how we live together should differ radically, too. Seeing ourselves as part of one family deluded by anxiety and fear dissolves our ideas around race and focuses us on the work of ending racism. All of the differences that we perceive between ourselves and others are truly, as they say, only skin deep; and yet, *belief in those differences* helps maintain a system of unnecessary, uneven, racially distributed suffering. If we could travel far enough back in time, we would find that we share the same human and pre-human ancestors across a vast, misunderstood, underappreciated history. And yet, we are disconnected from that history. Ultimately, we owe one another the care and concern that we would offer a brother, a sister, as we disrupt the patterns of power-over-others that cause surplus harm. We owe a politically adverse brother the same care that we would offer a beloved, easily understood sister; and we owe it to all of humanity to fight for a more just distribution of the resources necessary to live freely and with dignity. The cousin recently found sleeping on the street, or wasting in a jail cell, or abandoned to a mental institution, or beaten because of who she loves deserves the same level of care and concern, too.

CONTEMPLATING ALL HUMANITY AS ONE FAMILY

Take your seat.

Breathe in deeply and settle into natural peace.

Rest and relax, allowing yourself to open up to the great mystery of your life.

Now call to mind your mother. Even if you were not able to grow up with her, or your relationship with her was a difficult one, imagine her in as much detail as you are able.

And now call to mind your mother's mother.

And then her mother, as best you can.

Imagine going all the way back through the generations and tens of thousands of years, until you arrive at our common ancestral mother among human populations—the woman whom anthropologists and geneticists tend to agree was the single female ancestor that all living human beings have in common, our great-great-great-great- . . . great-grandmother.

Now imagine looking over human history from her point of view and resting on the problems we face today.

What would *our* common ancestor see? How would she feel? What might she think?

Now imagine her gesturing to you to come closer. She wants to deliver a message to you, one that you will share as you engage with others in the struggle for justice for the rest of your life.

What is that message?

Lean in and listen.

Lean in. Listen. It may just be the only way that we will find our way home.

CHAPTER TWENTY-THREE

THAT EVERYTHING MAY HEAL US

❧

As we seek to bring our own selves into alignment with what we care about, we must remember that everything within us and around us—our own bodies' nervous systems, our neighborhoods, our economies, our social services, our national stories and aspirations and challenges—is in continual conversation. When we acknowledge still-open wounds like legacies of slavery, mass incarceration, Islamophobia, and anti-immigrant racism, we can see we need healing and transformation for individuals and for the larger systems we are a part of.

—DAVID TRELEAVEN[1]

Investigating Collective Suffering and Privilege

Innumerable race-related wounds fester in cultures that have been touched by white supremacy and colonialism. Where its dehumanizing ideologies and social and cultural practices have taken root, white supremacy divides the hearts of nations and communities. Sadly, these very old themes are resurgent today, reverberating through cultures across the globe, creating new injuries and reactivating old, frequently multigenerational ones. Many of us feel the pain in our hearts, spirits, and bodies, and suffer with those who are most directly harmed, but as we deepen our capacity for mindful inquiry, we experience more than empathy and compassion.

We begin to see that these efforts to divide humanity represent the confusion of living in the mindlessness of greed, the delusions of hyper-individualism, and the false notion that our harmful actions toward others do not matter in the long run. It is painful for us to keep our eyes focused on these realities long enough to deepen our understanding. And yet when we do, we can see that underneath the renewed racism, sexism, and other forms of violence is a sense of disconnection from the self, from one another, from the natural and built world, and the appeal of power-over rather than power-with as a way of relating with others. And so we are reminded that the struggle for racial justice, for a more equitable distribution of power and resources, is ongoing and interlocks with all other struggles against oppression. There can be no racial justice in a society in which sexism, homophobia, classism, ableism, mass incarceration, inadequate health care, contaminated water, housing insecurity, and other forms of social injustice reign. We need to see more clearly what justice requires for more robust understanding and action.

Focusing on the Vulnerable

Regardless of when or where we have experienced suffering, it lingers, festers, and creates a kind of quiet but overweening fealty to the culture of violence—both direct and indirect—in which we find ourselves today. The actions that cause harm to one person or group reactivate the pain of the wounds carried in the hearts, minds, and bodies of all others. For example, if we are the grandchildren of those interned during World War II, the idea of rounding up and housing asylum applicants in detention centers or military bases echoes the deep, intergenerational wounding of the WWII internment camps. We know that when we look at each of these policies, we see government-sponsored racial oppression. And deep within the DNA of those who have come to see themselves as white lie the embedded trauma of memories of violence against their ancestors as members of vulnerable ethnic groups across Europe—painful patterns of experience with dehumanization that no doubt fueled the oppressions of colonialism all around the globe. As we become more comfortable looking at racism and the dynamics of race-making in our times, we begin to explore more deeply how we came to this place.

In this chapter, we will look at how engaging with others with vulnerability, supported by compassionate awareness of self and others, improves connection and supports healing of both self and communities. Through these modes of healing, we find ways of working more effectively with others for change, exploring bold new models for working against injustice with the potential to transform the world.

Bringing Compassionate Mindfulness into Community-Based Engagement

On the day of the press conference at which the president of the United States argued that there were "good people on both sides" of the fight for and against white supremacy that had recently descended upon Charlottesville, Virginia, I was asked to facilitate a healing space for community members. It would only last an hour and I was also still reeling from the news myself, so I was not certain that I would be of any benefit. But I believed that I would be better off sitting with others than suffering alone, and that speaking with others in safety and from the heart could be of some benefit, seen or unseen.

Like many who showed up that afternoon, I was feeling tender, raw, and vulnerable. I leaned heavily on whatever I had done before to feel the ground beneath me as I took my seat in the circle. Feeling the pressure of the time constraint, I gathered myself. I decided I would, at a minimum, offer a supportive practice for sensing into feelings of kindness toward ourselves and others in the room. I would lead the group in a guided meditation and offer lightly facilitated conversation from there. I trusted that we would make the best of that hour.

I could feel the tension in the air. We could all feel it. Before beginning the self-compassion reflection, we shared welcoming reflections and a few guidelines to frame our time together.

"I admit that I'm feeling more emotional today than I thought I would be. It's been a hard few days, since the weekend's incidents and their aftermath. I believe that the only possible grounded optimism that may come from this is to see that we are now seeing many things that have been with us always, but we have not been willing to face.

"I should also say," I went on, "that I spent eight years in Charlottesville as a student at UVA, and so it has brought up a lot to see these images of my former home. This space is for hearing from you. I ask you to think about what emotions, thoughts, and sensations are coming up for you, right now, in your body. If you feel comfortable here, please speak of what you fear. And also, reflect on your hopes. Anything that comes up for you is okay in this space. It's not about answering the questions that we have, but for now, allowing ourselves to feel what we are feeling, to name the thoughts that are arising, and to share them in a supportive group of others struggling to make sense of what we have all just witnessed. You will probably want to reflect more afterward, so please make time and space to do so when you can."

I then opened the floor to hear from the people in the room. I could see the signs of settling in. A woman adjusting herself in her seat, dropping her arms to her sides, allowing herself to take up just a bit more room. A man letting out a deep breath and falling a bit more deeply against the back of the sectional. For a few moments, eyes faced downward, or closed. The air was heavy with the weight of emotion, reflection, and concern.

The first person who spoke was Liz. She was a bit older than me and one of the few other African-American women in the room. "I grew up in Atlanta, and my parents spent time up north in Virginia. I have family there and remember spending summers there. I've been talking with my friends in the South, and we all believe the same thing: our parents must be turning over in their graves."

A Jewish woman named Rose spoke up next: "It seems that all these months we kept thinking, 'This will be the thing that will wake people up and move us on from the level of support that Trump has.' And yet, nothing has shaken it. With this show of white nationalism, I don't even see it shifting now. I've never been so afraid in my life. And while I hope this will wake people up, I'm really scared that things will get worse."

Beth, a white woman, wondered aloud, "What will it take to make people really wake up?"

After a few moments of silence, Anouja, a South-Asian-American woman, spoke in response, "Yes, I was thinking the same thing. I've been feeling a lot of strong feelings about all of this, too. I'm from the South, so I have friends from there, and from here in the Bay Area. From what I can see, the people who really care about these issues are from the Bay Area. The rest of my friends are just posting articles from BuzzFeed, seemingly oblivious, and not caring. How can we get *those* people to care?"

I nodded, thanked her for her comment. We sat again in silence.

Kim, a queer black woman, said, "There are a lot of emotions running through me now, but I think I want to share what I'm feeling most, and that is fear. When I get on the BART, I get all kinds of reactions, and I feel fear. This isn't just something that is happening in the South. It is here, too.

"And so I just want to say to my white homies, 'Talk to your cousins! Start having these conversations about all of this with *them*, with your own people.' Because this isn't our problem, really. It's white folks' problem. And if you don't talk with your people, this won't end. I think that is all I want to say for now."

A white woman named Jewel spoke up: "I grew up in Texas. And I've come to realize that what I grew up with needs to be confronted. I went to a school with Confederate symbols on its mascot and as part of our school insignia. And it's still there. I've just been thinking about what I might be able to do to help in that community, to help spark a conversation about all of this."

Andre, an African-American man, spoke up next. In his voice was a sense of urgency. "I want to bring the sense of needing to be hypervigilant into this space, because that is what I feel all the time. I'm sorry, but I could not do the reflection. I don't have the luxury of reflecting. I have to be vigilant. Because as the sister said, whenever my black body enters a space, it can be an occasion for violence. We can talk about Trump or Charlottesville, but all of this is right here. And we need to be thinking about what we can do here to help make those whose bodies are seen as a reason for violence feel more protected. We also need to have people here who believe like the white nationalists do. Otherwise, we are just preaching to the choir, and that won't change anything."

A white woman named Audrey spoke: "When you talk about fear on the BART, I feel that, too. I am not trying to say that my fear is the same as or equal to yours. But I'm just saying that I, too, feel afraid on the BART, I feel that I am not safe."

"I understand that," Andre responded. "But what I am saying is that if you have been trained to feel that your safety, your sense of being safe, is facilitated by me being oppressed, and you don't see that, it leaves me more vulnerable still."

Audrey nodded.

Then Jack, a middle-aged white man spoke: "All of these statues that we're looking at—Robert E. Lee, General Jackson—these are about white supremacy. They are not about heritage or history. They are about the desire for symbols that reflect the politics of white supremacy. And I think we need to be very clear about that and not get distracted. This is what we are dealing with, and what we must stand against."

Darren, a young white man spoke: "I also went to UVA. And when I saw those pictures coming out of Charlottesville, I first thought, 'This isn't the school I went to,' and I was concerned that the school and city that I knew was being misrepresented. But then I started to think about it, and I could see that there were some less obvious ways that these themes were still there. I'm not sure what to make of it, but that's why I came today."

Our time together had nearly come to an end. As we closed, I thanked everyone for coming. I reminded the group that we were here, that no one had to carry this alone. And I wished for their well-being, peace, and safety.

I came away full of my own emotions. I certainly wasn't sure that this time had been worthwhile, and felt frustrated about the possibility that I was simply helping the institution take part in a "performance of engagement" before returning to business as usual. I shared my concerns with a colleague, and she agreed that working within organizations like this and seeking to make change from within was always difficult.

Still, I found myself thinking about how we might be making some difference, even if we couldn't point precisely to how in this moment. We might see our work as one small effort, among many, across the span of many years. Over the course of my career, I'd facilitated more conversations about race than I could count. What did I know for sure had come of them? I knew that people who engaged in those conversations had, even if only for a short while, been touched by a sense of community. I knew that such experiences change us in ways we cannot always name. And I knew that being in that kind of community—what Martin Luther King and others called "the Beloved Community"—was healing in a way that seemed necessary for the work of transforming the world.

Deepening the Path of Wisdom

Transforming identity-based bias and oppression, and dismantling the structures that maintain them, is lifelong work. Its success cannot be measured in the short run, though we may be able to see and feel some positive differences as we go. The long years it has taken to get mired in the problems of racism ensure that it will take many years to get us out.

And, as we have seen, it is not merely personal work. It requires that we take a long-term view of what it means to see, to be with, and to correct racist structures for the liberation of all people. Because structures of inequity remain, we must imagine ourselves continuing in the work of mindful social, antiracist justice for the rest of our lives.

The legacies of our historic commitments to inequality and caste run deep. Our ancestors' experiences may have been different, but if we take the time to explore our own histories as best we can, we will find that we all know something about social oppression, its causes and effects. Looking at each of our histories gives us a means of strengthening our capacity to stand in the depths of where we come from, of how we enter into the stream of racecrafting, have participated in it, been harmed by it, or benefited from it. Only from that place might we begin the work of healing that includes our families, our peoples. We can then join together on the journey toward repair, redemption, and restoration for all.

Turning the eye of inquiry toward my own family history, I call to mind how identities and suffering intersect. My maternal grandmother was born in 1906, just seven years and a short distance away from a riot by white supremacists in Wilmington, North Carolina, that decimated the once-prosperous Reconstruction-era-established black middle class there. She was not permitted to attend school after the first grade. Instead, as a child and through much of her adulthood, she worked tobacco fields alongside a changing array of extended family.

The deprivation of education, the denial of opportunities to excel, the relegation of so many to subservient, economically exploitable conditions, and the corresponding unjust enrichment of others are what the often violent system of white supremacy and privilege that we call— somewhat euphemistically—"segregation" required. It was considered normal because segregation was sanctioned by law and culture, which made it hard for those privileged under the system to see it as an evil. Thus, many, if not most, white people during that time believed that the vast amount of suffering that this system laid bare before everyone's eyes was no one's fault—how could one's ancestors have been monsters? They came to see segregation as the "natural order" of things. Even, apparently, when it led to lynching and other forms of lawless violence.

And yet, an extraordinary encounter could challenge the foundation of this notion of the "natural order" and set a person on a path to righting the wrongs society made. The following story, told by the late, great legal strategist and law professor Charles Black, who helped up-end state-sponsored segregation in *Brown v. Board of Education*, gives us a vivid example of this. As a sixteen-year-old freshman at the University of Texas at Austin in 1931, young Charlie went to hear jazz played by the great Louis Armstrong. Years later, Black described the experience this way:

> Steamwhistle power, lyric grace, alternated at will, even blended. Louis played mostly with his eyes closed; just before he closed them they seemed to have ceased to look outward, to have turned inward, to the world out of which the music was to flow. . . .
>
> He was the first genius I had ever seen. . . . The moment of first being, and knowing oneself to be, in the presence of genius, is a solemn moment; it is perhaps the moment of final and indelible perception of man's utter transcendence of all else created. It is impossible to overstate the significance of a sixteen-year-old Southern boy's seeing genius, for the first time, in a black. . . .
>
> You don't get over that. You stay young awhile longer, with the hesitations, the incertitudes, the half-obedience to crowd-pressure, of the young. But you don't forget. The lies reel, and contradict one another, and simper in silliness, and fade into shadow. But the seen truth remains . . .
>
> Through many years now, I have felt that it was just then that I started toward the [*Brown v. Board of Education*] case, where I belonged. . . . Louis opened my eyes wide, and put to me a choice. Blacks, the saying went, were "all right in their place." What was the "place" of such a man, and of the people from which he sprung?[2]

My grandmother grew up in a world made by those who believed, as Charles Black had been taught, that blacks were "all right in their place." It was a world in which there was a place for black people, red people, brown people, and yellow people—and it was a limited and subservient one. Such a world *created* the sense of whiteness and blackness and Otherness of many shades. Whiteness was a form of embodied power and entitlement, compared to "coloredness" as one shade or another of deprivation. Because those who fought against the social practices and ideologies that created this hierarchy were generally deemed un-American, the culture embedded biases deep into the consciousness of our identities as American. Reflecting on the consequences of such practices and policies can assist us in deepening our capacity to see their legacies in our own communities, life experiences, and points of view.

Charles Black was able to overcome the trainings of his time by seeing—really seeing—the truth that a whole culture had been constructed around the practice of denying. But seeing things rightly did not instantly change the world. For that, Black joined together with brilliant black lawyers such as Charles Hamilton Houston, Thurgood Marshall, Pauli Murray, and a host of others working to change the laws to create new realities for all of us, dismantling the legal, political, and social structures of segregation. He would be joined in body and in spirit in this work against injustice by others, like Ruth Bader Ginsburg and Sonia Sotomayor, who have inspired generations to link arms and to do our part in the same.

MINDFUL REFLECTION

What do you need to turn toward, to see more clearly, to enable you to get actively involved in the work of racial justice? What social practices, habits, patterns, and conditioning do you need to move past or break through to be of greater service in the world?

CHAPTER TWENTY-FOUR

HEARTS WITHOUT BORDERS:
DEEP INTERPERSONAL MINDFULNESS

☙

Ain't no such thing as I can hate anybody and hope to see God's face.

—FANNIE LOU HAMER[1]

The law has occasionally opened the door to revolutionary change, creating a more equitable world, followed by the inevitable backlash against those changes. That swing to and fro has not been easy for us to understand. We don't always realize that we must work continuously to make real the promise of liberating human interrelationship. Even less often do we have the skills to do this work together. Indeed, we have lacked the consciousness necessary to see our potential together and to lift ourselves up to a new plane for being in relationship with one another in ways that do not depend on power-over, but rejoice in power-with.

So while a lot of people struggled together to disrupt the power structure, to rewrite the culture, to make the systemic changes that ultimately make my own journey to this moment with you possible, none of that happened quickly enough for my Grandma Nan's life to change much.

Looking back at my childhood in Kinston, it's easy to see the failings and virtues of the individuals who shaped my path, but it is much harder to see the racist systems that underpinned their stories. Many find it difficult to see that individual or community-wide weaknesses are tied to intergenerational structures of oppression that we have been given to believe no longer exist. It is often difficult for people today to see how a national culture constructed by a long period of white supremacy, male dominance, and the exploitation of working people continues to limit the potential of people trapped in Kinston and many similar neighborhoods across America.

While I came to see education as a way out of the limitations of the community in which I had been raised, I also saw that various systems of oppression would continue to impact my life. When I was a student at the University of Virginia, a landlord—a woman who had herself only recently moved to the U.S. from her native country in South Asia—told my two white classmates that she wouldn't allow me to move into their home when they had an extra room to rent. Although the young white women told me they would fight against the landlady's racism if I wanted them to, they did not necessarily see the value in doing so on their own, to fight for their own right to select the roommate of their choosing. I found another place to live.

Things on campus were not always much better. One of my law professors blithely made light of the fact that Supreme Court Justice Hugo Black (no relation to Professor Charles) was a member of the KKK ("Why, at that time, everyone who was anyone was a member. It was like being a member of the Kiwanis Club!"). I felt safest in regulated spaces such as classrooms, and most vulnerable in unregulated spaces, such as frat parties, bars, and anywhere on the streets off campus after night fell.

My successes, such as they were, did not prevent my being singled out for slights and comments that were tinged with race-bias and left me feeling like a perpetual outsider. Graduating from a good law school where I'd had the distinction of serving as an editor of the *Law Review*, passing one of the most difficult bar exams in the country on the first try, and landing a job with a firm in California shielded me from the worst implications of working-class vulnerability. But none of that protected me against racialized sexism or gendered racism.

I have known since I was a child that the ways in which I had been trained to see myself were not reflective of who I really was. I somehow knew, at an early age, that the identity given to me by the social world was not nearly big or deep enough to hold the mystery-in-plain-sight that I was—*that we all are*. We have a sense of ourselves as racialized and gendered beings in specific cultural contexts, living as convention demands, but at the same time, some of us know, instinctively, that there is something much more to who we are. And yet, we have not been trained, for the most part, to talk about ourselves and our "labels" as both real-and-fixed-and-limited *and* not-real-and-relative-and-vast-beyond-words. It is also difficult to communicate this complexity to others.

The sense of ourselves as fundamentally separate makes it difficult to see our inherent connections with others. Combined with demographic changes, this may lead to distress and negative social consequences—reawakening of the desire for physical segregation, the tendency toward hate, and the inability to imagine a world that works for all of us.

Admittedly, other forms of identity can supersede our racial conditionings. For example, someone's identity as a police officer may become their primary identification, superseding their identity as black or Latino. If racial identity does not seem to define your existence, this may be especially important to reflect on and investigate. We are often defined by racial identity, even if it shows up most in the ways we deny or resist its relevance in our lives.

Whatever your level of comfort with these reflections, deepening your understanding requires that you bring mindfulness to your own race-specific experiences. Again, we know that for many of us, looking closely at our experiences of race will be painful. Some of us have had extremely hurtful experiences of racism that we find hard to let go. Some of us have had painful experiences on a regular basis. The commitment to open engagement will be important in sustaining growth and increasing the capacity to engage with challenges over time.

More Complex Race Stories, Shared with Less Attachment

My ancestors include black, white, and very likely "Other" people. My black ancestors were most likely brought over from Africa during the period of enslavement, although I have seen no detailed records, and they may not even exist. The situation with my probable white ancestors is also both ambiguous and incomplete. Ancestry.com reports that I have a fourth great-uncle, Josiah Sugg, a former officer in the Confederate army who served in the North Carolina Senate during the period of the Reconstruction. What I do not know is whether Mr. "Sugg," who apparently owned some of my black ancestors (consequently known by the subtly possessive name "Suggs"), was also genetically related to one or more of them.

This complicated, obscured, incomplete, racially "mixed" background contains more truth than does the standard story of single-race ancestral history that many if not most black Americans with roots in the South hold as "our story." And this means that the same is true of most *white* Americans with roots in the South as well. For me, this leads me to an important insight: however we have been taught to think of ourselves in terms of race, whatever the labels we find ourselves using or that have been applied to us, *the actual truth of our heritage is, without question, vastly more complicated than most of us can even fathom.*

What comes up for you when you reflect on this statement?

Might a closer look at your own history, going back several generations on both of your parents' sides, reveal intersections with cultures and races previously unknown to you or your family members, whether from heritage groups here or abroad?

Homo sapiens sapiens, the species we call human, evolved some 250,000 years ago. And yet most of us are lucky if we can trace our heritage in any detail back a few generations. What of those ancestors going back over the tens of thousands of years of human history before the written record, to what anthropologists call our common ancestor? Who are our cousins, our family when seen from this broader perspective? Why do we cling to such relatively narrow stories about our heritage, going back, at the very most, a thousand years, when the deeper human history is literally unknowable, and yet by definition contains multitudes?

Take a few minutes to sit with these questions, your thoughts and emotions in response to them, and their implications.

Mindfulness of Community

RECOGNIZING THE EXPERIENCE OF COMMUNITY

This is a guided meditation aimed at helping us become more consciously aware of and conversant about our nuanced experiences in community. This practice is focused on the recognition part of the RAIN acronym (Recognize, Accept, Investigate, and Non-Identify).

We begin by looking deeply at how our sense of being separate and apart has been reinforced by the particular communities in which we were raised.

Call to mind places where you have lived.

Reflect on how experiences of living in particular communities are known deeply in your body. Reflect on how your experiences of community and the cultures that form them are carried forward into the world through your interactions with others.

For this practice, we are focusing on physical places where we have lived, the sense of community that we found there, and how these environments shaped our sense of self.

Begin by visualizing the neighborhood surrounding one of your earliest homes.

What do you see when you visualize that neighborhood and the community there?

Whom do you see? Who were some of the people who stood out as members of the community? Who were the leaders? Who were the teachers? Who carried out the labor and service work? For each of these categories of people, what race would most likely apply to them?

How did it feel to be in that community?

In what ways did you feel like you belonged?

In what ways did you feel like an outsider?

Call to mind what you know about feeling like or identifying others as outsiders in that community. Allow yourself to really experience the thoughts, emotions, and sensations that accompany what you know about not being included. Allow these feelings to dissolve.

Now consider what you know about *how* this community was formed.

Do you know any formal or informal boundaries—legal, cultural, or otherwise—that determined who was accepted and who was not?

If so, how does it feel to know this?

If not, how does it feel to not know more about this aspect of the community?

Once again, allow yourself to experience the thoughts, feelings, and sensations that accompany this reflection. Let the feelings dissolve.

As we draw this meditation to a close, bring your focus to the sensations in the heart region of your body. If you are feeling any painful or stressful emotions as a result of this practice, please also complete this brief self-compassion practice:

Placing one hand over the heart, and one just below the belly button, silently recite these phrases to yourself:

"In this community, I and others suffered discomfort, pain, or loneliness from the sense of not fully belonging. Suffering in this way is a part of the human condition. I and others deserved compassion then, and I offer compassion to myself and toward others now."

Now, come back more fully into awareness of the sensations of breathing and sitting. Sense into the ground beneath you.

Connected at the Heart

Moving from color blindness to ColorInsight requires the will to see things differently, to act differently as a result, and to stay committed to doing so for the rest of our lives. We start to look for hidden aspects of the story of race. Consider the following informal reflection prompts:

What have you gained from your connection to the so-called Other (whomever you were taught to think of that way)?

What have you given to Others?

What difficulties have you caused to Others?[2]

How are aspects of your life now linked to or sustained by the suffering of Others?

What are the borders you have placed around your heart to make this suffering okay?

What are you willing to let go of, what borders are you willing to dissolve, in the struggle for justice?

Beginning Again

Bianca came to me out of curiosity. As a recent immigrant to the United States from Eastern Europe, she was aware that not everyone in her adopted culture was accorded the same level of respect. Drawing on what she had learned while growing up in her home country, she recognized the general pattern—there were groups who were preferred and privileged in the dominant culture, and others who were not. But for Bianca, the particular biases in the United States were new and more than a little puzzling.

She told our class community that race wasn't as significant in her home country, where most people looked more or less like she did. Yet she could see immediately that race mattered in the United States in ways that she desperately wanted to understand.

Citizenship also meant something altogether different in her home country, compared to the United States. In her home country, no one held the idea of citizenship in particularly high regard. Rather, they associated it with senseless bureaucracy and with the hypocrisy of a false nationalism. Here, citizenship seemed to signify belonging, and served as a dividing line.

In sharing these things, Bianca helped us to understand how the meaning of concepts like race and citizenship vary from place to place, culture to culture, context to context. Bianca realized that groups that she had been raised to see as different in her home country, such as the Roma peoples, were the object of cultural projections not present here. In order for us to see the powerful but arbitrary ways in which cultures mark and marginalize different groups of people, we had to share our cross-cultural stories.

Bianca confided with us that she was, inevitably as a result of living in the United States, learning what it meant to be white here, a designation that was so much more important in this country than in her own. It didn't make sense to her that whiteness seemed so much more valuable a commodity in the United States than it had in her fairly homogeneous home city (comprising primarily white people) in Eastern Europe. Because she had not been raised to value whiteness especially, she was surprised by and critical of the ways she was being invited to identify with whiteness and to dis-identify with so many others.

Bianca could also see her own biases. After reflecting on some of the ways she had been trained to think about the spectrum of possible mates, she was surprised at how limited she had been. Before long, she was dating a South Asian man.

"I would never have thought this even possible before having taken this course with you," she wrote to me on a postcard some years later. On the front of the card was a photo of her with her new husband and their infant.

Confronting Fear on the Path to Public Justice

In order to engage in anti-oppression-focused social justice work, we must be in ongoing conversation with people who have differing views. The more effective we are at encouraging, inspiring, and enacting real change, the more resistance we are likely to encounter. Often, people we disagree with will not be equally committed to compassionate engage-ment or mindfulness. In those moments, we must remember the re-sources we have developed to live by our values and to stay true to our intentions despite being met with intense reactivity or worse.

Ultimately, each of us must discern how we wish to engage with peo-ple during intense disagreement. Certainly, when there are threats of physical harm, we have the right, if not the responsibility, to withdraw from such conversations. But short of that, we can continue to explore ways of bringing mindfulness to bear directly on the experience of fear, anxiety, and fragility. Meeting conflict with connection and mutual re-spect is itself a form of transformative justice. And we must stay present and engaged in processes that transform our formal systems of legal response and redress—including law, law enforcement, and politics—bringing the view of radical interconnectedness and the practices of mindfulness there, too.

Recently, at the invitation of Jamie Bristow of the Mindfulness Initia-tive in the United Kingdom, I had the honor of presenting on mindfulness and social justice to members of Parliament in London. Over dinner with a few legislators, I heard a full range of reactions to my presentation, from skepticism to appreciation to wonder. Skepticism was expressed by a member who had been fighting for social justice for immigrants of color and other marginalized communities for years. She wondered whether we could actually fight entrenched injustice using the soft practices of mind-fulness. Appreciation came from a member who had lost a son to a nation-ally galvanizing instance of racist violence, a case that, as a result of her own steadfast and persistent efforts, and those of many whom she in-spired, led to police reforms. She wanted to know how awareness prac-tices might support her in sustainably staying in the struggle over time. And one member was particularly interested in the question of how such practices could support members of Parliament and Lords in the day-to-day work of making more just and effective laws and policies. She was concerned about the tendency of negotiations to break down and the difficulties that members had in hearing one another's different perspectives and finding common ground during the epic battles kindling European politics in these times.

Indeed, I've joined and supported quiet conversations about social justice, egalitarianism, and their links with mindfulness and compassion practices that are taking place in centers of power in the United States, Canada, Europe, South Africa, and elsewhere. While they do not in and of themselves mean that change is happening, these engagements represent the *potential* birth of something new. We are living in an age where, as Representative Tim Ryan (D-Ohio) suggests in the title of his recent book, *A Mindful Nation*, mindful national political movements may become real.[3] At a time when we are seeing our systems stretched to the near-breaking point by fear-based calls for a return to the politics of division and domination, the very possibility that structures of political power in the West may be transformed by mindfulness-based interventions may sound far-fetched. And yet the shifts in perspective that mindfulness brings are having an under-reported impact already.

Compassionate Accountability

Where intentional physical and psychological harm has happened, how do we think mindfully and compassionately about a response? Compassion for someone who has caused harm must coexist with transformative justice.

A few years ago, I joined Charles Halpern, former director of the Berkeley Initiative for Mindfulness at the University of California Berkeley School of Law, and others at a national gathering on transforming the justice system through mindfulness practice. We structured it to include everyone from crime victims to former convicts, from defenders to prosecutors and police officers, from judges to correctional officers and prison policy makers. I was heartened to hear about programs that were changing people's lives for the better, bringing mindfulness to thousands of prisoners, wardens, and probation officials. Famed activist Angela Davis's sister Fania shared about the restorative justice work she had helped bring to the public school system in Oakland, California, a program now serving thousands. Former convict Dr. Fleet Maull shared how his Engaged Mindfulness Institute had taken him beyond bringing mindfulness into prisons nationwide, and into local communities where it might minimize entry into prisons in the first place. I was particularly inspired by a state-level prison auditor who was doing what he could to bring compassionate policing into the system through his responsibilities for oversight and review. I came away convinced that efforts are under way across the country to change how we respond to crime right now.

In the process, we took away one clear insight: the criminal justice system is broken on every level, from community-level policing to government oversight. However we might go about it, we promised to continue to raise awareness of the ways that the system was broken and do what we could to change or replace it. Many mindful lawyers support incorporating restorative practices rather than retribution into legal education and the administration of law. We applaud efforts by Bryan Stevenson, of the Equal Justice Initiative, and others to raise awareness of the racism in our history that is the deeper cultural context for the disproportionate impact of harsh policing practices on poor black communities. We seek new, creative responses to violence and injustice, responses aimed not at criminalizing the poor, the dispossessed, or the persecuted from the other side of the border, but at correcting, making amends, and healing. And we know that because of the disproportionate application of criminal law against people of color, criminal justice reform or alternatives to incarceration would themselves promote racial justice.

Perhaps even more than seeking to restore, I support approaches to racial justice that help establish caring connections and relationships where they were not explicitly present before. I look for approaches that blend accountability with the goal of healing traumatized communities and families. None of this is easy. The work is ongoing. But we are making a difference by bringing awareness again and again to the social practices through which injustice is made, by developing the will to address them, and by working to respond to injury in a way that repairs and awakens at the same time.

A few years ago, I received a call from a former student of mine. Now a member of the San Francisco District Attorney's Office, she was helping the DA connect more effectively with various communities in his district. The *San Francisco Chronicle* had recently reported that members of our police force had exchanged text messages containing racist and homophobic language. My former student invited me to a meeting of community members, and out of that grew a request that I work with the DA's office to hold a space for community reflection and feedback on the impact of this revelation on them.

I agreed to assist. My first suggestion was that every effort be made to bring together representatives of *all* members of the community, including the police. Doing so would go a long way, I thought, toward moving from an adversarial approach to a restorative one. Unfortunately, we were not able to make that happen. But we were grateful that representatives of the district attorney's office and community members from a variety of diverse backgrounds were joined by former San Francisco police from other jurisdictions in a healing circle. We'd been scared that no one would show.

On one side were tables for gathering in small groups. We served food to create a sense of genuine welcome. On the other side was a large circle with cushioned seating for everyone. More than sixty people came, and nearly all stayed the whole day. I opened with a few minutes of guided meditation and reflection. We then spent most of the time listening to one another's reflections.

There was a young Latino man who spoke about explicit racism he'd experienced while serving time in a California prison, and how the text messages brought it all back. "We need less policing, less incarceration. Because the prison system perpetuates racism."

There were many activists—mothers, grandmothers, fathers, and grandfathers—who had been part of the movement for justice in San Francisco for years. One white woman explained why she had come: "I am committed to working with and exposing whiteness," which she saw as tied to the harsh policing trends bearing down on black and brown communities. She had recently learned about a five-year-old black child who'd had the police called on him three times while in school, and she believed that something needed to be done.

There were young black men, from high school students to lawyers, who had been victims or witnesses of violence. "I realize that my voice needs to be in this conversation," said one, as he described community-grounded efforts, like ours, to raise political consciousness. Another shared poetry that captured his anguish about the over-policing of his community.

Prosecutors lamented the bias in the system, and defense counsel, some nearly in tears, shared how their work followed incidents of police brutality. Over the course of five hours, the feeling in the room shifted palpably toward a sense of safety and community. A key to the event's success was simply creating space for each person's voice to be heard. Our guidelines ensured that people listened to one another mindfully, with compassion and respect.

Bringing mindfulness to such a gathering had a powerful effect on participants. "In the open circle, it was healing to hear everyone express how they feel," reported one participant. Another said, "Sometimes it is important to just have a space to speak from the heart and not try to move a structured agenda."

We convened a follow-up event to which more than forty community members returned. This event was more focused on identifying solutions, but even there, a community member came up to me at the beginning and requested that I bring in "The Pause." "Your mindfulness is one of the reasons I'm back," she whispered to me as the clock nearly tolled the start of our session, smiling genuinely and making her way swiftly to her seat. We could not promise the end of racism. But the connections we made and the hugs we shared rippled with a deep sense of possibility.

Racism as Concentrated Trauma

I would venture to guess that people who have disproportionately experienced racism up close are also more likely than those who have not to have experienced other forms of trauma, including physical violence in the home, alcoholism, and sexual abuse. As a child, perhaps I was special. I experienced all three.

As I've mentioned before, I lived in a town that was racially segregated as a legacy of generations of white supremacy beginning in the era of slavery. This means that I was raised by people who were confronted daily, throughout their lifetimes, with race-based indignities, from personal to structural. My family was not among the fortunate few during that time to garner education and other substantial resources. For us, the struggle was not an abstraction.

Being relegated to positions that would have been reserved for enslaved people in an earlier time set the stage for a variety of foreseeable, negative consequences. Battling a diminished sense of herself, my mother married and divorced one man, my father, who had suffered just as much, if not more. Unfortunately, she then married another man who carried at least as much inner pain and unleashed it on us. I didn't know it then, of course, but I later learned that each of my parents had suffered abuse and neglect, both in the broader social world and while growing up in their homes. It would be no surprise, then, that increasingly over the years, my brother, sister, and I lived in a home that was not safe for children.

It is often very difficult to bear witness to pain, especially as a young child. Indeed, the man who became the Buddha was, throughout his young adulthood, assiduously sheltered from witnessing suffering. But if those who experience great suffering somehow manage to survive intact, they likely have learned something of value that is worth sharing with the world. We know firsthand something about how our vulnerability, weathered faithfully, builds resilience.

As all of the stories presented in this book have revealed, racism itself is traumatizing. It creates symptoms that researchers say are common in sufferers of PTSD, including hypervigilance against the threat of more racism.

To survive and to thrive despite disadvantages like these, we must see beyond our circumstances. I had to see my life through a larger lens. Maintaining a sense of my own well-being meant getting to know the habits of my own mind that kept me trapped in the experience of the trauma, and seeing the humanity all around me, even if sometimes through tears.

Trauma researchers have shown that learning to recognize thoughts that do not serve us and to interrogate these thoughts ("Is it true?") helps in the healing process. Mindful reflection, journaling, joyful conversation practices and movement can assist in these efforts to reframe our traumatic experiences in ways that support true healing.

In addition, getting to know precisely how trauma shows up in sensations in our bodies is essential. Mindfulness of the body can increase our capacity to come home to the sensations that mark our ongoing experience of trauma and lead us to experiences that can help to free us.

Finally, the ability to reflect on our experiences of trauma under conditions of safety helps us retrain the body and repair that part of our brain and body that holds the traumatic experience in place.

In some cases, healing requires the assistance of therapists, but mindfulness- and compassion-based community engagements also aid in the healing of trauma in our neighborhoods, schools, workplaces, and broader social world, especially when people trained in recognizing trauma and incorporating trauma-informed supportive practices are part of the process.

We live in a world full of distress—where we see systemic suffering, the consequences of harsh immigration and policing practices, public policies that deny people dignity and health care, and more. In such a world and time as this, it is all the more important that we are able to face each moment with deep mindfulness. We simply must find new ways of being in the world together. Mindfulness meditation practice helps us through these times by building our capacity for emotional awareness and robust clarity in the face of our fears. We can learn to stay with the painful sense of anxiety, of not knowing, of possibly losing ground as the world changes around us. We learn to stay present to what triggers our fight-or-flight reaction as long as necessary to see, investigate, and deepen our understanding. And what's even more is this: as we learn to let go and relax into the supportive ground beneath us, we may heal the sense of disconnection from the luscious host we have call the earth and come to know, again, the great gift of simply being alive.

Mindfulness as Resilience

With mindfulness practice, we deepen the resilience necessary to stay with suffering over time—our own suffering and that of our friends, family, and others we will meet along the way. We have already seen how difficult it is to train ourselves in the capacity to be present, especially when it comes to issues of identity-based suffering. It is difficult for many of us to realize that our efforts to redress these harms will require daily work. Indeed, this work may not be appreciated by any other than ourselves. It may appear to somehow facilitate a loss of comfort or status in the dominant culture. And so with mindfulness practice, we are building the capacity to stay with it, to be mentally strong enough to handle the challenges that come with continually waking up to injustices and to offer a soft landing for those who need it as we go. We develop the will, the concentration, and the capacity to support ourselves and one another along the way, often by pausing when necessary and then coming back to the work when our clarity and energy are renewed.

Using the tools of mindful inquiry, we see where we are attached, aversive, or ignorant about things that we simply need to explore. This helps us understand how others, despite living what seem at a glance to be very different lives, might just be experiencing much of the same. We notice our tendencies to reach for palliatives—saying, "Things are getting better"—when what we really need to do is play a greater part in making sure that they do. We see that beneath hate and anger is most often some version of fear. We begin to wish to learn more about how we become triggered or overwhelmed and despairing.

What are the root causes of the fear around us? What can we do to meet it all with kindness? On the surface, fear seems to take many forms—the anxiety, even terror, rising up from the thought of losing our country to immigrants, for example. We have been asked to believe that immigrants south of the U.S. border are most likely criminals. We hear that immigrants are coming to take away our jobs. Deep down, we may fear a loss of status for ourselves and for our children. And beneath that, given the hard time so many have just making ends meet, some of us may fear not being able, literally, to survive. This is what I have heard often in person and online. What if we were able to address these fears directly, rather than indirectly assuage them by being "tough on immigration"? Might we be able to develop more effective and humane policies that actually work for the people and families of the United States and for the most vulnerable immigrants, too?

Addressing problems such as these will, no doubt, be difficult, and even stressful. Many prominent mindfulness training programs include teachings about just how this stress affects our bodies. Mindfulness-based stress reduction was designed to help us move away from reactivity to responding with mindfulness. Research shows that mindfulness can help reduce the negative health effects of stress. As Jon Kabat-Zinn and others have reported, stress-hardy, or psychologically hardy, people do exist.[4] They are characterized by commitment, control, and openness to change. We demonstrate commitment when we engage wholeheartedly in whatever we are doing. We experience a sense of control when we believe that we have some impact on the world around us. And we can confront challenges with more of our inborn power when we act with awareness that change is the only constant in our lives.

Over the course of this book, we have been working to develop the commitment to deepening our awareness and understanding to work for our own healing as a part of the work for racial justice, day after day, and moment to moment. To practice mindfulness is also to demonstrate our belief that we have control over some aspect of our lives. As we work for clarity in our own lives, clarity inevitably reverberates around us. Our interdependence with others means that what we do to shift our own awareness and to become more resilient is contagious. Our own mindfulness and compassion practices actually serve all those around us. And at the very core of traditional teachings from which contemporary mindfulness practices emerge is the idea of the inherent impermanence of our experiences. Mindfulness can help us embrace change, so we can move through it with more grace and ease, exhibiting courage, letting go when necessary, and jumping for joy every chance we get, because we know that despite the challenges we face, we were built for that, too.

The Role of Resilience in the Struggle for Justice

Like many of you, I know about the importance of resilience. As a child, I was immersed in the residue of centuries of structural racism and sexism, experiencing what psychologists call multiple adverse childhood experiences or complex trauma. And yet, as I reflect on my experiences, I know that there is a little girl inside of me who grew up concerned with things like food scarcity, the arbitrary violence of an alcoholic, and ever-present vulnerability in a home with a sexually and psychologically abusive stepfather. Although research shows that people who suffer from adverse childhood experiences are more vulnerable to a range of long-term health issues, including obesity and morbidity,[5] I am not imprisoned by statistics. For one thing, I know that mindfulness practices have been shown to increase well-being and health in those who have suffered potentially devastating experiences such as these.[6] In other words, people who have experienced familial and social injustice may be most likely to benefit from mindfulness. And for another, I know this: being aware of the infinite beauty in every heart that I meet, and of the unrepeatable glory of every sunrise and sunset is the only true wealth, sustainable health, and most complete freedom.

Whiteness and Its Blind Spots in Communities of Practice

Despite the fact that people of color stand to benefit greatly from mindfulness, and have relied on awareness and compassion practices to build up resilience since the dawn of time, most spaces in which mindfulness is practiced in group settings in the United States are predominantly white.

Pause and Reflect

What does it mean that mindfulness spaces and trainings have traditionally been developed by teachers who are predominantly white? What does it mean that they have typically been delivered in such spaces?

What do you think it means for the full range of those interested or engaged in mindfulness teaching, training, and practice?

What stories of suffering might flow from this fact?

Because much of what we think of as mindfulness has been largely shaped by white experience, the affect and culture of Western mindfulness appears consistent with characteristics of whiteness, valuing individualism over collectivism and brain-centeredness over heart-centeredness. Most programs and apps on mindfulness focus on a solo personal practice that can be entirely taken up by oneself, alone, and almost wholly disconnected from the communities that originally gave birth to the practices and the communities in which we currently live and breathe. Research on mindfulness primarily focuses on the individual (and traditionally, the white individual). In this golden age of neuroscience, research is also generally focused on the individual, decontextualized human brain.

Perhaps as a consequence of this focus on the individual, we see in the Western mindfulness movement only a glancing focus on the importance of community well-being. This is so despite the fact that mindfulness arose from centuries-long traditions in which community-grounded practices were central. Indeed, the Buddha himself reportedly told his close disciple, Ananda, that practicing alongside friends and living mindfully in community was not merely half of the holy life, but all of it.

Most of what I've learned about the benefits of mindfulness in the work of racial justice has been tested in real communities, where people have come, sometimes on a "one-off" basis, sometimes weekly, to learn the skills necessary to address bias in ourselves and others. Often right in the thick of the city, at a school or in a cultural center's library, we allow mindfulness of the sounds of life around us—the heavy traffic, the children learning tae kwan do—to envelop us and carry us home. When the groups really gel, something of the African ancestors in all of us breaks out during our final sessions together: when we are happy, we sing, we dance; when we are sad, we sing, we dance. Using those skills in diverse community often produces the kind of radiant joy that comes from acting in alignment with our values and connecting with others to make the world a better place. This is the hidden story of what mindfulness in community can bring. It turns out, then, that the work we do to be able to take in the suffering of others can be the ground for not only deepening our resilience, but also for being available to connect in loving community wherever we are.

A PRACTICE FOR EVERYDAY GROUNDING:
ENGAGED CALM ABIDING

Have you ever felt physically exhausted, heavyhearted, or tempted to smoke or drink after simply reading news headlines? Trying to take in an update on the latest political skirmish, a police shooting of an unarmed man or woman, or the actions at the southern U.S. border? Gentle practices like this one provide support for staying grounded as you open up to information that might cause pain.

Take a deep breath and turn your intention inward, resting your attention on the in-breath and the out-breath, following the flow as best you can.

On an in-breath, breathe in for a count of 4, and then hold your breath for a count of 7.

Next, release the breath for a count of 8, through the mouth. Repeat once.

Then settle into a natural rhythm, maintaining awareness of just how deeply and fully you are breathing. Rest along the river of the long, broad, and deep now.

Call to mind your desire for peace and well-being for yourself and for others.

On the next in-breath, consciously focus on the love that exists in your heart.

As you breathe in, bring greater awareness to that love, its warmth, its softness, or other characteristics unique to your experience of it. As much as possible, allow yourself to completely feel the compassion in your being for everyone who is suffering, wherever they are in this very moment.

And as you breathe out, consciously send loving support toward all those you believe to be in need of it in this very moment.

CHAPTER TWENTY-FIVE

STEPPING INTO FREEDOM

∽

For the first time in years, I feel free.

—ADAM, AFRICAN-AMERICAN PARTICIPANT IN A COMMUNITY-BASED
MINDFULNESS FOR SOCIAL JUSTICE COURSE

Breathing Again

When Adam signed up for a seven-week mindfulness-based course that I offered in his neighborhood, he was skeptical. He had been a civil rights advocate, community organizer, and entrepreneur for most of his life, and he was now in his seventies. He had made a comfortable, respectable life for himself, which is not an especially easy thing to do as a black man in San Francisco. Most of what he had achieved, he attributed to his willingness to work hard, despite the challenges against him, including racism. Not surprisingly, he was skeptical of the idea that taking time to "do nothing" could be of benefit to him.

And yet, by the end of the course—in which he experimented with various forms of meditation, such as sitting in silence, walking meditation, body scanning, and mindful listening and speaking—he had a profoundly different view.

"For the first time in years, I feel free," he said.

When people recognize how powerful systems unfairly limit the potential and diminish the joy of vulnerable populations, they often feel a responsibility to share what they have seen with others and to take up the work of creating a more just world. For such people, taking time to pause, to get clear, to better understand what measures to take can seem a bit frivolous.

And yet, taking time to see through the fog of our everyday lives is essential to attaining anything like freedom. We need a taste of solitude and for seeing in ways not packaged for mass consumption. We need to see reality through lenses not shaped by the soul-crushing dictates of the systems that got us here.

The first step to seeing clearly is breathing again, coming home to the body. It is coming home to moments in which we are not driven by yesterday's thoughts, nor even this morning's. It is from here that we can begin to answer the question "Who am I, really?" in a way that connects us more fully to our brilliant, nearly unfathomable miracle that is life manifesting in each and all. We ultimately develop the capacity to relax a little. It is from here that we might imagine ways of changing the world with lasting potential for new freedom for everyone.

Reconnecting with Love

Research suggests that our sense that race is real is not inborn. Indeed, recent studies indicate that we learn to favor people who look like us during our infancy, starting at about three months of age.[1] But what's even more interesting is this: studies suggest that just as quickly, at about nine months, we tend to be more prone to favor looking at those who appear different from us.[2] Perhaps this is a result of our inborn curiosity, before we are taught to fear what we do not know.

The biases that we hold, then, are learned rather than innate. They are the logical reactions to the manifold pressures to think as others have thought, and to behave as the broader system deems appropriate. We have been trained away from our interest in novel faces and the broader world. We have been trained away from our sense that the world is a safe and trustworthy place. We have been trained to fear, to be on the lookout for threats to our safety. We have directed our fears toward one another.

Looking deeply into our existence is a way to reconnect with our instinct to learn about others and to care for one another's well-being. Living with awareness is one means of experiencing, again and again, the love and the joy that keep us coming back. As we engage in mindfulness meditation and mindful social engagement, we see things differently. We begin to see that our own answers to the question "Who am I?" may vary quite a bit from moment to moment. And we can appreciate the vastness of who we are and of what we're capable of being and experiencing in the world.

Thus, we recognize that our social identities are not fixed. We can acknowledge that they are relevant at some times, but not others. When our social identities fall away, they give rise to a sense within us of being at one with the deeper ground, the mystery from which we arose at birth and into which we will one day return in death.

Mindful Social Identity Development

Our particular social identities—whether as men, women, people of color, LGBTQ, or otherwise—are ways of intentionally pointing toward narrow bands of our experiences in the world. Mindful engagement with identity, then, is a means of living in color, in race, in the various ways we see each other in the world. Mindful living with ColorInsight means being aware of how color, race, and other forms of identity have caused and continue to cause unnecessary suffering in the world, and to live out a commitment to stand against racism.

Through transformative mindfulness, we appreciate the previous generations that shaped us. We humbly learn about the people and cultures we come from, as well as those around the globe that have impacted us. Examining our particular heritages, we see the scope of their struggles, name their failures, and honor their successes. We learn what we might owe to others as we take intentional steps toward redeeming our ancestors' transgressions. We can reach backward and forward at once.

Our lives are infused with a large purpose—that of redeeming our ancestors' journeys to this point and living with a sense of oneness and common humanity.

At the heart of the work of mindful racial justice is a commitment to doing no harm, to healing the wounds of injustice through caring—through a fierce, courageous, and far-sighted love. There is something radical about giving what was not given to me, about healing myself so that the harm stops here, and about offering love and compassion in ways that heal the world and protect future generations. Calmly, clearly, and with love, we do what we can. And then we let go and let be.

Mindfulness and Serenity

Many of us are familiar with the serenity prayer: *God, grant me the serenity to accept the things I cannot change, courage to change the things I can, and wisdom to know the difference.* Mindfulness develops in us the inner resources to accept what we cannot change long enough that we may approach the things we can change with wisdom.

We move from accepting the prevalence of racism to exploring ways to learn more about it and how to disrupt it. We move from simply witnessing bias to figuring out how to be a resource for those fighting to end racism. We move from avoiding our sadness or burying it with distractions and addictive substances, to allowing the pain to guide us toward more emotionally intelligent, healthier, and generative relationships with ourselves and others. Thus mindfulness and compassion practices help us to identify and take wise, ethical action in the world, putting us on the path to our own freedom and toward the greater liberation of others.

Deep awareness leads to gratitude for what we are and to freedom. The stories of our suffering, even our most favorite and cherished, have less and less appeal. Like Adam, we *feel* free. From there, we can access the wherewithal to help ourselves where we need it and to help others as we feel our capability to do so. Each day, we realize anew that, despite all evidence seemingly to the contrary, there really is enough for us all. And we realize something more: that in our healing and being, we reveal the power within each of us to help create the conditions for more healing and freedom around the world.

EXPLORING COLLECTIVE MINDFUL SOCIAL JUSTICE PRACTICE

The next time you gather with others to address a particular social justice issue, whether related to immigration, housing, environmental, or criminal justice reform, bring awareness to the whole body as you enter into the work with others.

What feelings have you experienced as a result of the rhetoric associated with this issue?

How would you support yourself in discussing how racism affects understanding about this issue?

Where might you get stuck?

What thoughts, beliefs, teachings, conditions, or habits would you have to break through in order for you to feel better able to bring the topic of racism into the conversation?

What course of study—as an allied discipline alongside your mindfulness practice—might support you in doing this work more effectively? How might you engage in it with stable, grounded love?

Love's Liberating Resistance

Working to end social suffering has not always been seen as a central part of living mindfully. For the most part, mindfulness in the West has been presented as a personal improvement practice. We have not been taught to view mindfulness as a pathway to active social engagement for the benefit of others.

And yet, the traditional teachings on which mindfulness is based make it clear that practitioners must reflect on the ethical implications of their actions in the world. The thrust of this teaching highlights the need to become aware of the ways that our actions define us and, in a real sense, create us. It turns out that our actions toward ourselves and others hold the keys to our liberation.

As we examine the nature of suffering, we see that to a large degree it arises out of our own habits and conditioned ways of thinking and behaving in the world. Coming to greater awareness of this habitual mind*less*ness, we start to see the potential we have in each moment to relate to the world anew. As we recognize the connection between actions that cause our own suffering and those that we take in the world, we begin to see the imperative to bring mindfulness to our actions. We see our interconnectedness with others near and far. Everything we do matters. As my GranNan used to say it, "You reap what you sow." With each act, we literally create the world anew.

The traditions from which mindfulness emerged sometimes use the word *karma* to describe the relationship between our actions and our well-being—a word often taken to suggest that our circumstances in this life are tied to something we experienced in a past life. But the teachings of the Buddha suggest a very different meaning for the word. Karma more accurately translates into the word *action*, or even better, *work*. Karma entails work or actions that we take each day to live in a way that brings about an end to suffering in our own lives and in the lives of others. Having read this far, you are very likely committed to alleviating the suffering associated with racism and other forms of injustice. Even as you make time to reflect on these things, you are opening up your consciousness in a way that is already part of the solution.

From Personal to Collective, Transformative Justice

Justice begins with our daily practice of coming home to our senses in the present moment, bringing love to our work with others to change harmful systems, and pushing the refresh button to begin again. From the place of awareness, justice looks like compassionate action to reconnect what has been artificially separated and to maintain those connections throughout our days. Rather than engage in adversarial arguments that focus on shaming and punishing, we look to ways of seeking accountability while maintaining a sense of ourselves as part of an integrated whole. We seek, in other words, a deep and revolutionary mindfulness with the capacity to awaken us to our role in the suffering of others and support us in enacting transformative justice—again and again, wherever we are. We practice a mindfulness strong enough to resist the siren song of the world's confusion, separations, over-attachment to outcomes, and ability to live comfortably off the excess afforded by the systemic suffering of others.

Senator Bobby Kennedy's visit to the Mississippi Delta region in 1967, described briefly in the closing pages of chapter nineteen, opened the eyes of America to a region many people had never had the chance to see, and to the stark suffering caused by racial oppression there. But I know of one black man who didn't need Bobby Kennedy to tell him about racial oppression in Mississippi. My father, Edward Magee, had lived in Mississippi until he was just old enough to leave it behind. Born in Biloxi in 1938, he had escaped the place that historians called the most racially restrictive state in the country, the state with the largest recorded number of lynchings ever, for the comparative freedom of the U.S. Marine Corps during a time of war. At twenty-nine years old, he was living in North Carolina. As Kennedy toured the Delta, my father was settling into an apartment in Kinston with his wife and young son. And he was looking forward to a new baby girl. He and his wife would name her Rhonda Varette. And though I grew up mostly without him, I've come to learn of the vicious segregation he faced growing up. For the simple pleasure of wading into the waters of the Gulf Coast as a young man, he could well have lost his freedom, if not his life.[3] When he died in 1986, a veteran of Vietnam, he took with him the stories he might have shared with me and with the world about his years growing up there. But he left behind a daughter who would somehow come to see that, for all of his imperfections, and for all those of the Southerners who could not look upon my father's young bright face and see him as family, we are all called to see ourselves and one another rightly in the fullness of our common humanity.

Starting in 2003, I began writing about an approach to law and policy that emerges, for me, from mindfulness and compassion practice. I called this approach "Humanity Consciousness":

> We *see* interconnectedness.
> We *feel* the suffering of others.
> We *discern* what action might help alleviate the suffering
> and harm.
> We *take action* and reflect on its impact.[4]

If we are able to see one another clearly, we are able to see the value in each person we are privileged to meet. If we can take on their pain as ours, we might, together, be able to disrupt the patterns that led to that pain. We do not do it out of anger or bitterness. Our efforts to create a world in which we are more alive and well are driven by positive care and concern.

One of the most celebrated civil rights heroes of our day, Colin Kaepernick, makes it plain: "We resist out of love."

Kaepernick echoes the sentiments of untold numbers of people over the millennia of human history who have seen the impact of violence on real human lives when he describes his motivation for bringing awareness to injustices and for taking action to resist them.

So many of us fight for racial justice because of the love we feel in our hearts—love that burns like fire for those who have been harmed or killed by racism, and those whose lives have been diminished by the stories they have internalized.

For me, the love that kindles the fire for justice in this very life is also for those who feel so disconnected from their fellow human beings that racism finds a home within their hearts and minds.

I have suffered enough. You have suffered enough. We have *all* suffered enough.

May we bring ourselves into continual conversation with one another and with the racial injustices here and now, ending the suffering and making things right—one moment, one risk, one luminous reconnection at a time.

ACKNOWLEDGMENTS

Doing my part to bring this book and its teachings into the world has been a small, partial repayment of the great debt I owe to this interdependent world, including, of course, many more people than I can name who have helped and supported me in ways large and small.

First and foremost, I thank my family—those who held my hands through joy and pain, showed me how to turn tears into laughter, and shared their creativity and caring ways with me since my earliest days in Kinston, North Carolina—my mother, Ruth, sisters Shonda and Toni, and brother, Everette.

Next, I thank my first mindfulness practice community, the Center for Contemplative Mind in Society's Working Group for Lawyers, anchored by Norman Fischer, former abbott of the San Francisco Zen Center, and Charlie Halpern, formerly of the Initiative for Mindfulness and Law at the University of California at Berkeley. And I thank my colleagues at the University of San Francisco for their support—especially Dean Susan Freiwald, Tristin Green, Tim Iglesias, and Joshua Rosenberg; and trailblazers in the broader mindfulness and law movement, especially Peter Gabel, Angela Harris, Scott Rogers, and Judi Cohen.

I thank the Project for the Integration of Spirituality, Law, and Politics; the Center for Contemplative Mind in Society; the University of Massachusetts Center for Mindfulness; the Mindfulness Center at Brown; the Mind and Life Institute; UCLA's Mindful Awareness Research Center; the Engaged Mindfulness Institute; and the Search Inside Yourself Leadership Institute. For making your communities mine, I am eternally grateful.

I offer my deepest gratitude to my teachers and friends in the mindfulness community. I thank my grandmother Nan Suggs, who found her light, let it shine, and held it aloft through even the darkest days. I thank

Jon Kabat-Zinn, whose inspiring teaching and generous mentoring over the years has been nothing short of revolutionary. And deepest thanks to these important colleagues and friends: Zoketsu Norman Fischer, Sharon Salzberg, Richie Davidson, Roshi Joan Halifax, Jack Kornfield, Mirabai Bush, Arthur Zajonc, Mushim Patricia Ikeda, Larry Yang, Konda Mason, Zenju Earthlyn Manuel, Lama Rod Owens, Angel Kyoto Williams, Dan Siegel, Elissa Epel, Diana Winston, David Zimmerman, Barry Boyce, Daniel Barbezat, Rose Sackey-Milligan, Saki Santorelli, Florence Meleo-Meyer, Soren Gordhamer, Michael Craft, Susan Bauer-Wu, Chuck Lief, Rich Fernandez, Amy Gross, Carrie Bergman, Angel Acosta, Angela Rose Black, Mays Imad, Ali Smith, Atman Smith, Andre Gonzalez, Abri Holden, Lisa Baker, Heather Sorensen, Rose Felix Cratsley, George Mumford, Jaime Kucinskas, Tara Healey, Helen Weng, Amishi Jha, Tova Green, Gary Gach, David Forbes, Ron Purser, Ed Ng, Lone Fjorback, Simon Whitesman, Jamie Bristow, Lisa Freinkel, Jennifer Harper Cohen, Anne Bettencourt, Christopher Corts, Chris Fortin, David Treleaven, Liz Roemer, Jayesh Goyal, Bill Duane, and Rand Rosenberg. And I am grateful to the broad network of writing inspirations, mentors, and cheerleaders on the road to book publication, including James Gimian, Jennifer Banks, Josh Bartok, Camille Hayes, Melissa Valentine, and my dear San Francisco neighbor, Leyza Yardley.

Despite the invaluable influences of this incredible circle of scholars, practitioners, innovators, and leaders, there would have been no actual book in your hands without my publisher, TarcherPerigee, and my editor, Joanna Ng, whose supportive colleagues included Marie Finamore, Dorian Hastings, Marlena Brown, and Sara Johnson. Joanna, thank you for cutting what deserved to be cut and clearing space for my voice. And thank you to Lindsay Edgecombe of Levine, Greenberg, and Rostan Literary Agency for taking a chance on a first-time book author, believing in the message you heard me trying to say, and working with me on the proposal that found this book a home at TarcherPerigee.

To the incomparable Jessica Wallace, my dear friend: as you know, your advice, counsel, faith, and love are at the very heart of this book. Thank you for all that you do to inspire in me a sense of grounded but grand possibility.

And most important, I thank Nitin Subhedar. This book would probably never have come to life without the years of support and everyday care that I have enjoyed with you, my partner in life and in meandering, often too-late-at-night conversation. I thank you for giving me a home to return to and an ear to bend after countless trips and presentations; for reading drafts early and late and providing expert editing; and for your love. And I thank my extended family on Nitin's side—Mom, Dad, Tina, Arvind, Nikhil, and Ilina—for your encouragement and loving support as well.

Finally, I dedicate this book to two different groups, who no doubt in many ways overlap and intersect.

To the generations of courageous human beings of all ages, cultures, and heritages who have experienced disrespect, impoverishment, slurs, threats, psychological violence, physical violence, terrorism, or systemic subordination because of racism—those beaten, enslaved, wrongfully convicted, removed, or subordinated through slavery, human trafficking, segregation, deportation, reservations, resource-limited ghettos, and other interlocking parts of the systems devised for building the political community and international empire that we know as the United States of America. May our healing continue! And may we in the process witness the yet-to-be-born New World—the one that so many have suffered in this one to help build, the one based on the compassionate action that is the only wise response to the awareness of our interconnectedness.

And even more, I dedicate this book to you, dear reader. Thank you for calling this book into being. May your willingness to look without delusion at racism in our midst right now help us all to know and to feel that this new New World is actually possible—in fact, is already coming into being—*precisely because of (y)our being and having been here*, with courage, dignity, steadfastness, and love. And may we together have the courage not merely to perceive it, but to link hands and transform the racial, social injustice of this very life—whether on behalf of brown families in custody in border towns in Texas and Arizona, or black men facing the guns of police and racist vigilantes on streets across the country, or black and indigenous women suffering inadequate maternity care; or ourselves or anyone else.

May the ocean of our healing
your river meeting mine
bring peace,
renew the places and spaces we share,
and strengthen the currents running through us
of justice,
of just this.
Unceasingly.

NOTES

Epigraph

1. The line in quotes was written by an unknown author.

Chapter 1. Pausing and Reckoning

1. Martin Luther King, Jr., "I Have A Dream . . ." (1963), text available at the National Archives website: www.archives.gov/files/press/exhibits/dream-speech.pdf.

2. Ta-Nehisi Coates, *Between the World and Me* (New York: Spiegel & Grau, 2015), 7.

3. Toni Morrison, *Playing in the Dark: Whiteness and the Literary Imagination* (Cambridge, MA: Harvard University Press, 1992).

4. James Pennebaker, *Writing to Heal: A Guided Journal for Recovering from Trauma and Emotional Upheaval* (Oakland, CA: New Harbinger Publications, 2004).

Chapter 2. Sitting with Compassionate Racial Awareness

1. Reverend Angel Kyodo Williams, Lama Rod Owens, and Jasmine Syedullah, *Radical Dharma* (Berkeley, CA: North Atlantic Books, 2016), 203.

2. Sharon Salzberg, *Real Love: The Art of Mindful Connection* (New York: Flatiron Books, 2017), 75.

3. "Court Watchers Tell Bill Moyers: Justice Scalia Has Used His Platform to Mobilize GOP Base," Raw Story website, July 11, 2014, www.rawstory.com/2014/07/court-watchers-tell-bill-moyers-justice-scalia-has-used-his-platform-to-mobilize-gop-base/. Compare Parents Involved in Community Schools v. Seattle School Dist. 1, 551 U.S. 701 (2007), Supreme Court Chief Justice John Roberts: "The Way to Stop Discrimination on the Basis of Race Is to Stop Discriminating Based on Race."

4. Robin DiAngelo, *What Does It Mean to Be White? Developing White Racial Literacy* (New York: Peter Lang, 2016).

Chapter 3. Honoring and Remembering

1. Anna Julia Cooper, quoted in Patricia Hill Collins, *Black Feminist Thought* (New York: Routledge, 2009), 46.

2. See Jon Kabat-Zinn and other wisdom teachers for the notion of foundations of mindfulness.

3. Elissa Epel et al., "Can Meditation Slow Rate of Cellular Aging? Cognitive Stress, Mindfulness, and Telomeres," *Annals of the New York Academy of Sciences* 1172, no. 1 (August 2009): 34–53, http://doi.org/10.1111/j.1749-6632.2009.04414.x.

4. David Treleaven, *Trauma-Sensitive Mindfulness: Practices for Safe and Transformative Healing* (New York: W. W. Norton, 2018). See also Peter A. Levine, *Healing Trauma* (Boulder, CO: Sounds True, 2008).

5. Resmaa Menakem, *My Grandmother's Hands: Racialized Trauma and the Pathway to Mending of Our Bodies and Hearts* (Las Vegas: Central Recovery Press, 2017).

Chapter 4. Mindfulness Practice as ColorInsight Practice

1. Ralph M. Steele, "A Teaching on the Second Noble Truth," in Hilda Gutiérrez Baldoquín, ed., *Dharma, Color, and Culture* (Berkeley, CA: Parallax Press, 2004).

2. The quote is "The past is never dead. It's not even past"; in William Faulkner, *Requiem for a Nun* (New York: Random House, 1951), 91.

3. James Baldwin, "As Much Truth as One Can Bear" in *The New York Times Book Review*, January 14, 1962; reprinted in Randall Kenan, ed., *James Baldwin: The Cross of Redemption, Uncollected Writings* (New York: Vintage, 2011).

Chapter 5. True Inheritance

1. Michele Benzamin-Miki, "To Love Unconditionally Is Freedom," in Hilda Gutiérrez Baldoquín, ed., *Dharma, Color, and Culture* (Berkeley, CA: Parallax Press, 2004).

2. Ex parte *Shahid*, 205 F. 812, 813 (E.D.S.C. 1913), (Syrians Are Not White); and In re *Najour*, 174 F. 735 (N.D. Ga. 1909), (Syrians Are White).

Part 2. Seeing

1. Charles L. Black, Jr., "My World with Louis Armstrong," *Yale Law Journal* 69 (1979).

Chapter 6. Looking at the Reality of Racism

1. Thich Nhat Hahn, "The Nobility of Suffering," in Hilda Gutiérrez Baldoquín, ed., *Dharma, Color, and Culture* (Berkeley, CA: Parallax Press, 2004).

2. William McNamara, as quoted by Walter Burghardt, "Contemplation: A Long, Loving Look at the Real," *Church* 5 (Winter 1989): 14–17.

3. *Race: The Power of an Illusion,* 3 episodes, executive producer, Larry Adelman (San Francisco: California Newsreel, 2003), DVD; first aired on PBS, April 24, 2003.

4. ER Services website, online course, "Teaching Diversity: The Science You Need to Know to Explain Why Race Is Not Biological," available at https://courses .lumenlearning.com/suny-wm-readinganthology/chapter/teaching-diversity-the -science-you-need-to-know-to-explain-why-race-is-not-biological/, accessed March 9, 2019. See also Michael Yudell, Dorothy Roberts, Rob DeSalle, and Sarah Tishkoff, "Taking Race out of Human Genetics," *Science* 351, no. 6273 (February 4, 2016): 564–65, available at https://www.sun.ac.za/english/faculty/healthsciences/cmel /Documents/taking%20race%20out%20of%20human%20genetics.pdf.

5. Michael Omi and Howard Winant, *Racial Formation in the United States: From the 1960s to the 1990s* (New York: Routledge, 1994).

6. Paul Cavaco, "Rihanna: Her Allure Photo Shoot," *Allure*, February 24, 2009, https:// www.allure.com/gallery/rihanna-2008.

7. Megan Gannon, "Race Is a Social Construct, Scientists Argue," *Scientific American*, February 5, 2016, https://www.scientificamerican.com/article/race-is-a-social -construct-scientists-argue.

8. Jennifer Lee and Frank D. Bean, "Reinventing the Color Line: Immigration and America's New Racial/Ethnic Divide," *Social Forces* 86, no. 2 (December 2007): 561–86.

9. Raj Chetty, Nathaniel Hendren, Maggie R. Jones, and Sonya R. Porter, Race and Economic Opportunity in the United States: An Intergenerational Perspective, NBER Working Paper No. 24441, March 2018; reported by Emily Badger, Claire Cain Miller, Adam Pearce, and Kevin Quealy, "Extensive Data Shows Punishing Reach of Racism for Black Boys," *The New York Times*, March 19, 2018, available at https://www.nytimes.com/interactive/2018/03/19/upshot/race-class-white-and-black-men.html.

Chapter 7. Deepening Insight Through Compassion

1. Ta-Nehisi Coates, *Between the World and Me* (New York: Spiegel & Grau, 2015).

2. 1790 Naturalization Act; *U.S. v. Ozawa (1922); U.S. v. Bhagat Singh Thind (1923)*; 1965 Hart Celler Act; see https://history.state.gov/milestones/1921-1936/immigration-act and https://cis.org/Report/HartCeller-Immigration-Act-1965]; see Ian Haney Lopez, *White by Law: The Legal Construction of Race* (New York: New York University Press, 1996).

3. Mahzarin R. Banaji and Anthony G. Greenwald, *Blindspot: Hidden Biases of Good People* (New York: Bantam, 2016).

4. Theodore R. Johnson, "Black-on-Black Racism: The Hazards of Implicit Bias," *The Atlantic*, December 26, 2014.

5. Patricia Williams, "Not-Black by Default," *The Nation*, April 21, 2010.

6. Richard G. Wilkinson and Kate E. Pickett, *The Spirit Level: Why More Equal Societies Almost Always Do Better* (London: Bloomsbury Press, 2009).

7. Rucker C. Johnson, "Long-Run Impacts of School Desegregation and School Quality on Adult Attainments," National Bureau of Economic Research Working Paper no. 16664 (2001, 2015). See also "The Benefits of Socioeconomically and Racially Integrated Schools and Classrooms," The Century Foundation, April 29, 2019, https://tcf.org/content/facts/the-benefits-of-socioeconomically-and-racially-integrated-schools-and-classrooms/.

8. Wilkinson and Pickett, *The Spirit Level*, n. 17.

9. Shai Davidai and Thomas Gilovich, "The Headwinds/Tailwinds Asymmetry: An Availability Bias in Assessments of Barriers and Blessings," *Journal of Personality and Social Psychology* 111, no. 6 (December 2016): 835–51, http://dx.doi.org/10.1037/pspa0000066.

10. Paul Rozin and Edward B. Royzman, "Negativity Bias, Negativity Dominance, and Contagion," *Personality and Social Psychology Review* 5, no. 4 (2001): 296–320, https://doi.org/10.1207/S15327957PSPR0504_2.

11. Juliana G. Breines and Serena Chen, "Self-Compassion Increases Self-Improvement Motivation," *Personality and Social Psychology Bulletin* 38, no. 9 (2012).

12. Frances W. Jones Magnet Middle School, in Hampton, VA; see http://jon.hampton.k12.va.us/school-information/jmms-history. In 1977, this building was dedicated as Francis W. Jones Junior High School. Unfortunately, the need for the school was

short-lived and the building eventually became home for the administrative offices of the school system. In 1998, this building was rededicated as Francis W. Jones Middle School.

13. Supreme Court Chief Justice John Roberts, "The Way to Stop Discrimination on the Basis of Race Is to Stop Discriminating Based on Race," *Parents Involved in Community Schools v. Seattle School Dist. 1*, 551 U.S. 701 (2007).

Chapter 8. Seeing Implicit Bias

1. James Baldwin, "Unnameable Objects, Unspeakable Crimes," in *The White Problem in America, Ebony* magazine, eds. (Chicago: Johnson Publishing Co., 1966).

2. Anita Hill is a lawyer and academic currently serving as university professor of social policy, law, and women's studies at Brandeis University. She is best known as the woman who accused Supreme Court nominee Clarence Thomas of sexual harassment while working with Thomas at the U.S. Equal Employment Opportunity Commission, an accusation that Thomas has consistently denied.

3. Paul DiMaggio, "Culture and Cognition," *Annual Review of Sociology* 23 (August 1997): 263–87, doi:10.1146/annurev.soc.23.1.263.

Chapter 9. RAINing Racism

1. Bonnie Duran, "Race, Racism, and the Dharma," in *Dharma, Color, and Culture*, Hilda Gutiérrez Baldoquín, ed. (Berkeley, CA: Parallax Press, 2004), 165–68.

2. David A. Treleaven, *Trauma-Sensitive Mindfulness: Practices for Safe and Transformative Healing* (New York: W. W. Norton, 2018); Resmaa Menakem, *My Grandmother's Hands: Racialized Trauma and the Pathway to Mending of Our Bodies and Hearts* (Las Vegas: Central Recovery Press, 2017).

3. Ibid.

4. Karen E. Fields and Barbara J. Fields, *Racecraft: The Soul of Inequality in American Life* (London: Verso, 2012).

5. *Milliken v. Bradley*, 418 US 717 (1974), docket no. 73-434.

6. See Vijay Prashad, *The Karma of Brown Folk* (Minneapolis: University of Minnesota Press, 2001).

7. Brendan Nyhan and Jason Reifler, "When Corrections Fail: The Persistence of Political Misperceptions," *Political Behavior* 32, no. 2 (June 2010): 303–30, https://doi .org/10.1007/s11109-010-9112-2; and see also Thomas Wood and Ethan Porter, "The Elusive Backfire Effect: Mass Attitudes' Steadfast Factual Adherence," *Political Behavior* 41, no. 1 (March 2019): 135–63, https://doi.org/10.1007/s11109-018-9443-y.

8. James Baldwin, "Unnameable Objects, Unspeakable Crimes," in *The White Problem in America, Ebony* magazine, eds. (Chicago: Johnson Publishing Co., 1966).

Chapter 10. Developing Mindful Racial Literacy amid Complexity

1. Zenju Earthlyn Manuel, *The Way of Tenderness* (Somerville, MA: Wisdom Publications, 2015), 3940.

2. Anālayo, *Satipatthana Meditation: A Practice Guide* (2018).

Chapter 11. Making the Invisible Visible Through Mindfulness

1. Jon Kabat-Zinn, *Mindfulness for All: The Wisdom to Transform the World* (New York: Hachette Books, 2018), 13.

2. *Perez v. Sharp*, 32 Cal.2d 711 (1948).

3. See Derald Wing Sue et al., "Racial Microaggressions in Everyday Life: Implications for Clinical Practice," *American Psychologist* 62, no. 4 (May/June 2007): 271–85.

4. Reva B. Siegel, "Why Equal Protection No Longer Protects: The Evolving Forms of Status-Enforcing State Action," *Stanford Law Review* 49, no. 5 (May 1997): 1111–148, doi: 10.2307/1229249.

5. Mahzarin R. Banaji and Anthony G. Greenwald, *Blindspot: The Hidden Biases of Good People* (New York: Delacorte Press: 2013).

Chapter 12. Mindful Social Connection

1. Larry Yang, *Awakening Together* (Somerville, MA: Wisdom Publications, 2017), 216.

2. John Paul Lederach, *The Moral Imagination: The Art and Soul of Building Peace* (New York: Oxford University Press, 2005).

3. Mari J. Matsuda, "Looking to the Bottom: Critical Legal Studies and Reparations," *Harvard Civil Rights and Civil Liberties Law Review* 22, no. 2 (1987): 323–400.

Chapter 13. Personal Justice

1. Rhonda V. Magee, "The Way of ColorInsight: Understanding Race and Law Effectively Through Mindfulness-Based ColorInsight Practices," *Georgetown Law Journal of Modern Critical Race Perspectives* 8, no. 2 (January 2016).

Chapter 14. Entering a Room Full of People (and Elephants), and Leaving a Community

1. Rosa Parks quotes available at http://rosaparksfacts.com/rosa-parks-quotes.

2. Helen Y. Weng et al., "Visual Attention to Suffering After Compassion Training Is Associated with Decreased Amygdala Responses," *Frontiers in Psychology* 9 (May 22, 2018): 771, doi: 10.3389/fpsyg.2018.00771.

Chapter 15. From Identity-Safety to Bravery

1. Deb Morrison, Subini Ancy Annamma, and Darrell D. Jackson, eds., *Critical Race Spatial Analysis: Mapping to Understand and Address Educational Inequity* (Sterling, VA: Stylus Publishing, 2017), 13–17.

2. Bruce Perry, cited in Think:Kids website, "Regulate, Relate, Reason," available at: http://www.thinkkids.org/regulate-relate-reason/.

Chapter 16. Particularity as the Doorway to Empathy and Common Humanity

1. Robin DiAngelo, *What Does It Mean to Be White?* (New York: Peter Lang, 2016).

2. The ALICE (Asset Limited, Income Constrained, Employed) Project research report, available at United for ALICE: https://www.unitedforalice.org/national-comparison.

3. Data available at United Way of Northern New Jersey, ALICE Michigan Report, 2017 Update, p. 8, https://static1.squarespace.com/static/52fbd39ce4b060243dd722d8/t /58e2fc51bf629a13c2cf176d/1491270749317/16UW+ALICE+Report_MIUpdate_3.24.17 _Hires.pdf.

4. Audrey G. McFarlane, "Operatively White: Exploring the Significance of Race and Class through the Paradox of Black Middle-Classness," *Law and Contemporary Problems* 72, no. 163 (Fall 2009): 163–96.

5. Shoshana Zuboff, *The Age of Surveillance Capitalism: The Fight for a Human Future at the New Frontier of Power* (New York: PublicAffairs Books, 2019).

6. See Project Implicit, a nonprofit and international collaborative network of researchers, https://www.projectimplicit.org. The related Implicit Association's Test (IAT) is available here: https://implicit.harvard.edu/implicit/iatdetails.html. See also Banaji and Greenwald, *Blindspot: The Hidden Biases of Good People.*

7. See Jerry Kang, *Implicit Bias: A Primer for Courts*, National Center for State Courts, August 2009. https://www.ncsc.org/~/media/Files/PDF/Topics/Gender%20and %20Racial%20Fairness/kangIBprimer.ashx.

Part Four. Doing

1. Angela Davis at UCLA Social Justice Summit, C-SPAN, January 12, 2019, https:// www.c-span.org/video/?456737-1/angela-davis-common-ucla-social-justice -summit.

Chapter 17. "Fuck!" and Other Mindful Communications

1. Ruth King, *Mindful of Race* (Boulder, CO: Sounds True, 2018).

2. Ray Charles, "You Are My Sunshine LIVE," YouTube comment, available at www .youtube.com/watch?v=a8040s6Um6g.

Chapter 18. Deconstructing Whiteness and Race

1. Naturalization Act of 1790, Annals of Congress, First Congress, Sess. II, Ch 3, see at https://legisworks.org/sal/1/stats/STATUTE-1-Pg103.pdf.

2. *Prestige*, directed by Tay Garnett (1932); *Kitty Foyle*, directed by Sam Wood (1940). Andre Heisel, "The Rise and Fall of an All-American Catchphrase: 'Free, White, and 21,'" *Jezebel* Pictorial, September 10, 2015, https://pictorial.jezebel.com/the-rise-and -fall-of-an-all-american-catchphrase-free-1729621311.

3. Robin DiAngelo, *What Does It Mean to Be White?* (New York: Peter Lang, 2016).

Chapter 19. Color-Blind Racism and Its Consequences

1. Audre Lorde, "Age, Race, Class and Sex," in *Sister Outsider: Essays and Speeches* (Berkeley, CA: Crossing Press Feminist Series, 1984).

2. Eduardo Bonilla-Silva, *Racism Without Racists: Color-Blind Racism and the Persistence of Racial Inequality in America* (Lanham, MD: Rowman & Littlefield, 2006).

3. Ibid. See also Reva Siegel, "Why Equal Protection No Longer Protects," p. 1113: "The ways in which the legal system enforces social stratification are various and vary over time. Efforts to reform a status regime bring about changes in its rule structure and justificatory rhetoric—a dynamic I have called . . . 'preservation-through-transformation.'"

4. Richard Rothstein, *The Color of Law: A Forgotten History of How Our Government Segregated America* (New York: Liveright, 2017).

5. Elizabeth Winkler, "'Snob Zoning' Is Racial Housing Discrimination by Another Name," *Washington Post*, September 25, 2017.

6. John Freese, "Dependent Origination of Racism 3 of 3," available at https://www.youtube.com/watch?v=ecIOOlaR33s.

7. Rothstein, *The Color of Law*.

8. Ibid.

9. John Freese, "Dependent Origination of Racism 2 of 3," available at https: www.youtube.com/watch?v/mcCdFBxe21c.

Chapter 20. The Wolf in the Water

1. David Treleaven, *Trauma-Sensitive Mindfulness: Practices for Safe and Transformative Healing* (New York: W. W. Norton, 2018).

2. Dan Rather, interview on *The Rachel Maddow Show*, July 29, 2016.

3. Elizabeth Blackburn and Elisa Epel, *The Telomere Effect* (New York: Hachette Books, 2017).

4. Ibid.

5. Adam Leuke and Bryan Gibson, "Mindfulness Meditation Reduces Implicit Age and Race Bias," *Social Psychology and Personality Science* 1, no. 5 (2014).

6. Marshall Rosenberg, chapter 10, *Nonviolent Communication*, Center for Nonviolent Communication, https://www.cnvc.org.

Chapter 21. In Living Color

1. Jon Kabat-Zinn, *Mindfulness for All: The Wisdom to Transform the World* (New York: Hachette Books, 2018).

2. Daniel J. Siegel, *Aware: The Science and Practice of Presence* (New York: TarcherPerigee, 2018).

3. Wallace Stevens, "The Final Soliloquy of the Interior Paramour," from *The Collected Poems of Wallace Stevens* (New York: Alfred A. Knopf, 1954).

4. Y. Kang, J. R. Gray, and J. F. Dovidio, "The Non-Discriminating Heart: Lovingkindness Meditation Training Decreases Implicit Intergroup Bias," *Journal of Experimental Psychology: General* 143, no. 3 (June 2014): 1306–13.

Part Five. Liberating

1. Jon Kabat-Zinn, *Wherever You Go, There You Are* (New York: Hyperion, 1994).

Chapter 22. Walking Each Other Home

1. Thich Nhat Hanh, *You Are Here* (Boston: Shambhala Publications, 2009).

Chapter 23. That Everything May Heal Us

1. David Treleaven, *Trauma-Sensitive Mindfulness: Practices for Safe and Transformative Healing* (New York: W. W. Norton, 2018), 205.

2. Charles L. Black, Jr., "My World with Louis Armstrong," *Yale Law Journal* 69 (1979).

Chapter 24. Hearts Without Borders

1. Fannie Lou Hamer, quoted in June Jordan, *Civil Wars* (New York: Simon & Schuster, 1981).

2. Adapted from the ToDo Institute, "How to Practice Naikan Reflection," http://www
.todoinstitute.org/naikan3.html.

3. Tim Ryan, *A Mindful Nation: How a Simple Practice Can Help Us Reduce Stress, Improve Performance, and Recapture the American Spirit* (Carlsbad, CA: Hay House, 2012).

4. Jon Kabat-Zinn, *Full Catastrophe Living: Using the Wisdom of Your Body and Mind to Face Stress, Pain, and Illness*, rev. ed. (New York: Bantam, 2013).

5. Shanta Dube et al., "The Impact of Adverse Childhood Experiences on Health Problems," *Preventive Medicine* 37 (2003): 268–77.

6. David Treleaven, *Trauma-Sensitive Mindfulness: Practices for Safe and Transformative Healing* (New York: W. W. Norton, 2018).

Chapter 25. Stepping into Freedom

1. David J. Kelly et al., "Three-Month-Olds, but Not Newborns, Prefer Own-Race Faces," *Developmental Science* 8, no. 6 (November 2005): F31–F36, doi:10.1111/j.1467
-7687.2005.0434a.x.

2. Shaoying Liu et al., "Development of Visual Preference for Own- Versus Other-Race Faces in Infancy," *Developmental Psychology* 51, no. 4 (April 2015): 500–11, http://dx.doi
.org/10.1037/a0038835.

3. https://www.history.com/news/how-civil-rights-wade-ins-desegregated
-southern-beaches.

4. Rhonda V. Magee Andrews, "Racial Suffering as Human Suffering: An Existentially-Grounded Humanity Consciousness as a Guide to a Fourteenth Amendment Reborn," *Temple Political and Civil Rights Law Review* 13, no. 2 (2004); Rhonda V. Magee Andrews, "The Third Reconstruction: An Alternative to Race Consciousness and Colorblindness in Post-Slavery America," *Alabama Law Review* 54, no. 2 (2003): 483–560.

INDEX

shame, 77, 78, 111, 112, 123, 126, 152, 164, 181, 184, 193, 204, 206, 222, 252, 253, 257, 260, 261, 288, 293, 332
Shela's story, 55–58, 66, 67, 68
Shellette's story, 166–73
Siegel, Dan, 105
Siegel, Reva, 132, 236–37
Skillfulness of Compassion for Self and Others practice, 158–60
slavery, 3, 51, 66, 69, 74–76, 129, 218, 243, 248, 308, 318
social connection, 141–56
social construction(s), 7, 13, 67, 68, 70, 71, 72, 79, 96, 209–10, 211–12, 216, 245, 291
social identity, 72, 73, 96, 119–20, 121, 153, 194, 204, 225, 328–29
    See also identity-based bias
social injustice, 36, 147, 189, 227, 296, 323, 338
social intelligence, 151, 222
social justice, 20, 21, 32, 154, 198, 233, 241, 312–14, 330
    See also racial justice
Sotomayor, Sonia, 304
Spiral of Healing, 45–46
spiritual bypassing (Welword), 49
stereotypes, 82, 92, 101, 110, 111, 112–13, 133, 183, 211–12, 224, 246–47, 292
    See also bias
Stevens, Wallace, 272
Stevenson, Bryan, 315
STOP (Stop, Take, Observe, Practice), 262
STOP for Mindfulness in Sticky Situations practice, 261–63
stress, 5, 17, 35–36, 38, 44–45, 110, 113, 133, 150, 153, 190, 253–54, 262, 310, 321–22
structural racism, 52, 83, 84, 91, 186, 189, 191, 193, 195, 198–99, 209, 223–24, 227–28, 318, 322
    See also racism
Sugg, Josiah, 308
systemic dimension of racism, 7, 14, 22, 24, 50, 67, 69, 75, 76, 80, 83, 84, 85, 91, 107, 113, 115, 127–28, 132, 142, 147, 148, 171, 185, 187, 190, 192, 193, 198, 217, 218, 223, 237, 240, 243, 244, 293, 302, 305–6, 313, 314, 315, 316, 317, 319, 326–27, 331–32
    See also racial justice

transformative justice, 7, 87, 239, 245, 276, 313, 314, 331–34
trauma-releasing practices, 44–47

trauma, responses to, 105–6
Treleaven, David, 44
Trump, Donald J., 299, 300
trust, 154, 168, 181, 182, 187, 188, 221, 222–23, 247

ubuntu practice, 168–69, 173, 178–79, 194
United Nations, 66
Universal Declaration of Human Rights, 66
U.S. Department of Homeland Security, 244
U.S. Supreme Court, 23, 56, 97, 109, 306

Values-Identification practices, 273–74
violence, 2, 5, 23, 75, 83, 86, 89, 144, 171, 186, 235, 242, 251, 263, 296, 300, 302, 313, 315, 317, 318, 322, 333
Virginia, 11, 12, 14, 108, 166, 183, 237, 251, 297–301
vulnerability, 2, 5, 6, 14, 25–26, 66, 75, 82, 85–86, 87, 97, 111, 113, 130, 144, 145, 147, 152–55, 161, 166, 171, 176–77, 180, 181, 182, 184, 186, 187, 190, 192, 209, 217, 221, 224, 227, 238, 241, 242, 247, 253, 260, 276, 277–78, 281, 288, 290, 296–97, 300, 306, 319, 321, 322, 326

Welwood, John, 49
Western cultures, 20, 28, 66, 208, 218, 220, 239, 323–24
white nationalism, 23, 81, 132–33, 183, 190, 299, 300
whiteness, 13, 57, 69–70, 74–76, 81–82, 84, 85, 89, 108, 132, 133, 164, 167, 175, 186, 187, 188, 190, 209, 211, 216–28, 217, 218, 219–20, 223–24, 230, 231, 236, 238, 239–40, 289, 304, 312, 317, 323–25
whites and racism, 7, 12, 13–14, 15, 16, 23, 74, 76, 81, 108, 114, 116, 117, 131–32, 148, 163–64, 232, 308
white supremacy, 14, 15, 21, 22, 83, 85, 88, 89, 90, 91, 118, 121, 129, 156, 184, 217, 224, 234, 239, 241, 242, 243–44, 289, 295, 297, 300, 302, 318
window of tolerance (Siegel), 105
Williams, Patricia, 79
working with strong emotions, 250–64
Woodson, Carter G., 119
World War II, 296

ABOUT THE AUTHOR

Rhonda V. Magee, M.A., J.D., is a professor of law at the University of San Francisco. Also trained in sociology and mindfulness-based stress reduction (MBSR), she is a highly practiced facilitator of trauma-sensitive, restorative MBSR-based interventions for lawyers and law students, and for minimizing the effects of social-identity-based bias. Rhonda has been a visiting scholar at the Center for the Study of Law and Society, a visiting professor of law at the University of California, Berkeley, and is a Fellow of the Mind and Life Institute.